CONFLICT AND RECONCILIATION

A Study in Human Relations
and Schizophrenia

HELM STIERLIN was born in Germany in 1926 and studied philosophy and medicine at the universities of Freiburg, Zürich, and Heidelberg. He was a psychiatric resident at the Sheppard and Enoch Pratt Hospital in Baltimore, and then became a staff member at Chestnut Lodge in Rockville, Maryland.

He now works at the National Institute of Mental Health in Bethesda, Maryland, and carries out research in the problems of schizophrenia and adolescence. He is a member of the American Psychoanalytic Association, and the author of several scientific articles published in English, French, and German.

CONFLICT and RECONCILIATION

A Study in Human Relations
and Schizophrenia

HELM STIERLIN, M.D., Ph.D.

ANCHOR BOOKS

DOUBLEDAY & COMPANY, INC.

GARDEN CITY, NEW YORK

1969

For Satu, my wife

"Das erste Moment in der Liebe ist, dass ich keine selb-ständige Person für mich sein will, und dass, wenn ich dies wäre, ich mich mangelhaft und unvollständig fühle. Das zweite Moment ist, dass ich mich in einer anderen Person gewinne, dass ich in ihr gelte, was sie wiederum in mir erreicht. Die Liebe ist daher der ungeheuerste Wider-spruch, den der Verstand nicht lösen kann, indem es nichts Härteres gibt als diese Punktualität des Selbstbewusst-seins, die negiert wird, und die ich doch als affirmativ haben soll. Die Liebe ist die Hervorbringung und die Auflösung des Widerspruchs zugleich; als die Auflösung ist sie die sittliche Einigkeit."

Hegel, *Rechtsphilosophie*, VIII § 158 Zusatz, S. 222

"The first moment in love is the fact that I do not want to be, for myself, an independent person and that I, were this the case, would feel defective and incomplete. The second moment is that I win my independence in another person, that I am affirmed in that person, and vice versa. Thus, love is the most formidable contradiction, which the mind cannot resolve. For there exists nothing as unyielding as this singularity of my self-awareness—which must be ne-gated and which yet I need to have affirmed. Love is both the creation and resolution of this contradiction; as its resolution it is moral communion."

Hegel, *Philosophy of Law*, VIII § 158, Addition page 222

INTRODUCTION

"Nothing can be understood in isolation."

Spinoza

"Something has vital force only when it contains contradiction; it is a measure of this force that the contradiction can be grasped and endured."

Hegel

Conflict and reconciliation are central to human adaptation and growth. They are central also to the ways in which we acquire and organize our knowledge about the latter. We gain such knowledge, I believe, through participating in a dialectical process. In this process we become exposed to conflict. We must endure this conflict, grapple with it, feel it in our insides. But then we must reconcile the conflicting elements—only to find ourselves embroiled in new conflict. In this process we achieve ever new levels of complexity of insight. We both gain and outgrow knowledge. And we change.

In the following essay, I have tried to convey some of the dynamic intensity of this process. It reflects what Hegel called the "effort of the concept" (*die Anstrengung des Begriffs*), which, in a relentless push, tries to relate the part to the whole, the whole to the part, and which strives for clarity while simultaneously asking: What is the meaning of it all?

This effort, we learn from Hegel, must be sustained. Only when the dialectical process has unfolded can its full impact be felt. Only when the conceptual movement has left its traces, can the implications of the original propositions become apparent.

Although Hegel provided important ideas for this work, it does not deal with him or his concepts. It deals with human relationships, as seen from a psychotherapist's point of view. And it deals with schizophrenia.

I shall start with a description of the psychoanalytic situation. I do not intend a critique of this situation, but shall try to show how conflict and reconciliation provide a theme which elucidates a variety of human relationships. This exploration will lead us to focus, among other things, on the nature of the mother-child relationship, on the concept of schizophrenia, and on the therapeutic relationship needed with the schizophrenic patient.

The concern with schizophrenia derives from my psychotherapeutic experience and interest. But also, it reflects my belief that this condition, probably like no other, reveals those extremes of human existence and relatedness which allow us to see the more ordinary in perspective.

Many friends, teachers, and patients aided me in developing the ideas here presented. Some of them will be mentioned in the text, others cannot. I am indebted to all of them.

HELM STIERLIN, M.D., PH.D.

CONTENTS

I

THE PSYCHOANALYTIC SITUATION

The psychoanalytic situation, with which we are familiar, grew out of the relationship between doctor and patient as developed in our Western culture. Two elements characterize this relationship.

TECHNICAL VS. HEALING ORIENTATION

The first of these may be termed the *"technical orientation."* The physician, in this relationship, is understood to be a technical expert. Medical problems for him are technical problems. This means above all two things: first, the problem in question is looked at and treated as limited in scope, as circumscribed. It is delineated within the framework of a certain technical competency. The technician, in this sense, is a specialist. He is competent for and therewith limited to certain problems of bodily function—in the manner in which a dentist is concerned with and limited to problems of teeth. Second, the physician is qua technician related to his problems with a certain matter-of-factness: he maintains emotional distance. It follows from this attitude that the "emotional core of the patient's personality" is left untouched by this technical procedure.

Both these facts, the narrowing of the expert's attention to a special realm of competency and, along with this, his distancing matter-of-factness, make the technical approach highly learnable and transmittable. It is "technique" of this kind, characterizing a certain type of knowledge and approach to problems—easily made available and

leaving untouched the emotional core of the personality—
which is the subject matter of schools in the narrower
sense of the word, of what in German is called "*Fachschu-
len*." Many aspects of our modern industrialized society
inextricably are tied to the dissemination of the "technical
orientation," as here defined.

Yet the same Western tradition allots the physician another role than that of mere "technical expert." Besides
being a technical expert, the physician is considered a
"healer." The healing vehicle—from this point of view—is
not his technical expertness but something which his personality radiates. This "something," though, is elusive. We
speak of the physician's bedside manner or, in slightly different contexts, of his charisma, his appeal, his personality.

This side of the physician's role and approach reflects
the counter-position to the technical orientation as described above. While the technical orientation is characterized by clarity, distance, delineation of a realm of competency, the "healing orientation" implies elusiveness,
emotional entanglement, and generality of approach.

This dichotomy is highlighted by our focusing on the
kinds of personal interaction which these two orientations
bring about. The physician's relationship to his patient qua
technical expert is fashioned after a *contract*. The model
for the contract is found in the business interactions of the
modern industrialized society. A contract defines the kind
and scope of such interaction. Out of a vast continuum of
possible interactions, the contract cuts out a piece. This
piece is then more narrowly delineated and made transparent. Then it is made binding for both partners. The rest
of the scale becomes irrelevant. Thus, a surgeon is paid for
relocating and restituting a fractured leg, applying, in the
process, his expert knowledge. Both his task and remuneration, his obligations and rewards, are rather clearly
defined.

But the physician qua healer is measured with a different yardstick. Instead of being viewed as just another species of businessman and technician in our industrial society, he becomes the target for special expectations. He is

expected to serve his patient selflessly and, in a wider sense, mankind. Regarding this healing function he is not unlike a minister. Instead of working under a contract, freely arranged, he is viewed as responding to an appeal, transcending the nature of a business venture. It is implied in such a view that this remuneration must remain equally unmeasurable. Partly he is expected to reap it in the form of increased prestige which is due such a selflessly serving agent.

Inevitably, in thus being accorded a special position, which is both privileged and demanding, he makes himself vulnerable to various projections. In particular, he is easily placed into the role of a more or less omnipotent father, with the consequent focusing on him of wishes—in the patient and in others—to be treated by him as children, but also of envy and rebelliousness. To the degree that these feelings are not tolerated in awareness, the ambivalence felt toward him might be marked.

This is the doctor's position in our Western society, and his relationship with his patients reflects thus conflicting expectations. They give evidence of a dichotomy which appears built into his role as this is shaped and sustained by tradition: to be both technical expert and healer, a contractor for services which he, at the same time, is held to give selflessly.

It is out of these conflicting elements that Freud distilled what has come to be known as the "Analytic Situation."

Freud, we must remember, strongly stood in the medical tradition of his time. He was a practicing neurologist before he became a psychoanalyst. Thus, he could not help but be heir to the two conflicting tendencies which are part of this tradition. He, too, had to be both technical expert and healer.

Confronted with these conflicting roles, Freud found a new solution: He further extended the realm of the technical orientation. But he extended it in a manner which signaled a break with what had been essential in this orientation.

The technically oriented physician, we just saw, tends

to narrow down his interest to a circumscribed area of organic competency. In thus proceeding, he circumvents the emotional core of his patient's personality. Just this Freud—and that is centrally important—did not do. Far from circumventing this core, *he brought the technical approach, as outlined above, to bear on it with full force.* He applied, in other words, the principles of the technical orientation to illuminate those areas of the patient's life which up to then had been excluded from such rational, scientific penetration. These areas, we know by now, comprise the realm of dreams, that which since Freud has come to be understood as the "Unconscious," and spheres of feeling, motivation, and moral judgment. Freud dared to tackle these areas with disengaged scientific interest.

It is hard to over-estimate what this meant: Freud, in thus opening a new field to the technical approach, created an unique experimental situation for studying important areas of psychic life—that of the patient and that of the observer. From only such a stronghold that permitted experience and observation of that experience could present-day analytic theory and practice develop.

Freud, through the analytic situation, thus reconciled the two elements in the doctor-patient relationship which at first seemed irreconcilable: the roles of technical expert and healer. This he achieved by bringing the rational, scientific approach to bear on what had been the healer's domain: the "core" of the patient's personality, his seeming "irrational" psychic processes, fears, and expectations. What seemed contradictory and incompatible, he subjected to a creative confrontation and reconciliation. The analytic situation both structures and reflects such confrontation.

This *"creative reconciliation"* I shall now trace further. I shall try to show how, through this situation, two participants—doctor and patient—meet in a manner which creates a balance of forces. Both contribute to and maintain this balance, although in different ways and degrees. This kind of balance then indicates the reconciliation of seeming opposites. It also decides about the two persons' transactions, that is, it both structures and makes observable a characteristic relatedness. In illuminating various aspects of this balance, I shall thus, more deeply, illuminate the analytic situation. But also, I shall provide a base for the comparative study of other relationships which, in turn, will throw further light on the analytic situation.

THE DIALECTIC OF THE FIVE ANALYTIC BALANCES

I shall present this balance of forces through a series of dichotomies. These are interdependent aspects of the analytic situation. They are not the only dichotomies (or polarities) which can meaningfully illuminate this relationship. Others have been suggested and have been implied in the literature. I have chosen the following five dichotomies because, to me, they most clearly reveal the theme of conflict and reconciliation. Also, they seem to provide widest leverage for a comparative analysis of other relationships. The order of the following presentation is not arbitrary. I shall begin with that dichotomy which, in a sense, is most constitutive, and let the other dichotomies build on it.[1] Thus, I believe, the chosen sequence will come closest to revealing the essence of analytic relatedness.

The analytic situation unfolds and becomes effective *in time*. Time, therefore, will be the first and, in a sense, most

---

[1] A thinking in dichotomies (or polarities) seems most consonant with a dialectical approach that emphasizes conflict and reconciliation. It most immediately conveys the pull and counterpull of the dialectical process. However, there exist levels of conceptualization where such a thinking in dichotomies seems less useful or appropriate. For example, it may interfere with an adequate grasp of phenomena where the continuity of a scale is an important dimension, where—to speak with Hegel—a difference in quantity does *not* imply a change in quality and yet is important. Also, there are forms of multidimensional organization where a thinking in dichotomies would appear unduly narrowing.

constitutive aspect of this relationship. The balance of forces, from the point of view of time, presents itself as *the dialectic of* MOMENT *vs.* DURATION. This dichotomy, therefore, reflects the first pair of tendencies, which, in the analytic situation, are reconciled in a characteristic manner.

The importance of the moment shines forth in the term "timing." The analyst has to decide on the right moment at which to make his intervention. In hitting this moment, he matches his interpretation with the patient's optimal receptivity. This is similar to a physician who, for example, supplies vitamin D at a moment which is right—when the child's growing bones need it most to avoid rickets. But such hitting the right moment in the analysis, among many other things, requires long-term investment and commitment. It is only within a relationship that endures, which grows, that the moment can become meaningful. Only such enduring relationship can gain a quality of realness for the partners. Only with time can the analyst, in many important respects, become a reliable reference pole for needs to be kindled, for expectations to be aroused, confirmed, or betrayed. The duration of the relationship, therefore, must be seen as staking out a width, intensity, and meaning, against which the moment can become effective.

It is the structuring of the analytic relationship along the lines of technique and contract which also colors this dialectic of moment vs. duration. More than in other relationships, this dialectic has become subjected to conscious planning. This dialectic reflects the manner in which segments of human action are valued, made predictable and manipulable in our industrial society. The analyst, a part of this society, tends to regulate his life around the appointment book. His income and existence will depend on how his units of time are filled. The patient, a member of this same society, tends to bring forth expectations and values which match those of the analyst. He will, this means, become a party to the "analytic" evaluation and handling of time.

itself to those wishes and tendencies in the patient which, at the moment, carry greatest neurotic weight.

A patient at one point might attempt to intrude into her analyst's private life. She socializes extensively with a friend whom she knows to be a friend of her analyst's wife. Avidly she researches for details which reflect on her analyst's marriage. These voyeuristic interests of the patient may have to be frustrated. The analyst might advise her to stop this research. Yet in thus frustrating her, he helps her to reveal fantasies she has about her analyst's marital relationship. These fantasies might now enlighten her: They point to complex, rivalrous feelings she had toward her mother—feelings which are at the root of much of her neurotic trouble. At other times, when the main neurotic focus has shifted elsewhere, such frustration of intrusive and voyeuristic impulses may seem less important.

And such "strategic frustration," we notice further, is balanced by what may be termed "supportive gratification." For example, a patient's neurotic needs—such as wanting to turn the analyst into a suitor—may have to be sharply frustrated, yet her need to find a sympathetic, attentive, non-moralizing listener will be gratified. Therefore, gratification and frustration, though subject to certain basic rules, also will have to be reconciled in an ongoing balance as reflected in and guaranteed through the analytic situation.

The fourth dichotomy is STIMULATION *vs.* STABILIZATION.

The stabilizing influences partly grow out of forces earlier mentioned: of duration, sameness and frustration, as constellated in the analytic situation. They make for continuity and regularity. In a sense, they make operational the elements of rationality and predictability implied in the analytic contract. The analyst's office thus may turn into a haven in which the waves and currents of daily life tone down. The analyst, being calm and imperturbed, to some degree personifies reliable continuity. Many stimuli which normally cause distraction and agitation, seem excluded from this situation. Their absence appears to heighten a climate of steady rootedness which puts analyst and patient above the turmoils of the day.

This balance of stimulation vs. stabilization is reflected in the dynamic of "controlled regression." Controlled regression may be considered the ferment of analytic change. It denotes a loosening of a person's mental organization and a heightened receptivity to stimulation from the inside and outside. He becomes more tuned to and accepting of his inner imagery and normally repressed desires. Control of regression means that this regression is temporary and reversible.

It is out of the regressive loosening of mental processes and structures that the Phoenix of inner regeneration, of a better personality organization, and a new sensitivity might arise. The balance of stimulation vs. stabilization appears skillfully aimed at bringing about a regressive loosening that the patient can still manage. His reclining on the couch, his protection from (or deprivation of) distracting influences, his surrendering himself—with the encouragement of the analyst—to the soft breath of reverie and free association: these and other factors induce him to regressive loosening and receptivity. The analyst must then watch that this loosening does not get out of hand. He must, this implies, keenly gauge the patient's "binding" capacity—that is, his ability to keep in check, and thus reversible, his regression—and he must, based on such judgment, skillfully make use of the stabilizing instrumentarium which the analytic situation puts at his disposal. His "technique" thus will reveal his skills in keeping workable the analytic balance of stimulation vs. stability: in using it to initiate and maintain "controlled regression."

The fifth and last dichotomy is CLOSENESS vs. DISTANCE.

Seen epistemologically, distance and closeness are always related to each other. As relative measurements the two concepts require each other in order to be meaningful. The closest closeness which still warrants this term also presupposes some distance between two objects. Where this minimum distance is lacking, closeness fades into fusion and the term is no longer applicable.

Many animals have their so-called "individual distance" observable, e.g. in penguins nesting on a beach or in crows sitting on wires between telephone poles. Hediger, who coined this term and studied many aspects of this phenomenon, defined such individual distance as the animal's spatially advanced body boundary. If this boundary is transgressed the animal reacts as if it were attacked in its own body: it either flees or fights.

In human situations many spatial arrangements have been instituted and ritualized in order to indicate and safeguard distance. It is, in particular, concern with deference, respect, and awareness of social hierarchy that easily translates itself into concern with distance. Correct distance thus may find its way into diplomatic protocol.

As human relations became more varied and complex, it became necessary to handle distance flexibly and selectively. The methods for establishing distance, therefore, had to become more varied and subtle. Any social role and formula which indicates a difference vis-à-vis another person thus also came to signal and create distance. For example, the German use of the informal *"Sie"* (Thou) and of cumbersome titles reflects a social distance instrumentarium as do the dresses of different sexes and ages. The individual, in each case, turns into his distance shield what society offers him.

Psychological distance, however, reflects a boundary setting primarily relying on mental mechanisms. These seem relatively independent of defined social situations. The work of selective distancing replaces objective distance with subjective detachment. We manipulate our attention and image of the other person so as to prevent him from meaningfully touching us, from letting him get beneath our emotional skin. Through such mental operations we keep this person in a place from where he cannot threaten our boundaries. Instead of primarily relying on outer distance, we structure the field of relatedness so as to create *"inner distance."*

In our modern society such selective detachment is a matter of self-protection. We otherwise would be swamped with indigestible interpersonal stimuli. As a result, we are bound constantly to support and use all those conventions, formulas, and accepted hypocrisies by which society institutionalizes distance while, at the same time, it makes less abrasive our intercourse with each other. The philosopher Kant, out of such insight, defended the need for social etiquette and, hence, for sanctioned hypocrisy.

Yet selective distancing facilitates a further important function which is central to analysis: It enables us to see things objectively and in perspective. In order to clearly see and count the buildings of a city, writes Nietzsche, we must step out of its confines. We must observe it from the outside. Psychological—meaning "emotional"—distance allows us to see the other person *sine ira et studio*. Being uninvolved, we can afford to notice attitudes and behavior in the other person against which our emotionality would otherwise blind us.

The analytic situation, typically, places a premium on the analyst's interpersonal detachment. This detachment, in a sense, raises the analyst above the patient's private turmoils and entanglements. This detachment, again, is an element which Freud found prepared in the traditional role of doctor qua objective, functionally oriented expert. This detachment, rooted in his professional attitude, reflects and supports the differences in roles (as evidenced in the balance of sameness-difference), and it strengthens the elements of frustration and stabilization mentioned earlier. It guarantees, above all, relative neutrality and objectivity of observation. It ensures, on the part of the analyst, an attitude of scientific, reflective curiosity. This will then set the tone for the work to come. It will encourage and train the patient to subject his experiences, feelings, and attitudes to analytic self-scrutiny. It will help to unite analyst and patient in the mutual endeavor at clarifying what goes on between them, at finding their interpersonal truth.

But this detachment, crucial as it is, differs from the detachment required in other fields of scientific inquiry. For this detachment is, so to speak, constantly embroiled with the forces of personal involvement. Unlike the detachment of a mathematician contemplating the logic compatibility of arithmetic systems, analytic detachment has to concern itself with processes which diametrically seem to oppose it and, in a sense, which tend to negate it. "Unbounded" needs, wishes, and feelings are bound to be stirred up as the analysis evolves and, with its evolution, a certain regressive loosening in the patient gets under way. These processes indicate and foster interpersonal entanglement. They seem destined to draw the two participants into each other's emotional orbit. This detachment, therefore, is inseparable from a certain involvement. Both involvement and detachment constantly have to reassert *against* and reconcile *with* each other.

The distance, inbuilt into the analytic situation, is correspondingly balanced by closeness. This closeness, among other things, is evidenced in a characteristic "analytic intimacy," reflecting trust, a feeling of freedom and the ability and willingness to reveal ourselves as we are. This intimacy thus inextricably is tied to and colored by the distance as constantly reestablished in the analytic situation. This intimacy is perhaps the most important and precious outgrowth of the continuing reshuffling and reinstituting of the analytic boundary balance: that is, the ongoing reconciliation of closeness and distance.

It is the interplay and balance of forces, as revealed in these dichotomies, which further illuminate some central features of the psychoanalytic situation. With these features I shall now deal.

TRANSFERENCE

The first of these is *transference*.

Since Freud, we denote as transference the reenactment of attitudes and patterns of behavior (including thinking, feeling, wishes, etc.) which, in the given context of relatedness, are inappropriate. They tend to trap the individual in relationships that arrest growth and prevent flexible adaptation. When recognized as inappropriate, these patterns can be traced to their origins (i.e. the specific early constellation of relatedness) and eventually be corrected. Everyday life offers many examples of behavior and attitudes that are understandable in terms of the individual's formative experiences but have become obsolete vis-à-vis adult and "normal" situations and requirements. If such attitudes deviate strikingly from expected attitudes and norms and seem resistive to corrective insight, we tend to label them neurotic. In this sense, daily life abounds with transference phenomena.

A secretary, for example, began to take a special interest in an older woman in her office who suffered from mild emphysema. She related to the woman as if the lady were on the brink of collapse. Without being solicited, the secretary spent much time procuring drugs and medical advice. She insisted the older woman stop smoking. At the same time, she brought her flowers and other little gifts. The latter soon felt smothered by so much uncalled-for concern. Finally, she asked to be transferred from the office, which left the secretary desolate and indignant. It was only through a later analysis—during certain phases of which she acted similarly solicitous toward her analyst —that this secretary began to understand the transference aspects in her behavior toward the older woman: She had reenacted a relationship she once had with an aunt who took her mother's place after the latter had died in a car accident. This aunt was suffering from emphysema. The young girl in her distress had felt very ambivalent toward her aunt and her strong hostile impulses—meeting with much guilt in her—had become transformed into an excessive concern with her aunt's health.

Transferences are, therefore, not restricted to the analytic situation.

The analytic situation, however, has an impact on transference in two specific ways. It distributes, first, the weights of relatedness so that transference develops and deepens. Secondly, it counter-balances such pampering and reenactment of neurotic patterns by a setup that also highlights their present inappropriateness. The waves of transference are thus both raised and broken.

This dual function of the analytic situation results from the balanced interplay of forces as outlined above. In particular, it depends on a careful staking against each other of gratifying acceptance, regressive loosening, and intimacy on the one side, and of stability, frustration, and distance on the other.

RESISTANCE

The second of these features is *resistance*.

Resistance, as brought to light in the analytic situation is, like transference, ubiquitous in human relationships. Any deepening relationship at one point or another will require, at least in one partner, a reorientation and reshuffling of mental mechanisms and personality traits. Yet any change in familiar patterns and adaptations is bound to stir up anxiety and, hence, will be resisted—the more so as it threatens to upset the bases of our self-esteem and security. But, unlike analysis, such "resistance" in daily life seldom becomes a topic for relatively unimpassioned scrutiny. The nature of our personal entanglements with each other prevents us, as a rule, from both experiencing resistance qua resistance, i.e. as resistance to insight and self-change, as well as from seeing this resistance in its genetic perspective. Yet both would be necessary to overcome, to outgrow resistance more thoroughly.

Resistance thus denotes the tenacity and skill with which certain invested defensive patterns are upheld by the patient. In this sense, it marks the power and strategy which keeps entrenched specific transferences. And this power will have more impact the greater the patient's neurotic stakes, and the sharper his skills and intelligence wherewith to defend them.

The analytic situation now influences resistance similarly as it does transference: It brings, we might say, to a maximum its power and special quality, but it also provides the setup to break it. It fosters and, in a sense, makes clearly palpable its impact on both analyst and patient, but it then turns this impact into fuel for corrective self-understanding. It sets the stage for a struggle that, instead of becoming disruptive and leading to the defeat of either partner, turns into a loving struggle.

Again, in order that such "loving struggle" might ensue, the balance of forces, as earlier described, must expertly be brought into play.

THE ANALYST'S SPECIAL POSITION

The third feature, newly illuminated through this interplay of forces, is the *analyst's special position*.

This position I defined earlier as that of a medical expert required to deal with personal core problems. Having outlined the dialectic of the analytic dichotomies, I can now more clearly point out the quality and dimension of this task: the analyst is both chief participant and regulator to this interpersonal dialectic: *he is the guardian of the analytic balance*.

Many aspects of the classic analytic arrangement can now be seen as supporting the analyst in his dual role as both participant and chief analytic pacesetter. Some aspects, for example, indicate inequality between analyst and patient: e.g. the patient must say what comes to his mind, the analyst need not. But other aspects—e.g. the patient's exposure to many of the analyst's idiosyncrasies, revealed in the analytic transaction—encourage realistic knowledge about the analyst and, hence, confirmation. The analytic situation thus seems tailored to "hold" the analyst in his dual position. It supports him in being both frustrating and gratifying, detached and involved, different and like the patient. It provides, in other words, the needed structure and support for this duality.

The analytic situation, in brief, ingeniously appears devised to enable the doctor to become an analyst. But—and this is important—the analytic situation alone, as just outlined, will not suffice to achieve this end. Not every doctor who enters this situation can make it operational. More is required. To illuminate this "more," we must turn to the *wider analytic situation*.

THE WIDER ANALYTIC SITUATION

In order to better understand the analyst's special position, we must see the analytic situation in a wider framework. Essentially, we have to deal with three interdependent elements. To the analytic situation itself—the first and most important element—must be added two others: the analyst's non-analytic life-situation as the second element and, finally, his personal qualifications as the third. In a wider sense, all these elements form part of the analytic situation. They influence, in their interdependence, the five balances as well as the play of transference and resistance, as these were outlined above.

How will it affect his dual role as participant and chief analytic pacesetter? The analytic situation exposes the analyst to unusual temptations as well as frustrations. It is in the light of these temptations and frustrations that his non-analytic life becomes important. To master them, the analyst should be able to draw strength from this life. This life should have a balancing impact. Providing real satisfactions and self-esteem, it should make him less susceptible to the dangers of non-analytic entanglements with his patients. Successfully anchored in life, he can be expected not to overtax the analytic situation, that is, not to overstrain its inbuilt safety devices. His current life, giving him meaning, gratification, and self-worth, becomes an additional system of checks and balances enabling him to function as an analyst.

This system may be called the analyst's non-analytic network of relatedness. Defects and disturbances in this system inevitably will reverberate into the analytic situation itself. For example, the balance of sameness-difference may be greatly threatened when, because of insufficient anchorage in his wider professional world, the analyst cannot afford to be sufficiently different, meaning here: professional. Further: erotic hunger, unsatisfied in real life, may spill over into the analytic relationship and then endanger the balance of gratification-frustration. And so with all the other balances. From a certain point of interference on, the analytic process will be adversely affected.

The analyst's personal qualifications—the third element in the wider analytic situation—appear in a special light. These personal qualifications both sustain and complement the balancing impact of his non-analytic life, described above. They sustain this impact insofar as many of the same qualities which allow the analyst to function qua analyst will also enable him to live successfully. They complement this impact insofar as these qualifications may balance defects and disturbances in his non-analytic life. They can compensate for shortcomings in his non-analytic network of relatedness. They may keep functioning the analytic situation despite stressful extra-analytic vicissitudes.

These personal qualifications, we might say, allow him to keep "operational" the analytic situation even in the face of forces that tend to strain and/or dilute it. Instead of only relying on the reconciling and balancing forces inherent in the psychoanalytic setup, he will also rely on his own *"reconciling power."* This reconciling power will thus relieve the analytic situation from "holding" him and, instead, will make himself "hold" a greater share of the analytic situation.

This reconciling ability helps the analyst to check responsibly the interpersonal power he wields. It contributes to his relative freedom from "blind spots": he must be aware of motives and tendencies in himself which might interfere with the patient's analytic expansion and self-examination. This reconciling ability also reflects his being able to manage his counter-transference. His reconciling ability will thus guarantee that his attitude vis-à-vis the patient will remain intransitive, as Lewis B. Hill has defined the term. That is, the feelings and interests awakened in the analytic situation—such as fatigue, irritation, compassion, sexual curiosity, etc.—must be prevented from becoming burdening to the patient. The patient may feel the presence of these interests in the analyst, but they must not squelch, or unduly engage him. This becomes possible through the analyst's reconciling ability which permits immediate emotional reactivity and, at the same time, its subtle buffering and modulation. It is, above all, this reconciling ability which the personal training analysis seeks to foster.

Such reconciling ability will always, for each person, remain a matter of degree. It is an ideal attitude to be striven for but never fully realized. Each person's powers at reconciliation, in other words, are limited. These powers are limited by the situation in which he may find himself —compare this with what was said earlier about the analyst's non-analytic life—and by the time of his life. And he may, further, be better at reconciling certain tendencies than others.

Still, there seem to be moments when this reconciling ability seems to shine forth purest. Then it can be compared to certain heights of artistic achievement where long years of struggle and of striving for perfection suddenly seem to culminate in a miraculous effortlessness. Such effortless near-perfection Kleist, the German playwright and novelist, has depicted in his essay on the marionette theater. The hard struggle with the material, the painstaking learning of technique then seem to translate themselves into genuine artistry.

Freud has given a name to that state in which the analyst's reconciling ability reveals itself most strikingly. This state he called "free floating attentiveness." It indicates an optimal tuning to the unconscious streams emanating from the patient. At the same time, it indicates their control through critical awareness. This state, thus, reflects maximal participation and intransitivity; a sensitive, receptive relaxation and sharpest concentration. It is that state in the analyst that optimally seems to match and sustain the analytic intimacy, earlier described, a form of relatedness which, above all, reflects trust and freedom to reveal ourselves. At this point a new light falls on the man who created the analytic situation. We get a glimpse of what must have been Freud's reconciling power, its intensity and special quality.

This power, I believe, most clearly becomes transparent in the story of Oedipus, whose name, since Freud, became a pivotal term in analytic thinking. The legend of Oedipus has many implications. Among the better known aspects associated with the Oedipus complex are those that are illuminated through analytic theory and practice. Oedipus' name thus was tied to a drama of relatedness inflicted upon each individual and having its climax around the age of four and five: The child, at these developmental crossroads, while incestuously close to the parent of opposite sex, turns into a feared and hated rival of his parent of the same sex. I shall later deal with this aspect of the Oedipal situation.

In the light of my present considerations, another aspect of the myth stands out: Oedipus' radical curiosity. This curiosity directs Oedipus to understand what, once understood, may break him. Oedipus' attitude and fate thus become synonymous with a search for truth which, instead of liberating us, may turn out to be more than we can bear. This truth, characteristically, concerns our basic relatedness. It has to do with the emotional stakes we have in the persons who are closest to us.

It is Oedipus' very entanglement with and closeness to his parents that cause him to be blind in an area where the blind Tereisias, a relatively unentangled and distant observer, is seeing. Yet Oedipus, in the attempt to see himself fully in this area of personal importance, ends up by blinding himself. He cannot endure the sight of what he enquired to see. In pitting his searching curiosity against his lifelines of relatedness—the nature of his tie with his parents; what these did to him and he to them—he tragically overreaches himself.

In order to sustain such radical curiosity, a special quality seems required. I have called it "related loneliness."

It signifies, in the broadest sense, the capacity to be deeply and meaningfully invested in persons and ideas but, at the same time, to be ready to investigate the sources of this investment and to live without illusions. It is a quality which may be called the primary reconciling power: that power which, in a sense, anchors and holds together all the forces mentioned earlier. And it seems to be this quality which thus foremostly qualifies an analyst to be the guardian of the analytic balance. We know that it was just this power which Freud himself revealed in many aspects of his life and work.

THE PATIENT'S SPECIAL POSITION

The fourth feature is the *patient's special position*.

This position I defined earlier as complementing and sustaining that of the physician. The patient, suffering and having problems, contracts for professional help. His problems are personal core problems. In order to let these reveal themselves he, like the doctor, must actively participate in the dialectic of the analytic dichotomies. He is not the guardian of the analytic balance, but his cooperation is as important as that of the doctor.

Many aspects of the classic analytic setup can now be seen as insuring and supporting the patient's cooperation as much as they support the physician. Given this setup, the patient, in many respects, knows what to expect. The very factors that professionalize the doctor's position, that put a premium on an understanding objectivity which is non-moralizing, accepting and problem-oriented, make for a reliability and reassurance rarely found in life. Thus, just as the analytic situation can be seen as tailored to "hold" the analyst, to back him in his dual position (as participant and chief analytic pacesetter), it must be viewed as "holding" the patient also, as strengthening his role as a responsible partner to the analytic balance. We may compare the analytic situation to an institution such as a school which, through its very presence and structure, supports the child in his role as a learner.

But just as the school is not enough to make the child come and learn, so is the analytic situation useless unless a patient fills it. The support he receives through the analytic situation will not suffice.

Just as was the case with the analyst's special position, that of the patient now must be seen in a wider framework. Also, the patient's role qua patient must be viewed as being supported by two further systems: his life-situation outside the analytic hours and his personal qualifications and contributions. These systems, again, are interdependent and, in a sense, reflect different aspects of the total situation.

This patient, though legitimately becoming more dependent on the analyst than the latter may become on him, still needs a life-situation which supports him. A certain order and stability in this life-situation is desirable. His professional life and his network of non-analytic relatedness to a degree must "hold" him in the analytic situation, supplementing the "holding features" of the analytic situation itself. A base of "real" satisfactions and self-esteem, anchored extra-analytically, must make bearable the temptations and frustrations awaiting the patient in analysis.

The patient's personal qualifications—the third relevant system—must again be seen as both sustaining and complementing this second system. These personal qualifications of the patient make possible his reasonably successful anchorage outside the analytic situation and also may compensate for disturbances in his life. All together, they enable him to maintain, on his part, the analytic situation. They reflect on his ability to participate *responsibly* in the psychoanalytic partnership.

Many aspects of his responsibility seem obvious: he must learn the rules of the analytic game and must abide by these rules. He must regularly pay the arranged fee, etc. In this sense, he must do what is required of any partner in a business transaction. He must take upon him his part of the bargain. Thus, he ensures, on his part, that transferences can deeply unfold and so yield maximal benefit in terms of meaningful, corrective insight. He ensures, further, that the resistance which is bound to come will finally yield to an understanding of its repetitive, defensive, and presently inappropriate nature, and so he helps to turn the analysis into a loving struggle that engenders between doctor and patient an ever deepening respect and openness with each other.

Clearly, the patient needs the abilities and skills at relating. The patient must be able to use a relationship which is confined to four or five weekly sessions. He must be able to store, carry around, and digest what has transpired during these sessions without letting it greatly upset his everyday life. In a sense, he must slip at command into states of regressive loosening and dependence, that is, he must control and keep reversible these states. He must be able to bear inner tensions without immediately acting on them. This, in turn, requires him to be able to delay, "brake," and modulate impulses. He must, to a degree, be constantly aware of what part of his inner life, of his feelings, fantasies, expectations belongs primarily to the analytic situation and what part has chiefly to do with his network of extra-analytic relatedness—despite the fact that the two realms continually interact. He must have what has come to be known as a strong observing and cooperating ego.

And all this he must have in addition to, or in spite of, the personal problems that caused him to seek analytic treatment. No wonder that Freud himself considered only a small group of people suitable for psychoanalysis.

These abilities and skills of the patient can thus—and this seems important—be seen as matching what I described as the analyst's reconciling power. In other words, that which can be described as a strong, observing, and cooperating ego (the ability to keep regression reversible, to maintain boundaries while being flexibly adapted, etc.) in the patient, seems to reflect an ability to reconcile that corresponds to a similar state in the analyst. This ability will be developed, strengthened and supported through the ongoing analysis, but a good deal of it must be there in the first place. It is then through this matching of corresponding abilities and attitudes in the patient and analyst that the analytic situation becomes the analytic process, that it turns into a working relationship.

To summarize:

The analytic situation grew out of the doctor-patient relationship as this developed in our Western world. It thus reflects important elements of its social climate and structure. In particular, it brings a spirit of rationality to bear on a relationship between two people. Freud's genius then forced into a confrontation this rationality with the realm of personal irrationality: with drives, dreams, the unconscious, our emotional lifelines. This he did by staking out an experimental setup—the analytic situation—that defined and channeled the contributions of each partner. These contributions thus could support and propel onward a characteristic interpersonal dialectic as revealed in the balance of analytic dichotomies. Within this setup a unique process of understanding participation could unfold. The physician's own feelings and actions could, to an uncommon degree, be made the object of reflection and be used as indicators for what went on in the patient. Within this setup, therefore, the dynamic play of transference and resistance could evolve and could be studied. It is this process which since Freud has come to be viewed as the axis of psychoanalytic theory and practice.

II
PSYCHOANALYSIS AND THE
PSYCHOTIC PATIENT

About half a century has passed since Freud put his seminal ideas before the scientific world. These ideas have since become incorporated into existing ideologies. They have become popularized and diluted. In one way or another they have taken hold of our imagination, of the way we think about ourselves and others. They have—more or less quietly—revolutionized many educational practices and social mores, such as sexual instruction, attitudes toward masturbation, toilet training, etc. These ideas, in other words, have proven powerful in transforming our social matrix, that is, the institutions, norms, and expectations which shape our lives.

In these same fifty years many other forces left their imprint on this social matrix. A rapidly expanding population, the abundance of consumer goods and leisure, the accelerating industrial revolution, the science of the atomic age and the modern technology of communication, among other factors have, in a complex interplay, influenced man's social environment. And these forces have interacted with the ideas which sprang from psychoanalysis.

Today we notice many an outgrowth of this interaction: psychoanalysis, at least in the United States, has become powerfully institutionalized. It has found itself backed and needed by a growing sophisticated, interpersonally-minded middle class. A social outcast at the time of Freud, psychoanalysis now presents itself proud and respectable. Along with this rise in status, the panorama of analyzable symptomatology imperceptibly seemed to change. The classic psychoneuroses of Freud's time, many observers noted, appeared to recede, while psychosomatic diseases and character problems became prominent. Many individual analyses grew longer. At the same time, psychoanalytic viewpoints found their way into other therapeutic approaches. Analytic group therapy began to flourish. The family became a focus for investigation and treatment along analytic lines. Psychoanalysis, further, fertilized comparative anthropology, opening transcultural perspectives and putting into a new light many of our own ways to feel and think. A bridge was finally built to the field of instinct and learning, as revealed through animal psychology. The child's early years of life—the period when man is still most animal and least human—became the fascinating meeting place for theories and insights of how man compares to his animal ancestors.

All these developments, we must remember, stemmed from the analytic situation. But all these developments, also, were bound to affect, in turn, the analytic situation—this unique amalgamate of social circumstance and Freud's personal contribution, this home base of relatedness wherein analytic theory and practice are rooted.

How then—and that is the central question—appears this home base in the light of the developments it made possible?

It is with this question in mind that I now want to turn to one development not yet mentioned. It is that development to which I, through my own work and experience, became most closely exposed. That is the study and psychotherapy of so-called psychotic and borderline people. Like the developments outlined above, this study and psychotherapy is unthinkable without Freud's pioneering efforts. But even more than the other developments, it forces us to reexamine the psychoanalytic situation itself. Along with such reexamination, it both challenges and promises to deepen our understanding of the bases of relatedness.

THE CONCEPT OF THE PSYCHOTIC PATIENT

Psychotic people in our Western culture came to be viewed and treated as medical patients. But though this view and practice is upheld by tradition and common expectation, it is contradicted by certain facts. It is even doubtful whether the psychotic patient can, in a meaningful sense, be called a patient at all.

The term "patient" evolved in the context of occidental medicine. It denotes a person who suffers (in Latin: *patiens*), and who, as a rule, acknowledges such suffering and seeks competent medical help to alleviate it. There may be cases when he is unable to seek such help himself. He may, for example, be made unconscious by an accident, but then his basic agreement to being treated can sensibly be assumed.

The concept "patient" thus is related to that of the doctor (or therapist) who, actually or potentially, recognizes the patient's suffering and attempts its remedy. Both concepts—that of patient and of doctor—in a characteristic balance require each other in order to become meaningful. The analytic situation, we saw, heralded a shift in such balance. It caused a certain transformation in the positions of both doctor and patient.

The neurotic patient who classically fitted the analytic situation in many respects ceased to be a medical patient in the traditional sense of the word. But in certain respects it still made sense to view and treat him in the framework of traditional medicine. This patient, even when only mimicking the symptoms of bodily ill patients, subjectively often suffered from these symptoms. He was, to some degree at least, aware of having problems. He could, therefore, concede to become a patient of sorts. Hence he could, out of his own will, participate in a doctor-patient alliance—the psychoanalytic situation which, though deviating from the traditional doctor-patient relationship, still bore many of its imprints.

The ordinary psychotic patient, in contrast, hardly fits even such an attenuated medical situation. He fulfills few or none of the last mentioned conditions. Others may consider him odd, confused, out of touch with reality, lonely, and helpless. But he himself frequently does not care or does not want to agree to such views. He often denies or is unaware he suffers. It often seems senseless to talk to him in terms of his problems. Such talk to him would appear inappropriate or plainly meaningless. He is unwilling or unable to recognize himself as a patient. He, implicitly or explicitly, flaunts those agreements and conventions which make operational a doctor-patient relationship. Having sidestepped and invalidated the accepted modes and systems for the validation of meaning he can, in the end, only submit to the superior power of those who declare him insane.

Who wields this power which casts him into the role of medical patient—despite his manifest unwillingness and/or inability to fill this role?

It rests, essentially, with the legal authorities, e.g. law-making bodies, courts—*and* with the medical profession. Thomas Szasz has described this situation. While the legal authorities more overtly apply this power (by decreeing, in given cases, insanity and ordering commitment) the medical profession uses it more covertly. This profession, with society's sanction, allocates the labels "health" and "illness" to certain groups of people. Given its general prestige, it thus channels into certain directions our views and expectations about the people so labeled. In particular it prepares the ground for viewing as patients those labeled as ill. These need not necessarily become actual patients, that is, be subjected to common forms of medical treatment. The believers in Christian Science, for example, can dare to disagree with the views of the medical profession and also, to a degree, avoid established forms of treatment. But such resistance to current medical opinion will become either less effective or impossible when there is no alternative ideology and no backing by others. But just this, as a rule, is the plight of the psychotic person. Having greatly invalidated the prevailing system of communication and reference, he is at a loss when it comes to asserting his rights within this system. He may refuse to accept the label "illness" or insanity which has been assigned to him. But, unable to take an effective stand against such assignment, he must submit to being treated as if he were ill. His situation is not unlike that of the Jews under Hitler who, once designated as Jews, had, being powerless, to suffer the consequences of such designation. They had to enter the concentration camps, just as mental patients are transported to so-called mental hospitals. (It is, we must remember, only a result of relative recent developments that most mental hospitals have become more like hopsitals in the ordinary, that is medical, sense of the word. Earlier they were, as Kraepelin among others has shown, in many respects closer to concentration camps than to hospitals.)

Notwithstanding the humanitarian climate of many modern mental hospitals, their inmates are captives to what those in power consider right for them. Yet this has greatly varied, depending on the geographic and historic situation and depending, foremostly, on what were considered the causes of the psychotic's predicament.

It became fateful for European psychiatry that these causes were, in the final analysis, believed to be material. So-called mental symptoms (such as disorders of speech, peculiar behavior, etc.) came to be equated with physical symptoms. There were strong reasons to uphold such a view: Progressive Paresis, a mental disease with flamboyant symptoms, was recognized to be due to syphilis of the nervous system. Other conditions of minor importance, such as Alzheimer's disease, could be traced to degenerative processes in the brain. Daily observation showed many drugs and so-called organic treatments (insulin, electroshock, etc.) as affecting psychotic symptoms in one way or the other. This evidence confirmed the so-called organic orientation of psychiatrists. And this organic orientation, in conjunction with psychiatrists' powers as medical experts, essentially led to the paradoxical situation stated above: That persons blatantly disqualifying as medical patients were, nonetheless, turned into such patients. As a result, mental patients were viewed and treated as patients suffering from physical ailments. They were housed in so-called hospitals that were modeled after hospitals for organically ill people. They were expected to share the privileges and duties which society bestows on its sick members—such as a lessened responsibility in certain areas, a certain right to be indulged, etc. And, most important, they were made to accept treatment from those persons whom society, with great expenditure of cost and effort, trains to take care of its sick individuals, that is, the doctors and the nursing personnel.

However, various developments during the last decades have tended to question and erode the organic orientation vis-à-vis the psychoses, and have cast into doubt the psychotic's status qua patient.

The one development is, in a sense, a lack of development: The two largest and most important groups of so-called psychoses—schizophrenia and the manic-depressive group—have not yet revealed their organic genesis as postulated by Griesinger, Kraepelin, Jaspers, and many others. There are hints that such organic bases may exist after all—these coming chiefly from various biochemical studies. But these hints seem overshadowed by the failure to nail down, until now, specific causes and factors—despite numerous efforts in all parts of the world. At the same time, central assumptions of the organic orientation have been questioned or invalidated for a number of reasons.

Some of the strongest reasons emerged out of the study of identical (or monozygotic) twins. It had been assumed until fairly recently that if one identical twin developed schizophrenia, the other twin most likely would do the same. The chances for this to happen were thought to be 80 to 90 percent. Recent careful investigations—by such authors as Tienari and Kringlen—have challenged this assumption. It is now held that the identical co-twin has no more than a 20 to 40 percent chance of becoming schizophrenic. This chance is still higher than that of non-identical co-twins or of ordinary siblings—while these siblings, in turn, have a higher chance than the average population (where less than one out of a hundred persons can expect to become labeled as schizophrenic). Still, these findings have weakened the case for the organic orientation which emphasized hereditary factors in schizophrenia.

As a result of such developments, the psychoses came into the twilight of controversy. The organic orientation had to compete with the functional point of view. Thus, while the organic orientation places the weight of theoretic relevance on material causes, including hereditary factors, the functional view places this weight, in one way or the other, on the individual's transactions with his important human environment. In this view the psychoses denote transactions which, in a sense, misfired.

At present these two views seem to have different geographic strongholds. The organic orientation is still prevalent in Europe, South America, Russia, and other parts of the world. The functional view is chiefly upheld in the United States.

When we try to weigh the merits of the organic versus the functional orientation, we must consider that, first of all, there can never be a question of taking a stand on a line that absolutely divides the organic and functional orientations. Human development is *always* determined by the interplay of biologic, constitutional factors on the one side and empirical vicissitudes on the other. The problem, therefore, is not when to take a stand but how to conceptualize this interplay. This conceptual problem is far from being resolved. Secondly, it can only be a question of *giving more or less weight* either to organic or functional (including psychodynamic) considerations—and not of excluding the one or the other. But it is exactly this giving more or less weight to either one or the other kind of considerations that so far has crucially shaped and entrenched attitudes toward the psychoses. This giving more or less weight has tended to effect a *Quellenscheidung* (a "parting of minds"): it reflected and—through circular reinforcement—confirmed a primary partiality in the selection of competing data. The more numerous the data in the field the more fateful such primary partiality will become. It will powerfully channel into certain directions our attentions and expectations. It will, in a sense, fixate the focus of our searching telescope, permitting us to take in certain facts and evidences while excluding others.

The disagreement between the above described organic and functional orientations thus, to a good deal, seems to be anchored in differently entrenched primary partialities. And these primary partialities essentially reflect the weight which is accorded interpersonal transactions. These partialities decide about how and how far interpersonal transactions are allowed to become sources of relevant data. While the organic point of view considers these transactions somewhat irrelevant, the functional orientation considers them essential.

How then could such sensitivity develop in the United States, in contrast to Europe and other parts of the world? In order to answer this question I must, first, return to earlier reflections about the analytic situation.

This situation, we saw, made possible a deepened sensitivity to interpersonal transactions. It was this situation which permitted interpersonal arguments to convince us. It tied, uniquely and thoroughly, insight to new life experience. Does this situation, therefore, hold the key also to that sensitivity which makes accessible psychotic experiences? Will it allow us to accept these experiences into our own cosmos of experience, to consider them as something which we could experience ourselves? Could it become the base for a relatedness which imaginatively spans the gap between the healthy and so-called psychotic world, that allows us to say, when confronted with the psychotic: this could have happened to me?

Can the analytic situation, therefore, accommodate also the psychotic and borderline patient? What openings does it offer these kinds of patients?

The answer, at first reflection, is clear: hardly any! In weighing the psychotic's fitness for the analytic situation, we must remember what was said earlier about the analysand's special position: this analytic patient, in order to become a responsible partner to the analytic alliance, must fulfill important requirements. His cooperative and observing ego must be well developed. He must have a reconciling power that can dovetail with that of the analyst's.

Psychotic patients fail blatantly in these respects. These patients, we saw, usually refuse to consider themselves as sick. They deny needing help and having problems. They thus refuse to deal "sensibly" with the doctor. They are, as a result, unable or unwilling to attend regular analytic sessions and to make use of the analytic moratorium. They are shakily rooted in reality. Their observing and cooperating ego is weak. They cannot abide by the rules of the analytic game. They are, at best, inept and forced partners in it. They make a mockery out of it and negate it from the beginning.

Freud, therefore, expressly denied these patients the access to the analytic situation as he had set it up. He excluded them from the group of people for whom he considered the analytic method suitable. Specifically he viewed them as unfit to endure and develop that kind of transference which is the springboard for insightful change. Their narcissistic self-absorption prevented, he found, any meaningful analytic relatedness.[1]

But—and this is important—the matter did not end there for the psychotic patients. These psychotic patients, though expressly excluded from the analytic situation, were bound nonetheless to feel its impact. The change of the scientific and interpersonal climate, triggered by the spread of analytic insights, could not but affect them also. And Freud,

---

[1] Karl Abraham, however, like other early followers of Freud, did not (always) share this opinion. He wrote in 1911, referring to a case of so-called simple schizophrenia: "The associative activity of these patients proceeds so far along organized paths that a psychoanalysis can be carried out with them just as well as with a psychoneurotic. Indeed, the work is even facilitated in such patients on account of the abolition of many inhibitions."

while explicitly doubting their analyzability, himself opened a back door for them. He initiated a development which, sooner or later, was destined to turn these patients into a therapeutic problem and challenge.

The reason for this development lies chiefly in certain theoretic formulations which immediately derive from analytic insights, that is, insights growing out of the analytic situation. These insights are tied to Freud's characteristic view of neurotic mechanisms. Freud made us see these neurotic mechanisms—such as repression, reaction-formation, isolation, obsessive undoing, etc.—as modes of psychic functioning which ensure momentary psychic security and stability at the expense of arrested experience, clear-sightedness, and growth.

Such a view of defense mechanisms differentiates between various degrees and manners by which security may be bought at the price of personal restriction. This bargain may seem extremely costly for a given individual: a shadowy security may have to be paid for with excessive disorientation and arrest. Certain security operations—such as denial and projection—then indicate an unusual disregard for and distortion of reality. In these instances urgent affective and security needs almost seem to annihilate any reality testing. These patients, accordingly, must appear as most difficult to reach and understand by more common approaches and modes of conduct.

But—and this is essential—such a view does not make these patients appear as categorically unreachable and un-understandable. There is, in this view, no difference in principle between neurotic and psychotic defense mechanisms. There are only different degrees of a self-defeating psychic bargain and, hence, of restriction and warped growth. No "abyss of abnormality" is placed between psychotics and more normal people. Psychotics are not, on account of their "madness," separated from the rest of mankind by a barrier of strangeness and otherness. They are seen as having gone a long way in destroying their bridges of relatedness. They appear entrapped in uncommon loneliness and confusion. Yet also they are viewed as suffering from a predicament that, given similar vicissitudes of early relatedness, could befall anybody. Neurotic and psychotic mechanisms, thus viewed, reflect an unbroken continuum of possible human modalities. Such a view, accordingly, must powerfully invalidate the central assumption of the organic orientation.

Analytic insights thus can transcend the analytic situation and illuminate psychotic experiences. And Freud himself gave the first practical lessons of such branching out of analytic insights beyond neurosis and the analytic situation proper. In a number of his writings he dealt with problems of the psychotic. And most importantly: He wrote his analysis of the case of Schreber, a high-ranking German judge, who had written an autobiographical account of his paranoid experiences. Today we may see in a different light than Freud did various aspects of Schreber's pathology. Still, this monograph remains a classic and pioneering work. The concept of defense mechanisms, Freud demonstrated, can accommodate what, since Kraepelin, has come to be seen as a central manifestation of schizophrenia: It can accommodate the paranoid condition. This paranoid condition Freud now depicted as the manifestation and result of mainly one mechanism called projection. He showed this projection to be an extreme but characteristic manipulation and distortion of one's meaningful interpersonal reality—including one's own and the other person's feelings, perceptions, and motives—carried out in the service of salvaging some sense of security and self-worth.

Thus, while not analyzing a Schreber in person, Freud prepared the ground that others like Schreber might therapeutically be met with deepened understanding. Inevitably, he paved the way for a development which on a new plane would tend to reconcile analytic insights and the psychotherapy of psychotic patients. This development, we know, has since come about, and the United States has become its center.

In the United States the expanding analytic insights found a social context in which an eager orientation to change and an uncommon social mobility prevailed, as well as distrust vis-à-vis authoritarian attitudes. These social forces, in conjunction with the more general tendencies mentioned above—such as industrialization, overabundance of goods, increase in population—made possible a different over-all approach to psychotic patients that was (and still is) typical of the European continent. For these forces tended either to erode or eliminate that intermeshing network of status considerations, authoritarianism, and classifying theory which, particularly in Germany, had entrenched the psychiatrist as distant observer. In Europe this distant observer, if himself reasonably secure, could often afford to become a benevolent patriarch. But only with great difficulty could he—because of the social context which both limited and supported him—become what Sullivan, one of the most seminal thinkers in American psychiatry, has called "the participant observer." This term denotes a therapist who, in contrast to the distant observer, proceeds from the assumption that mental illness is the natural, inevitable response to the events of the lifetime, past and present. He further dares to recognize his own experiences, actual or potential, in the patients with whom he deals, without excluding *a priori* certain groups of people.

Characteristically, Sullivan's concept of the participant observer grew out of his work with schizophrenic patients—the main group of patients so far excluded from the validation and examination of mutually shared experience in the doctor-patient relationship. He thus strategically changed the interpersonal status of these patients. Out of objects of detached symptom searching along organic lines he let them become partners to a special relatedness. Therein each person's interpersonal contributions became meaningful to both partners. The psychiatrist's position as participant observer, in other words, was both strengthened by, and made dependent upon, the concomitant breakdown of that barrier of otherness behind which the psychotic patient traditionally had been placed.

As a result, psychotherapy of psychotic and borderline

patients has been and is being practiced in many places of the United States. This practice has spread in recent years to Europe, and has become similar in its development to the American experience.

A NEW DICHOTOMY REVEALED

Thus, it is the psychotic patient who most clearly came to reveal the analytic situation as both necessary and in need of change. In order to understand and therapeutically approach this patient at all, the analytic situation had first to be developed. It had to become the base from which further steps could be made. But it must also be realized that to really understand and approach this patient, we must face the limits of this situation. This patient, in other words, now challenges us to explore and create the basis for a new situation, one which may or may not be called analytic, but one which *is right for him.*

This challenge, implicitly or explicitly, pervades present day approaches to psychotic and borderline patients. Characteristically, two central but opposing tendencies are reflected in these approaches. On the one side we notice a tendency to keep such approaches as clearly "analytic" as possible. This tendency reflects attempts to safeguard those aspects of the analytic situation which embody and facilitate what might be called the analyst's analysis-mindedness. This includes his conscientious scrutiny of what happens in the relationship, of what he does himself and why he does it. Various ways have been found to alleviate this task of fitting the psychotic and borderline patient into a psychoanalytic framework. So-called analytic psychotherapy (allegedly permissible for psychotic and borderline patients) *has been distinguished from classical analysis.* Also, a kind of mental guidebook has been developed which allows one to modify the analytic procedure under certain circumstances. This guidebook delineates some sort of model concept of the ideal goal, course, and technique of psychoanalysis. Psychotic patients, their special problems and liabilities, are seen as constituting special circumstances which require changes in this model concept. But these changes then must be clearly justifiable in each instance. They have to be treated as special parameters (Eissler), the pros and cons of which have to be carefully weighed.[2]

This general tendency, understandably, is emphasized by analysts whose training and background have been more classically analytic. They seem closer than others to Freud's original work and heritage. Hence, they tend to build further on the analytic situation as created by him. That is, they tend to enlarge and, if necessary, modify this situation, rather than risk its radical overthrow.

But this seems to characterize the proponents of the other main tendency as revealed in their dealings with psychotic patients. Many of these authors impatiently seem to discard the value of parameters and methodic subtleties. They emphasize, instead, the spontaneous clicking of needs of therapist and patient. Instead of focusing on the rationality of the analytic procedure, they stress the "personal encounter," the "I-Thou" relationship (Buber), the mutual commitment to growth. This has a paradoxical aspect: While they point to the basic humanity of all patients, be they neurotic or psychotic, they see psychotic and more normal analytic patients as differing so radically that they seek no common methodologic meeting ground. Therefore, these authors consider it futile to accommodate psychotic patients in the classic analytic situation.[3] Doing

[2] R. S. Wallerstein, while reviewing the current state of psychotherapy, has dealt with this issue in a much more thorough fashion than would fit the intent and scope of this essay. (Robert S. Wallerstein, "The Current State of Psychotherapy: Theory, Practice, Research." *J. Am. Psychoanal. Assn., 14:* 183–225, 1966.)

[3] Malcolm L. Hayward expresses a central tenet of this group when he states: "Freud said there is no transference in schizophrenia. I say that in the schizophrenic there is nothing but transference, and that is why we get so fouled up. *What you are trying to do is to reach a real experience*" (*Psychotherapy*

so, they argue, would channel our actions and preoccupations in a direction that leads us far away from what is essential in the relationship. It would interfere with or even kill that personal spontaneous interaction which alone counts.

Only this personal interaction—such is the reasoning—can bring about a durable and truly therapeutic reintegration of the patient's personality. Specific and limited analytic insights may help with these psychotic patients, but the main therapeutic accent must be placed elsewhere. In focusing on spontaneous interaction and mutual growth these authors, inevitably, tend to devalue technical considerations.

It is difficult to find a label for this second group. One reason is semantic: The analytic terminology, as developed by Freud and his followers has, at least in the United States, pervaded psychiatry and public life. Thus it offers itself to describe phenomena and transactions even when these grossly deviate from or negate the analytic situation. Therefore, for lack of a better over-all term, I shall call the second tendency "existential." It is, I believe, best represented by certain "existential psychotherapists." Some of these therapists most clearly seem to delineate the spontaneous and growth-producing encounter, from a more technical, analytic approach.

---

of Chronic Schizophrenic Patients, ed. Carl W. Whitaker. Boston: Little, Brown & Co., 1958, p. 158.)

In the United States such authors as Whitaker, Malone, Warkentin, and possibly Rosen, all experienced in the psychotherapy of chronic schizophrenic patients, could be seen as also belonging to this group. On the European continent I think of such therapists as Boss, Elrod, Siirala, Macnab, and possibly Laing. Recently several of these authors seem to have favored the family therapy of schizophrenia (particularly Whitaker and Warkentin), while Macnab from the start has concentrated on a group approach. Regarding the problematical situation of existential psychotherapy in Europe, see my article "Existentialism Meets Psychotherapy," wherein I examine Heidegger's overriding influence on this type of psychotherapy.

Let me, with these opposing tendencies in mind, turn back to the original components of the analytic situation. These were, first, the technical orientation that cast the physician in the role of a technical expert; and second, the healing orientation that emphasized the physician's charisma and personality. While the technical orientation was shown to denote clarity, distance, and delineation of a realm of competency, the healing orientation indicated elusiveness, emotional entanglement, and generality of approach. Freud then welded together and reconciled these two components. As a result he created the analytic situation. This analytic situation, in turn, helped to transform the social climate of our Western world. It has set in motion forces which tended to transcend and challenge it. And in the wake of such development, it has made the so-called psychotic and borderline patient into the cause of a new *Quellenscheidung*.

For we now realize that this "sicker" psychotic patient has, on a higher, more intricate and socially advanced level, brought into the open a similar dichotomy that was reflected in the doctor-patient relationship before Freud created the analytic situation. At that time it was the dichotomy of "technical versus healing orientation." This pre-analytic dichotomy now has given way to the post-analytic one of "analytic versus existential approach."

How can we attempt such reconciliation? What can the new situation be like? In trying to answer these questions let me take stock of what evolved in the last chapter.

The psychotic patient, we found, became a patient *contre coeur*. Historical developments, partly described above, caused two people to meet with each other—often for long periods of time: one the doctor, trained in the skills of the medical profession, heir to its attitudes and ethics; the other, the so-called psychotic patient, not really a patient but often society's outcast, trying to make the best of his ill-fitting patient role. It is this meeting of two people, strangely assorted, which became the basis for the present psychotherapy of the psychoses.

Seen from this angle, the two opposing approaches earlier described—the analytic and the existential—reflect attempts to cope with a unique, unforeseen situation. A relatedness seems required for which no guidelines and no conventional models easily offer themselves. And the two above approaches thus appear as those models, chosen from the available reservoir of frameworks of relatedness, which seem to come closest to what is required and what meaningfully can be conceptualized.

I shall examine a further model. This model has often been implied or mentioned. But it has seldom, as to its implication for the psychotherapy in question, been systematically explored. That model is the *relationship between mother and child.*

Various developments came together which suggested its pivotal role for the psychotherapy of psychosis. On the one side, several scientific disciplines—such as comparative anthropology, developmental psychology, sociology, ecology, and, in particular, the psychoanalytic study of ego-development—converged on the early mother-child relationship. As a result this relationship came to be viewed as that constitutive, fateful event in each person's life which decides our later sanity or insanity, our arrest or growth, our despair or hopeful acceptance of life. In order that true healing, growth, and integration might take place, some of the constitutive elements of the mother-child relationship must, in some way or the other, come into play also in therapy. On the other side, this therapeutic relationship, in its actual practice, in numerous ways suggested comparisons with the tie which exists between mother and child. As many of these psychotic patients did talk only little or not at all, much of the relationship had to unfold pre- and para-verbally. It had to rely on what has been termed the therapist's silent "holding" of the patient, on his immediate emphatic contact, on a sharing and soothing of the patient's anxieties, etc.—just as a mother is supposed to deal with her child, who cannot yet speak. While, in other words, the ordinary skills of the physician—diagnostic acumen, the use of words for differentiating and analyzing the problems of living, etc.—seemed to lose their value in this relationship, the ordinary skills of the mother, elusive as these may be, appeared to ascend in importance.

How then, can we examine this model?

Numerous ways are possible. I have decided on the following procedures: I shall first reflect on those features of early human development which are most fatefully affected by the mother-child relationship. This requires an outline of what I consider essential aspects of human individuation and, interdependent with this, acculturation. Second, I shall bring these aspects into clearer light by comparing the mother-child relationship with the analytic situation: I shall explore the former relationship in terms of the interplay of the positions and contributions of mother and child just as I explored the analytic situation in terms of the contributions of analyst and patient. I shall investigate the mother-child relationship chiefly in the light of the five above-mentioned dichotomies. Then, based on this investigation, I shall offer certain general formulations about the nature and dynamics of this relationship. Equipped with these formulations, I shall finally consider the problem of schizophrenia—from an etiologic as well as from a psychotherapeutic angle.

In following the procedure here outlined, I shall, in the next chapter, deal with those aspects of human individuation and development which are most crucial for an understanding of the child's early relations.

III

THE DAWN OF KNOWING
INDIVIDUATION

THE NUCLEAR EGO

Human individuation and acculturation build on man's
capacity to relate complexly to himself and to his world.
One concept, above everything, has illuminated this capacity: The concept of the ego. This concept is a creation of Freud. He put it before the scientific world in
1923 when he presented his structural model of man's
psychic apparatus.

Freud had mentioned the ego in his publications before
1923. He spoke of ego drives which he conceived as opposing and complementing sexual drives. In 1923, however,
he defined the ego anew. He distinguished the ego from
several other psychic agencies. On the one side, he delineated the ego against the id, that part in us which propels
us toward unrestrained drive discharge and pleasure; on
the other side, he separated it from the superego, commonly identified with our conscience. This superego fulfills a stabilizing, steering role. Like the id, the superego
operates largely in the unconscious. It can be compared
to an inner gyroscope which guides us in the light of
deeply internalized values: Those ethical or religious convictions which we learned so early that we have become
unaware of how we learned them. We feel their impact
most strongly through the guilt and pain we experience
in their violation.

Id, ego, and superego can be seen as representing complex systems within our psyche. All three are important
and powerful. Still, the ego, from the perspective adopted

in this essay, appears most significant. It appears as that system which enables man to adapt himself to a changing and complex environment. It allows him to modulate and "process" his drives in the light of such changing environment. It makes it possible for him to have not only an enlightened belief in his convictions, but also to challenge these convictions when necessary.[1] The ego, in brief, appears to provide the basis for man's reconciling powers.

We are foremostly indebted to Heinz Hartmann for having further illuminated the ego—its scope and functions. Hartmann, building on the basic discoveries of Freud, defined and elucidated the ego as a specific "organ of adaptation and organization." This "organ," like other human features and capacities, appears phylogenetically and ontogenetically determined. The ego appears phylogenetically determined in that its development can be traced through the history of the animal species. We can distinguish ego elements in various animals. (In rats, for example, we find a relatively high degree of adaptive flexibility; we might speak of "ego precursors in animals." Like men, rats learn rather easily through experience; they can therefore profit from the experience of other rats. Like men, they can thus adapt to new environments such as slum areas, ships, or marshlands. Konrad Lorenz has described this in his book *On Aggression*.)

The ego appears ontogenetically determined in that we can trace its development through the life phases of each growing embryo, infant, and child. The ego in man can be viewed as an outgrowth of his massive nervous system. But we must think of it as a psychic system—or organ—which is defined by its functions. These functions are many. Thinking, remembering, perceiving, are some of the most important. We can, in turn, classify these functions under a number of viewpoints. Hartmann adopted a viewpoint which emphasized the ego's "differentiating and organizing" functions.

[1] Nietzsche wrote in his diary: "A very popular error: having the courage of one's convictions; rather it is a matter of having the courage for the attack on one's convictions!"

I shall throw light on these "differentiating and organizing" functions when I introduce—in the latter part of this chapter—some general principles of human development and adaptation. At this point we might get some understanding of them by looking at a complex business corporation. This corporation must differentiate itself according to the functions it seeks to fulfill—such as devising, manufacturing, improving, selling, and advertising a product. All these functions, in a sense, can be compared to "executive" ego functions. However, we can see the manager (or managerial staff) as fulfilling special differentiating and organizing functions. He must ensure that all the diverse activities become functionally differentiated in the light of the company's over-all goal: e.g. making money or serving the community. But he must also make sure that the corporation, in its diversified complexity, remains united and organized, that its many activities and subsystems do not work at cross-purposes. This might require, among other things, that he establish a special agency for maintaining good public relations among all these subsystems and their various members, just as he must ensure good outside public relations. Understandably, the more complex the corporation grows, the more these differentiating and organizing functions will be taxed. (Nunberg elaborated in 1931 the concept of the "synthetic function of the ego" in a paper of the same title. Hartmann would like to see this concept replaced by the term "organizing" function.)

In the context of a complexly evolved psychoanalytic theory, Hartmann illuminated important genetic, dynamic, structural, economic, and adaptational aspects of the ego. For my present purpose, two concepts of Hartmann appear most important: His concept of the secondary autonomy of ego functions and—closely related thereto—his notion of the neutralization of instinctual energies. I shall bypass the complex theoretical issues connected with these concepts and, instead, use an example from daily life to illuminate their meaning.

In order to start a love relationship the partners need

highly developed ego functions. The young man, for instance, must assess himself, the girl, and their common situation on various levels. He must be aware of the girl's needs and personality. He can only pace his advances appropriately when he can gauge how he affects her. Seductive charm, like any other personality asset, implies an (unwitting) ego-ingenuity.

The boy's ego functions, as needed for winning and holding his girl, depend on certain operating conditions. First, his feelings and passions must not so overpower him as to interfere with his correctly assessing the situation and with his implementing a good strategy. In this case, it would be his id which could sabotage his ego. Second, he must not become unduly restricted in his maneuverability by harsh inner taboos. In this case, it would be—at least partly— his superego that could foil his ego. Therefore, in order to succeed in his task, the boy's ego must function in relative autonomy with regard to both his id and superego.

Such autonomy of the ego Hartmann called secondary, when it is the outgrowth of previous inner struggles (although he allows also for ego functions which are not born out of conflict but derive from a so-called conflict-free sphere of the ego). This secondary, conflict-born autonomy of the ego Hartmann conceives as being due to a neutralization of instinctual energies. Such neutralization, in other words, permits a smooth ego efficiency in human relationships which are taxing.

Such neutralization may break down, and the secondary autonomy of ego functions will be impaired. There will be a psychic dedifferentiation and the person will be less effective in his life tasks. Erotic (libidinal) as well as aggressive energies may become deneutralized in this manner: A person may become more crudely hostile or amorous.

To make this clear, let us return to the boy who wants to conquer his girl. At one point his sexual excitement may get the best of him. He becomes restless, sleepless, and can no longer think clearly. His work in school begins to suffer. But so—and this is important—does his work with the girl; that is, his work on the relationship. No longer is he able to gear himself sensitively to her needs and her personality. No longer can he pace his sexual advances successfully. On his part, the relationship has become much too eroticized. This defeats his goals. For this girl now finds him irritating, inept, and burdensome. Instinctual energies, which in neutralized form would have promoted a smooth ego efficiency, have become deneutralized in him. He has become a victim of his strongly aroused instincts. His ego's secondary autonomy seems—at least temporarily—in jeopardy.

For the purpose of the present study, we are chiefly interested in the *nuclear ego*. "Nuclear" here essentially means two things: The primordial, genetically early ego; and second, the core ego which now and later allows for effective differentiating and organizing functions as just defined.

René Spitz has traced many important steps in the development of the nuclear ego. He conceived this development as a field of forces within which certain "organizers of the psyche" become dominant centers of integration. Spitz tried to give the concept "organizer" a meaning in psychic development which is similar to the one it has in the embryo's bodily development. In embryology the organizer signifies something that acts as an inductor for the body's differentiation. The organizer requires an "organization center." That is the point (as the chordamesoderm of the dorsal lip of the vertebrate blastopore) in a developing embryo that serves as a focus about which the embryo differentiates.

Thus, psychic organizers install themselves during critical developmental periods. Later organizers, in order to exert a successful integrative pull, require well-installed earlier organizers. Each organizer highlights, consolidates, and provides new developmental push toward a new psychic complexity. Each organizer thus indicates crucial constellations in the evolving nuclear ego.

Spitz has distinguished three such organizers which indicate "a major change has taken place in the central steering organization in the ego." He used the "affective signal" of this change as the main criterion by which to spot and to delineate these organizers. These affective signals were for him first the "smiling response," occurring at the age of three months, second, the "eighth-month anxiety," and third, the beginning of speech, coming about at the age of about eighteen months.[2]

We may speak of crucial *phase-constellations* which, each time, signify the dominance of one particular organizer of the psyche. The period in which the three psychic organizers reign I shall call the *dawn of knowing individuation*.

By this term I want to convey what I consider crucial about this phase of human development: That, during this phase, man individuates himself by beginning *to know*. He begins to know about himself, about his world and about his own complex relation to the latter.

The smiling response truly ushers in human individuation. The nuclear ego begins to emerge out of the undifferentiated stage. This implies, according to Spitz:

1. The infant turns from inner sensation to outer perception.

2. He starts to test reality.

3. Memory traces are laid down and become available.

4. Directed object relations begin and can be observed.

In terms of psychoanalytic propositions this means the psychic apparatus divides topographically into a conscious and unconscious part; ego and id differentiate out of a stage of non-differentiation; thought processes occur in which memory traces are laid down.

At the same time when the second organizer, the

[2] Spitz's pioneering work has stimulated much research in the field of early child development, as a result of which his own conceptualization might have to be revised or further differentiated. Thus, John Benjamin has distinguished Spitz's "separation anxiety" from "stranger anxiety." And observations, made by Wells Goodrich and his associates, indicate that in addition to Spitz's organizers, several others might be important.

eighth-month anxiety, appears, "the ego has greatly changed from the elementary ego achieved at three months. It has developed a series of systems, like memory, perception, the thought process, the faculty of judgment . . . and ego apparatuses like the understanding of space, the social gesture, a little later the capacity for locomotion, all of which make the ego a more effective, but also more complex structure. We can say that now the ego has come into its own."

However, it is only with the advent of the third psychic organizer, the beginning of language, that the nuclear ego has been fully born. Therefore, I shall take the third psychic organizer as indicating a phase-constellation of particular importance: We are now in the middle of the dawn of knowing individuation. Already the nuclear ego has achieved an enormous complexity. But this complexity is now about to become infinitely more complex. Language from now on will decisively test the ego's capacities.

It is necessary to summarize those features of this phase-constellation which seem central to the nuclear ego's task. Essentially, this can be done by conceptualizing these features in terms of two concepts which denote interdependent aspects of one total field configuration. They are: Self-Polarization and Self-Demarcation.

SELF-POLARIZATION

The developing psyche must clearly have differentiated itself into a conscious and an unconscious realm. We may speak of its primary dichotomization. Once this has been achieved, a critical differentiating barrier has come into existence. Before the advent of this barrier, we can, in a sense, only speak of ego-tendencies, of ego-precursors, and ego-nuclei. Now we can say: The ego has been born (just as the infant is born only when he decisively and unmistakably has himself separated from his mother). This decisive differentiating barrier indicates the child has become able to repress certain unacceptable psychic contents. The barrier is effectively cathected; it has become invested (*besetzt*) with mental—or libidinal—energies. In the confrontation (and interplay) of ego and id, "conscious" and "unconscious," the psychic arena is being staked out for an increasingly subtle play of self-revelation and self-concealment.

The advent of this decisive differentiating barrier (and hence of repression as the primary and basic defense mechanism) signals the achievement of an *ordered, workable complexity within*. This achievement I call *self-polarization*.

Self-polarization, as a rule, begins by the age of three months and is accomplished by the age of eighteen months. However, certain vicissitudes beset the infant's quest for it. Repression, even when age-adequate, at the beginning appears rude, harsh, and radical, but also shaky and precarious. This dual feature, recently described by Anna Freud and Edith Jacobson, derives from the characteristics of this phase-constellation, a phase-constellation indicating both achievement and transition. This crucial differentiation of the child's psyche is not yet much consolidated; the nuclear structuring of his personality in many respects is still precarious. Wishful emoting still tends to interpenetrate and alternate rather freely and abruptly with a more realistic interpretation and acceptance of events. Primary processes—untamed impulses, wishes, images—still tend to dominate this child's world view and behavior. Therefore, in order to cope with such threatening preponderance of drives and primary processes, draconian measures seem indicated. They are needed to harness such mental lability. The needed repression will be tyrannical and overpowering.

Edith Jacobson points to "the enormous and rather disruptive influences which the processes of infantile denial and repression exert upon the formation of the self and the object world. Since these images arise essentially from the memory traces of pleasurable and unpleasurable experiences and are only gradually linked up with and connected by the perceptive memories which reflect reality, the cut-

ting out of a considerable section of unpleasurable memories by infantile repression eliminates a large amount of
unacceptable aspects of both the self and the outside
world. The defects caused by the work of repression may
be filled by screen elements, by distortions or embellish-
ments produced by the elaborate maneuvers of the ego's
defense system. Moreover, to the extent to which the repressed fantasies that have remained cathected in the
unconscious can find their way to the surface, they will
lend the coloring of past infantile images to the self and
object representations."

The usual amnesia for childhood memories, clearly observed and described by Freud, testifies to the relative
ruthlessness of early repression. Only later, when the personality has become more solidly and securely integrated
can the individual afford to loosen up on the tightness of
the repressive mechanism. Similarly, only a strong and
safely established democratic government, maintained
through a system of checks and balances, can afford to do
away with censorship and let grumblings and anarchic
tendencies come into the open.

SELF-DEMARCATION

While self-polarization denotes that the child has
reached an ordered complexity within himself, *self-
demarcation denotes such ordered complexity vis-à-vis the
outside world* of things and persons. In learning to demarcate himself the child learns to differentiate between inside and outside, me and not-me, inner happenings and
outer events.

Self-demarcation requires a mental apparatus with
which to differentiate—that is, it builds on a substrate of
other differentiations and integrations already achieved.
Capacities such as memory, perception, and motor coordination must have been formed. But self-demarcation,
further, requires a home base for self-reference. There
must have been consolidated some unquestioned center,

some unified, integrated whole, from and against which
the self can demarcate itself. We may call this center the
nuclear *self* (as to be distinguished from the nuclear ego).
(Hartmann also emphasizes the difference between self
and ego.) This nuclear self essentially is a body self. It
implies, among other things, the individual has established
a reliable body image. It implies that he has won a sense
of primary wholeness, a sense of unreflected me-ness, an
unquestioned certainty of being bounded, of being *one*
person.

The vicissitudes besetting the quest for self-demarcation
are comparable to those found in the quest for self-
polarization. The advent of self-demarcation, also, marks
an important achievement as well as a precarious transitional stage. Thus, at this stage crude attempts at self-
demarcation, at boundary setting, may be seen to alternate
abruptly and interpenetrate with states in which the de-
marcations seem to have become precariously loose and
indistinct.

The power of the nuclear ego as a differentiating and
organizing medium is reflected in what, leaning on Federn,[3] we might call the dialectic of ego boundaries. His
later ego concept, mainly elaborated through a kind of
phenomenologically enriched introspection, in many respects appears removed from the ego concept of Freud
and Hartmann. For one thing, it partly encompasses what
in Hartmann's thinking are aspects of the self *and* the ego.
Therefore, in the present context it might have been more
appropriate to employ the concept "self-feelings" and
"self-boundaries" instead of "ego feelings" and "ego
boundaries."

Federn's central concepts of "ego boundaries" and "ego
feelings" indicate and require the achievement and successful reconciliation of self-polarization and self-demarcation.

Our ego boundaries, in Federn's sense, in order to be

[3] Federn, one of the early Freudian analysts, was a pioneer
in the psychoanalytic study of the psychoses.

up to man's complex adaptational tasks, always must reflect a balance of stability and lability. In each moment of life this balance changes. To some degree, ego feelings and ego boundaries always fluctuate. For example, altered states of consciousness such as fatigue, falling asleep, and awakening, indicate changes in the quality and scope of ego feelings and, along with this, in experienced ego boundaries.

Further: This dialectic of ego boundaries unfolds in time. Federn found that ego boundaries in time tend to become more mobile and tend to encompass more functions and representations. This means that the stability and lability of ego boundaries must ever more complexly be reconciled, and in a matter of time, the nuclear ego's capacities will be tested even more severely.

TWO GENERAL PRINCIPLES OF DEVELOPMENT
AND ADAPTATION

In order to further illuminate human individuation and acculturation and the ego's role therein, I shall now present two general principles of development and adaptation.

The first of these is probably the broadest and most widely accepted developmental principle in biology and psychology: The principle of *Differentiation-Integration*. Heinz Werner has stated it as follows: "Wherever development occurs it proceeds from a state of relative globality and lack of differentiation to a state of increasing differentiation, articulation, and hierarchic integration."

To a degree, differentiation must always precede integration. Only after bodily or psychologic processes or capacities have become at least partially differentiated, can they become hierarchically integrated, organized, and related to one another. Thus, "part and whole, event and context, self and non-self, can become articulated" (Wynne). But, once the developmental process has come under way, an achieved integration tends to promote further differentiation. And so on. The relation between differentiation-integration is *reciprocal* and spirally expansive—that is, leading to ever new levels of developmental complexity.

However, a second principle seems required to grasp essential features of development and adaptation. This second principle partly complements the first principle of "differentiation-integration" by placing the latter into a dynamic, adaptational context. I should like to call it the principle of *Adaptive Reconciliation:* Any living organism, in order to survive, must learn to reconcile certain basic tendencies which seem opposed to each other and yet seem necessary. These tendencies present themselves as characteristic dichotomies. They require each other to become meaningful and denote different aspects of one transactional whole. Two such dichotomies stand out. These dichotomies are, first, *Doing-Undergoing* and, second, *Closure-Openness*.

Doing-Undergoing

John Dewey and, recently, Ernest Becker, among others, have stated and illuminated this dichotomy. In order to survive, even the lowest organism must be able to reconcile these two features: All living beings must *do;* they must exercise their powers. They must initiate action and actively impinge upon their environment. But all living beings also must *undergo,* they must make themselves accessible to being influenced, they must let this environment affect them. It is through the reconciliation of these basic tendencies that "learning through experience" is made possible. An organism which neglects the exercise of its powers will be dangerously at the mercy of its environment. It will tend to be swamped by relatively undifferentiated stimuli; its world will be less well discriminated, poor in clarity and quality. But its world will also be poorer when too much action blurs a reactivity to finer nuances and differences. Either way, a failure in (or an absence of) reconciliation of these tendencies threatens to wreck an individual's efforts at adaptation: "An excess of doing tends to empty experience of its content; an excess of undergoing tends to undermine power" (Becker).

While in the balance of doing-undergoing the *dynamic* aspect is emphasized in the individual's relationship to his environment; in the balance of closure-openness it is foremostly the *structural* aspect.

Closure-Openness

Each organism must achieve a minimum of structure which bounds and gives shape to its doing, its initiation of action. It must become a structural center to itself: It must achieve closure. But since an organism also needs its animate and inanimate environment (to have its needs fulfilled and to let essential experiences touch it), such closure also must leave room for an openness through which these needs can be satisfied and these experiences can reach it. A failure in reconciliation of the elements of "closure-openness" would be fatal: An excess of closure would mean an isolation made both need- and experience-proof and death, in the long run, would be inevitable. An excess of openness would extinguish any individuality and death would equally ensue.

I thus view human behavior as a circular, spirally expansive process, occurring in a transactional field which is constantly changing—partly as a consequence of this very process. This process has a developmental as well as an adaptive dimension. With the leverage given by the two above principles, "differentiation-integration" and "adaptative reconciliation," we will be able to trace important features of this process which reflect both these dimensions.

THE PRIMARY RECONCILING INSTRUMENT

The developmental perspective, here presented, highlights the importance of the nuclear ego.

In trying to trace the interplay of the above two general principles in human development, we face a panorama of staggering complexity: The most constitutive rounds of differentiation and integration take place in the earliest years of human life. A developmental dynamic of baffling speed is compressed into this time span. We may speak of a push toward increasing differentiation and integration, as triggered and sustained through numerous interdependent mechanisms. This push is set in motion at the time of impregnation; it gains momentum during the months of fetal life and enters a new phase after birth—the infant's physical separation from its mother. Then the push toward greater differentiation and integration seems to slow down in the sphere of organic growth and maturation. But in another sphere this push becomes more vehement and decisive. This sphere encompasses those processes which *shape the nuclear ego.* They occur during the *dawn of knowing individuation.*

This push toward differentiation and integration during the dawn of knowing individuation implies that the above described balances of doing-undergoing and closure-openness must be reorganized on ever new levels of complexity. Along with this growing complexity the *panorama of adaptational discrepancies* will widen. These discrepancies can be conceptualized (and often will be experienced) as conflicts. Such conflicts, first, may manifest themselves as conflicts within the developing psychic structure (e.g. in psychoanalytic terminology, as conflicts between id, ego, and superego), as well as between partial aspects of these sub-structures—Hartmann speaks in this context of inter- and intra-systemic conflicts.

Conflicts of the first kind—that is, inter-systemic conflicts—provided a dominant topic for the early psychoanalytic literature. The neurotic woman who is caught between sexual desires and her strict conscience would be a simple case in point. An example, again over-simplified, of an intra-systemic conflict would be provided by a man who is paralyzed by a conflicting superego. Having internalized certain values, he might be driven to work as a scientist. But other values, of equal superego force, possibly of a religious nature, might condemn his scientific curiosity.

Such conflicts, secondly, may occur between psychic

and somatic maturational requirements. A boy of sixteen —a rather frequent occurrence—may have the sexual maturity of a twelve-year-old. Consequently he feels little or no sexual drive; talk about certain aspects of sex is to him what talk about color would be to a blind person. Still, as a sixteen-year-old in a class with other sixteen-year-olds he, in one way or the other, must cope with sexual issues that excite and trouble his peers. For example, he may have to resolve the conflict between having and not wanting (or needing) to date.

Such conflicts, third, may occur between various relatively integrated needs, wishes, and requirements of the individual, on the one side, and his environment (human as well as non-human) on the other. A young man, musically talented, might seek a musical career. But his environment—such as an eighteenth century frontier community in the American Midwest—might oppose such aspirations. In this community (which may include his parents) these aspirations may be considered wasteful. They smack of libertinism and possible homosexuality.

All these different conflicts will either have to be resolved, or so endured or absorbed that reciprocal and spirally expansive developmental processes may go on— that new rounds of differentiation-integration may become possible and that the balances of doing-undergoing and closure-openness may be established on ever more complex levels.

I consider the ego the *primary reconciling instrument* destined to cope with conflicts in a manner which, again and again, makes possible these expanding processes. The nuclear ego—its quality and scope—in providing the basis for the mature ego, determines man's reconciling power.

In the light of the foregoing, I shall now illuminate some further aspects of the nuclear ego. The first of these aspects is *structural*. It is the principle differentiation-integration, in supporting the concepts self-polarization and self-demarcation, which brings this aspect into focus. It throws light on how the nuclear ego must be structured in order that it can fulfill its functions as an organizing and reconciling organ. We obtain a kind of blueprint of man's reconciling instrument.

The second aspect is *energetic*. It is less easily understandable than the structural aspect; therefore I shall attempt to explain it. It is the principle adaptive reconciliation, when brought to bear on these early phase-constellations, which brings into focus the energetic aspect of the nuclear ego. This energetic aspect supports and complements the structural aspects mentioned above.

In order that the two central dichotomies "doing-undergoing" and "closure-openness" can be made operational—and that means: can become reconciled—energy has to be expended and has to be adapted to different modes.

Let us first demonstrate this in the case of the balance doing-undergoing. Any interchange between organism and environment—aiming, for example, at the intake of food or at the intake of psychological stimuli which becomes material for learning—can, we saw, be conceived within this framework. Any such interchange also poses an energy problem: Energy, in each instance, is required to cathect and structure the organism's attention, to gear it to the context and wavelength on which this food or stimulus becomes a recognizable and graspable item. Energy is required to facilitate integrative switches. For example, attention must be shifted to different foci as this is demanded by the ensuing transactional sequences; the organism or parts of it must switch from a more actively searching to a more passively receiving mode, etc. Energy finally is required to achieve the storage and/or assimilation of these items. As a rule, the more complex the adaptational and transactional processes in question (and the more they have to build on a differentiation-integration previously achieved), the greater the expenditure of energy which is needed.

Equally, the balance closure-openness, in order to become operational, requires expenditure and transformation of energies. Federn, in indicating the dialectic of ego boundaries, also recognized therein the problem of con-

stant investment and redistribution of energy: ". . . maintenance of ego cathexis is necessary for all mental functioning, active or passive. Furthermore, the cathexis
necessarily increases with every functional effort, with
every claim from the outside world, and particularly every
task concerning adaptation and maturation."

We are now in a position to understand better the important interdependence of structural and energetic aspects
in the nuclear ego: the structural aspects—as evidenced in
the phase-constellations of self-polarization and self-demarcation—will crucially decide on the extent and modes of
energy expenditure by which forthcoming, spirally expansive developmental and adaptational processes will be
maintained and instigated.

The interplay between cathexis and structural constellation—and its role in either the propelling or blockage of
further developmental expansion may best be demonstrated by focusing on the dynamic of *attentional processes*.
Lyman Wynne has illuminated them. Attentional processes
are a crucial aspect of man's successful adaptation. They
are centrally implicated in doing-undergoing, as well as
in closure-openness.

ATTENTION

Attentional processes can be seen as being at the root
of the most simple and, in a sense, basic mental structure:
the memory trace. However, in order to understand the
relation between attention and the structuring of the memory trace, we are required to hypothesize an *attention
cathexis,* forming part of the energy of the ego. Freud, in
the seventh chapter of *The Interpretation of Dreams,* and,
later, David Rapaport have developed this hypothesis. The
mental energy available for attention cathexis, according to this hypothesis, is limited in quantity. Simultaneous
and continuous excitations, both from internal and external
sources, compete for it. Defenses, it is further hypothe-
sized, can diminish the quantity of attention cathexis

which is available. The mental structure—the memory trace—is built when a sufficient amount of attention is directed to and invested in a stimulus for a sufficient duration of time. Thereafter these structures retain only a small quantity of the energy that was needed to give rise to them and the energy used in the process then becomes available for new, other excitations.

Attention thus appears involved in creating a structure. But this structure, in turn, liberates new attention cathexis which now may be used to help to build new and more complex structures. And so on. We notice a circular expansive process.

This circular process is similar to other learning processes: in learning to drive a car, for example, at first much attentional investment is required. Once certain patterns of coordination and reactivity—Hartmann uses the term "pre-conscious automatisms"—have been established, attentional energy again is set free and may be used for talking or listening to the radio. Thus, in sum, a relationship seems to exist between mode and intensity of attention, and kind of attention-cathexis, invested over time, on the one side, and an adaptive, potentially expansive mental structurization, which reconciles both stability and flexible adjustment, on the other.

It is at this point that Hartmann's concept of neutralization becomes important. It helps us to understand better the dialectic between structure and cathexis in this circular expansive process: the structure must become maximally regression-proof and yet must minimally bind energy. The neutralization of instinctive energies, as conceived by Hartmann, appears to achieve this reconciliation: in making the structure resistive to regression it safeguards its relative (secondary) autonomy vis-à-vis the many stresses that are going to hit it. In keeping low its energy cathexis it ensures enough energy will be available for new structurizations and for new adaptive and reconciling tasks. The concept neutralization therefore appears the key to our understanding of the way in which cathexis and structure become two circularly reinforcing elements in an ongoing developmental and adaptive dynamic.

In principle, attentional processes and, along with them, the circularly expanding dialectic between structure and cathexis, have to occur on all levels of differentiation-integration. But with advancing differentiation-integration they occur within an increasingly complex framework.

Let us now turn to the framework that exists by the time the nuclear ego has been fully born. I have earlier described several of its important components and constellations under the terms self-polarization and self-demarcation. I must next turn to its—for the purposes of this study—most crucial outgrowth: language—the third psychic organizer in Spitz's meaning of the term. Through language attentional processes—and hence the interplay of structure and cathexis—acquire a new meaning and dimension.

LANGUAGE

Language in the widest sense of the word denotes our means and style of communication with ourselves and others. This comprises the language of images and pictures (as evidenced in dreams and artistic creations) and the language of clearly defined and differentiated propositions and concepts. It comprises the spoken and the unspoken language.

The possession of such language sets man apart from all other animals. Man becomes the "symbolic animal." Without language there would only be *die bewusstlose Nacht, die nicht zur Unterscheidung in ihr, noch zur Klarheit des Selbstwissens kommt*" (Hegel). "The night of unknowing, unable to distinguish within itself nor to become self-aware."

Language, in the dynamic of man's ongoing development and adaptation, marks a phase-constellation of new complexity. It mirrors a nuclear ego well established and functioning. It highlights and reflects man's unique reconciling potential and power. But also, it presents the threat of confusion, of unaccomplished reconciliation and of despair, to which no other animal is exposed.

In the following, I shall try to summarize briefly how language either promotes such complex reconciliation or endangers it. I shall view man's acquisition of language as crucially building on processes and achievements which encompass the first three years of life—although important features of language become only later fully manifest and differentiated. Again, in order to illuminate the reconciling function of language, I shall make use of the principles differentiation-integration and adaptive reconciliation as outlined above.

Piaget, Charlotte and Karl Bühler, Heinz Werner, Roger Brown, and many others have studied the development and acquisition of human language. Ethologists such as Lorenz have emphasized phylogenetic precursors. Ontogenetically, language grows through an intricate spiral of differentiating and integrating processes. It seems to grow similarly as does our body: from tiny inconspicuous beginnings the development leads to baffling complexity. Just as the fertilized egg is at the root of the adult organism with its billions of cells and specialized functions, so also the child's first unreflected stammerings of "mama" and "dada" will branch out into a rich array of words and symbols, from neighborhood colloquialisms to differential calculus, all these aspects having some relation to each other while, at the same time, signifying differences.

The phase-constellations "self-polarization" and "self-demarcation," in highlighting the achievement of a nuclear ego, also indicate important steps and constellations in the growth of language.

For the purpose of this study I shall distinguish two forms of language: propositional language and evocative language. In any given sample of language these two forms tend to become more or less reconciled. However, in order that we can understand the nature of, and necessity for, this reconciliation we must first grasp the differences between these two forms. These are differences in quality, function, and genesis. I shall begin with propositional language.

PROPOSITIONAL LANGUAGE

Propositional language essentially is conceptual language. It allows one to spell out and interrelate facts clearly and complexly. It is the vehicle of conceptual thinking. It is scientific language par excellence.

I shall, in the following, briefly illuminate principal features and functions of propositional language by focusing on certain developmental requirements that must be fulfilled in the ongoing process of differentiation-integration. The first of these requirements is the binding of space.

Binding of Space

An individual's life-mastery greatly depends on his ability to orient and anchor himself in a world of space. This anchorage he must to a large extent achieve by his own efforts. Piaget, above others, has illuminated conditions and vicissitudes in the infant's efforts at space-binding. The infant must learn to pattern his body movements. On his object world (constituting itself in these very developmental processes) he must bring to bear his increasingly surer coordination, his sense of touch and rhythm, his growing capacity to memorize and anticipate. Thus he builds and integrates his spatial world in which he—hopefully—learns to move comfortably. Space-binding, thus understood, to a great extent rests on automative body knowledge. "Sensory motor intelligence" as understood by Piaget reflects a solid and flexible space-binding at the age of eighteen months: The infant has become able to grasp spatial relationships in the range of his immediate perception and, within that range, to manipulate objects purposefully and inventively.

Binding of Time

The binding of time builds on, and is interrelated with,

the binding of space. Kant treated space and time as those forms of pure perception (*Formen der reinen Anschauung*) which, in a sense, constitute all human experience. Though Kant uses these concepts in a somewhat different sense than is intended here, he highlights their importance and interdependence: It is through his being anchored in a world of spatial and temporal relations, that man, endowed with his central nervous system, can successfully survive.

Time-binding, in building on space-binding, also builds on automative body knowledge. But, along with the higher level in differentiation-integration, it reflects a dimension of added intricacy. In addition to a sub-structure of bodily coordinations and ego functions successfully installed, it now requires the first elements of a differentiating language. It is through the availability of such differentiating language that essential space relations, recognized through the coordination of direct touch, grasp, and vision, can be translated into and maintained on the more abstract time-dimension. The differing spatial positions as indicated by the hands of a clock and as visually grasped, can now, with the help of certain storing, binding, and differentiating features of language be translated into time relations. The difference and sameness, which is experienced on the level of spatial relations, is therewith extended into a realm of a more complex and refined manipulability. Body language is being replaced by a symbol language which has an infinitely larger scope and potential. Time-binding appears as the pivotal feature of this symbol language.

Becker has excellently illuminated the significance of man's time-binding. "The human animal," he writes, "lives in a symbolic world of its own creation. Man is the only 'time-binding' animal, the only one who has a notion of past-present-future, a time stream in which he places himself and which he continually scans and appraises. Lower animals live in a continuous 'now,' troubled perhaps by sensory memories over which they have little or no control. But man controls his memories with the aid of his massive central nervous system. When the cerebral cortex became a central exchange for the regulation and delay of behavior, the stage for a consciousness of precise time was set. The organism could consciously delay response to a stimulus, and present in awareness several alternatives chosen from a memory; in this way a controlled time stream came into being." Thus, through the binding of time, man could manage to live in a highly predictable world. In connecting past events and past experiences with his plans and hopes for the future, he could, to a degree unthinkable in other animals, create and master his destiny.

Abstraction

Abstraction builds on time-binding. In order that man can abstract on a significant level, the differentiation and integration of language (and of its underlying psychic and bodily substrate) must have proceeded considerably. The capacity for abstraction reflects the predominance of secondary over primary processes, and hence of capacities and structures which delay and modulate the discharge of energies.

Through his ability to abstract man can neglect the individuality of things for the sake of what they have in common. This immensely extends the radius of his actions. For "to abstract is to refer an object to one's own intended use" (Becker). According to Baldwin, an abstract mental concept is less a mental picture than an expectation. "It is the possibility of a reaction which will answer equally for a great many particular experiences." Abstracting, man orders his world in the light of his expected requirements and adaptations. In the concept "wood" he counts only its expected use for making fires, for building houses, etc.; in the concept "snow" its value for skiing, for building igloos, its potential for getting wet feet. Through creating abstract concepts and constantly refining and interrelating these with other concepts, he creates a world of both easy and differentiated functionality. Man becomes the agile, anticipating animal.

Abstraction thus can be seen the core of a propositional,

conceptual language and hence of scientific language, which seems to have given man his greatest adaptational advantage over other animals, uniquely extending his possibilities for "learning through experience."

EVOCATIVE LANGUAGE

In distinguishing evocative language, I follow the example set by Th. French, W. Kaufmann, and others. In contrast to propositional language, evocative language appears closely related to primary processes: it appears highly body- and affect-tinged. It seems imbued with the immediacy of experience and seems minimally time-bound. It seems pleasure-oriented and magic-laden.

Evocative language is not—although it may resemble—a disintegration product of an advanced *conceptual language*. It builds on and responds to developmental requirements as does propositional language. Like the latter it reflects complex processes of differentiation-integration.

Evocative language, thus understood, optimally seems to serve drive discharge and tension reduction—functions of language and symbol formation, which were clearly described by Freud. This means it offers itself particularly well for libidinous and aggressive exploitation. Evocative language seems closer to man's organismic existence than propositional language, not only from the point of view of drive discharge but also in regard to the signaling function. It appears particularly receptive to his inner needs, to the stirrings of his vegetative undertows. It allows him to heed his needs for food, for sleep and relaxation, for sex, for the enjoyment of smell and touch, for feeling of regenerative warmth, in brief: for pleasure.

Thus, evocative language seems to store as well as transmit a good deal of the warmth, the impulsive vehemence, the richness, the regenerative power of man's organismic existence. It allows man to savor its spontaneity, to spot the clues and warnings arising therefrom. It helps him to live "embodied,"[4] in touch with his pulsating vitality. It ensures that a constant regenerative flow from within will not stop, that man, again and again, as did Antäus in touching the earth, may tap his replenishing reservoirs.

In order to fulfill such tasks, evocative language seems to build more strongly on certain (genetically early) instinctive and instinct-like processes than does propositional language. Specifically, it seems to have to do with such phenomena as resonance in the mother-child relationship (as described by Sullivan, French, and others) and as mood-inductions (*Stimmungsansteckung, Stimmungsübertragung*) in animals (as described by some ethologists and by Harold Lincke, a Swiss psychoanalyst).

Clearly, in the light of the above requirements, evocative language must lose in precision what it wins in color. Compared to the tightly and hierarchically organized propositional language, evocative language must appear loose, groping, rumbling, and circumstantial.

This very looseness allows it to sap and savor the etymological juice of words, to become sensitized to the nuances of smell, vision, and touch. By necessity, it must be largely an image and picture language. Thus, it can allow our associations, those unruly offshoots from the unconscious, organismic core of our personality, to assert themselves, to convey some of their spontaneous, unbounded, colorful quality.

Evocative language, thus understood, plays a central and well-known role not only in dreams, neurotic and psychotic symptoms (to be more fully elucidated later) but also in religious inspirations, in poetry and in imaginative writing. William Faulkner, for example, in order to convey psychological truth as *he* sees and experiences it, at times makes utmost use of evocative language. To convey the inner world of a castrated idiot (as in *The Sound and the Fury*), he deliberately robs language of many of its

[4] Ronald Laing, in his book *The Divided Self* (1960), has given a special meaning to this term.

abstracting, differentiating, space- and time-binding features. It becomes creeping, rumbling, repetitive, a morass of blurred images, of almost still-born associations.

PROPOSITIONAL AND EVOCATIVE LANGUAGE RECONCILED

In order that language can become operational, propositional and evocative language must be reconciled. This means that language can only serve adaptively as a reconciling medium when its propositional and evocative elements are integrated with each other in a manner that depends on the given linguistic task.

Such integration, however, is no easy matter. This is reflected on a most general, philosophic level. Certain hallmarks of propositional language, such as precision, logical stringency, hierarchic organization, etc., may tend to be installed as sole indicators of meaning and truth. Such meaning and truth soon become a dry, bare skeleton, when evocative language finds no or little place in this orientation. On the other side, an inappropriate buildup of evocative language soon becomes untenable also. Without an attempt at precision and hierarchic structurization there remains, in the end, only a vague, ineffable blur.

Wittgenstein and Heidegger, at the risk of great oversimplification, can be viewed as modern representatives of these two tendencies. Wittgenstein, at least in his *Tractatus logico-philosophicus,* while staking his hopes for truth and meaning on the exploration of the nature of logic (in a sense, the pure precipitate of propositional language) was led to the recognition that logic—in a most literal and banal manner—means nothing. It is purely tautologic in nature. The truth of a general statement adds nothing to the truth of individual statements on which it relies.

The "ethos" of propositional language, it seems, drove Wittgenstein to clarify the meaning of philosophic assertions, to deflate pretensions at truth-finding. Together with other members of the Vienna School of Neo-Positivism

(Schlick, Carnap, Reichenbach, etc.), he has perfected the logistic analysis of language. Heidegger, among others, offers himself as a target for such analysis. Carnap, in analyzing Heidegger's article *"Was ist Metaphysik"* ("What Is Metaphysic"), finds it to reflect a series of meaningless, unverifiable words.

Heidegger, on his part, can be seen as exemplifying the "ethos" of evocative language. For his *"dichtendes Denken,"* his poetizing thinking, appears highly evocative. While revering the power of a kind of homegrown language of his own, he scathes the abstract language of modern science. He appears to argue: The more language becomes abstract, differentiating, clear, and verifiable, that is, conceptual and scientific, the more it must miss out on what, according to Heidegger, is essential. Specifically, it must miss out on what, in line with the above considerations, might be called the private organismic realm. This organismic realm seems to shine forth in a conglomerate of colorful, felt uniqueness. Under the touch of propositional language, this uniqueness appears to evaporate. Never the twain seem allowed to meet. "At the very outset," writes Heidegger, "we never hear noises or sound complexes. We hear the squeaking car, the motorcycle. We hear the marching column, the north wind, the hammering woodpecker, the bristling fire."

How, then, does the ego integrate propositional and evocative language? In order to approach this question, the ego must be conceived as linguistically operating in two directions: language, first, must gear the ego to the *within,* to the self; and it must, second, gear the ego to the *outside,* to the non-human and human environment, including the man-made culture. The ego, in other words, has a dual linguistic front line.

On each front line the principle of adaptive reconciliation holds sway. This means in its dealings with the self, as well as in its dealings with others, the ego must reconcile doing-undergoing and closure-openness. I shall first describe the ego's dealings with the self.

Language Gearing the Ego to the Self

In order to achieve this task, language must help to organize and reinforce a stable frame of reference. In this sense, it must be closing and structuring. And such closing and structuring, on this first front line, seems to have priority. Amidst the constant flow and exchange of elements which constitute man's body, amidst the flux of life phases, of constantly changing moods and life-situations, language enduringly must constitute the ego vis-à-vis the self. This self-structuring aspect of language underpins what Hartmann has called the secondary autonomy of the ego. It fortifies the ego's resistivity to regressive pulls, and thus helps to ensure the ongoing neutralization of libidinal and aggressive instinctual energies.

Such structuring of the ego—indicating doing as well as closure—foremostly must rely on propositional language. It requires space- and time-binding, abstraction, etc., as these features were described earlier.

But more than such structuring is needed in the ego's intercourse with the self. The structure must not prevent the ego from being touched and, if necessary, stirred up by organismic happenings. It must, while being structured, remain open and undergoing vis-à-vis the body and its needs. Evocative language, we saw, is needed for this end.

Further, there seems to exist a hierarchy of elusiveness; the "deeper" our needs and strivings seem to be layered and the more profoundly they seem to arise from the core of our organismic existence, the lesser appear our chances of lifting them into the clear light of linguistic comprehension and the lesser, also, seems abstract propositional language apt to solve this task. The more elusive the wisdom of the body, the more we have to "trust" evocative language.

In brief: it is through reconciling the elements of propositional *and* evocative language that the ego can successfully relate to the self.

Language Gearing the Ego to the Other

Language not only must gear the ego to its inner reality,

but it also must tie it to its outer reality. Language as a reconciling medium facilitates intercourse not only with our inner processes, but also with our outer world. This outer world foremostly consists of other human beings, live and dead ones. It comprises the given culture.

Seen from this angle, language must build a network of lifelines. Through this network, we utilize what others have accumulated. We assimilate, through language, the experiences of countless people who lived before us and who are living with us.

Doing and undergoing, closure and openness have to be reconciled in the ego's dealings with the other as they must be reconciled in its dealings with the self. Language, this means, must ensure man's conceptual delineation as an individual vis-à-vis other individuals. It must provide him with a shelter for his individuality, with a set of consistent durational barriers. These bounding structures which guarantee the ego's secondary autonomy (in the sense indicated by Hartmann) will work two ways: not only will they make the ego resistive to threatening inner agents (e.g. instinctual demands which provoke regression), but also to outer agents (demands coming from other individuals and cultural institutions). In brief, also on this second front line language must be *closing* and structuring. And this, again, foremostly requires a well-differentiated propositional language.

Such closing and structuring indicates a predominantly defensive attitude vis-à-vis the other. But this defensive attitude alone will not do. In addition, active *doing* is required. And such active doing, on this second front line, appears all important. In interacting with his fellowmen and culture, man must conceive of himself as a locus of self-willed, responsible action. Language, therefore, must allow man to experience himself, as well as the other, as a unique action center. It must give a verifiable shape to his *I* do, *I* want, *I* make choices, *I* determine my destiny, *I* am ready to bear the consequences of my actions. It must provide him with a vocabulary of self-motivation, a vocabulary that allows him to think in terms of a causality which originates within himself.

Yet not only must language underpin and give shape to man's doing and closure, it equally must ensure his undergoing and openness. It must allow him to become an object for the causality originating in others and in the cosmos around him. For one thing, he could not incorporate new words or values if this were not so. The shielding, enclosing function of language must be balanced by receptivity and openness. This versatile openness must prevent the necessary closure from becoming either too premature, too rigid or both.

In order that undergoing and openness provide man with a wide integrative and adaptive radius, evocative language is needed as well as propositional language; both must find together to make language man's chief reconciling medium.

Language as an Imaginative Reconciling Effort

We are, at this point, in a better position to understand the demands which are made on language qua reconciling medium: any instance of language and symbol formation reflects an effort at a dynamic integration.

Heinz Werner and Bernard Kaplan, among others, have thrown light on this reconciling effort. They traced diligently how the child, step by step, learns to implant himself in his language. The culture provides him with a linguistic medium which has its inbuilt qualities and requirements. He learns to adapt this medium to his idiosyncratic needs and capacities; he also learns to respect the language as existing in its own right. This implies a constant imaginative struggle. Through this struggle, the child exploits and refines the evocative as well as propositional features of language. Werner and Kaplan give many examples, covering all age groups, of this linguistic reconciling effort. The following few examples concern very young children.

A three-year-old girl, speaking of a big orange, inflated her cheeks to represent the fat and round form of the fruit.

A girl expanded her chest when telling about a sailing boat. Piaget's daughter of two years and two months let some gravel trickle through her fingers and said: "It's raining." Another child (of Neugebauer) expressed size differences through intonational variation. He uttered the name for "stone" (in German, "*Stein,*" but the child pronounced it "*tein*") with a high, thin short sound when pointing to pebbles. But when he looked at rocks, his intonation was long and low. Another child (observed by Gabelentz) called his father "Papa." But he called him "*Pupu*" when the father had donned a big fur coat. (*Pupu* in the German language suggests something heavy, furry.)

The bodies of children seem to exert a constant evocative pull on the language. Postural sets, basic rhythms of movement, instinctual dispositions impose themselves on the linguistic materials and patterns supplied from the culture. The child's "bodily wisdom" and bodily spontaneity seem to impart themselves onto this language. They appear to instill it with melody and richness.

Werner and Kaplan speak of the child's organismic matrix which becomes welded into the vehicular form of the language.

The ascendance of propositional language, however, requires that the organismic matrix recede—at least to a degree. Along with the child's increasing differentiation and integration, he must learn to gain more distance from this language and must learn to treat it with less egocentricity.

Later, vehicular qualities and requirements almost totally appear to subdue the organismic matrix. Mathematical language, for example, sternly seems to force into a pre-established, outside-supplied mold what it is that the individual wishes to express. But a creative, dynamic reconciliation, Werner and Kaplan demonstrate convincingly, comes into play also in this latter instance. Also in these most abstract mathematical formulations we can discern highly modulated and refined patterns of a rhythmic, dynamic structurization, traceable to body-tainted rhythms and action patterns. In the language of the behavioral sciences, the organismic matrix will, by necessity, have much greater leeway in shaping communicated sequences.

Focusing mainly on the developmental vicissitudes of symbol formation, Werner and Kaplan partly cut across the distinctions (such as between ego and self, individual and culture, conceptual language and evocative language) which I employed for the context and purpose of this study. They nevertheless illuminate, enlarge, and corroborate many of its essential findings and conclusions.

The principle of adaptive reconciliation allows us to delineate characteristic "failing" constellations and to grasp their implications for the ego. In each of these constellations, there results an *alienation of ego from self*.

ALIENATION OF EGO FROM SELF

Let us examine a first "failing" constellation. The ego, vis-à-vis the self, shows an excess of closure-doing. In this instance, the ego will tightly and aggressively fence in the self. The self, accordingly, will be suffocated. Self-structuring may triumph, but at the cost of the ego's becoming isolated from its organismic matrix, from its reservoir of regenerative warmth and pleasure. Along therewith, the ego cuts itself off from the clues and warnings arising from its organismic substrate. It deprives itself of the "wisdom of its body." Conceptual language, in this constellation, tends to squelch evocative language. *Les raisons du coeur* have no chance of becoming *les raisons de la raison*.

Catherine L., a secretary, thirty-four years old and unmarried, may serve as an example. In all her life Catherine had exercised self-discipline. She had studied economics, but discontinued her studies when an influential politician offered her a job on his staff. She proved to be an excellent secretary, although groups of people disturbed her. She never cared to make herself attractive to men. A few times she had joined other unmarried women in guided tours to foreign countries. Following one of these tours, she started to change in a manner which made people concerned about her.

She began to work feverishly at her job and became invested in the right-wing cause which her politician boss espoused. She labored many nights, working out fund-raising campaigns, preparing and correcting memos, checking on speeches. Also, she suffered from back pains. Because of these pains, she consulted several doctors. As no medical cause for them was found, she was advised to see a psychiatrist.

The psychiatrist found her a brittle, spinsterish woman with hardened features. She talked intently. She was over-worked, she admitted, but this was due to the demands of her job. The more she talked, the more her alienation from her self became apparent. She spoke in tiring clichés. "One has to do one's job. Isn't it so? We must simply keep going. That's the thing. Keep going. And do a good job. Nothing more awful than all those people on welfare. . . ." She could not remember any dreams. Neither could she think of any daydreams. Idling she found disgusting. At one point she described her body as a piece of hard wood. It was as if her body, deprived of conveying its needs, signaled through the back pains that it still existed.

A second failing constellation is the following: The ego, vis-à-vis the self, is passive and open. There will result an over-boarding of primary processes, an unharnessed up-surge of archaic, organismic undertows. Without the ego's structuring and modulating counter-pull, evocative language will remain too diffuse and still-born. All this organismic fuel flickers away without purpose and aim.

Richard D., a twenty-four-year-old hospitalized student of architecture, eventually labeled as hebephrenic, may serve as an extreme case in point. Richard talked much of the time to himself, mixing bits from several languages. Passersby quickly attracted his attention. I remember him talking once as follows: "No rhyme or reason, *schöne Mädchen auf der Wiesen, ha Mädchen, Fräulein*—bla, bla, tits of goats, big tits, you want to see my tits, Doctor . . . ?" All this was said with a broad grin. He did not sustain his attention for me and went away mumbling to himself.

ALIENATION OF EGO FROM NON-SELF

Similar constellations come to play in the *Alienation of Ego from Non-Self*. A too rigid and premature closure of the language shield will not only deprive the individual of the wisdom of his body, it will also deprive him of the wisdom which the others and his culture can offer him. Such premature closure (when combined with an excess of doing) may be reflected in strongly invested and tightly knit systematizations, or it may (when appearing in conjunction with excessive undergoing) have a more uncoordinated, punctuated character.

I think of Spencer F., a thirty-three-year-old lawyer, as fitting the first description. As a member of a therapy group, he at first impressed the other patients as a forceful discussant. His logic appeared succinct. Everything was neatly explained. He could easily, it seemed, devastate his opponents. After a while, however, no one could help finding him tedious and repetitive. His lack of all humor was unsettling. He appeared always deadly serious. Never did a witty, fresh, or whimsical note shine through his discourse. Nothing new or unexpected could touch him. One patient in the group described his language as "newness-repellent."

His private life, I learned, had long become barren. His wife, whom he accused of being a Lesbian, had left him to spend an "open-ended" vacation with a distant divorcée friend. He spent countless lonely hours perfecting a system for manpower mobilization which he tried to sell to various organizations. Nobody, though, seemed interested; and he became indignant, embittered and began to feel persecuted. Eventually he was hospitalized with a diagnosis of paranoid schizophrenia. At the hospital he started at once to write numerous appeals and complaints protesting his unjust confinement. In Spencer F. we notice a deep alienation from the self—similar to the one found in Catherine L.—but the alienation of his ego from the non-self (the others and his culture) seems even more marked.

A constellation marked by too much openness of language may, under more favorable circumstances, particularly when paired with a good degree of doing, make an individual unduly responsive to and dependent upon emotional, evocatively amplified streams emanating from others. He may become an easy prey to demagogues who overplay the evocative powers of language. The Nazi language of "blood and soil" (*Blut und Boden*), skillfully amplified by such stage tricks as the mass chorus, the marching columns, the martial songs, etc., can be seen as catering to such vulnerability. The individual with an excess of openness and passivity toward others may thus become a kind of interpersonal driftwood: His language does not provide him with that minimum of structured boundaries which is indispensable for any kind of goal-directed, decisive action. He cannot assert himself vis-à-vis others and the culture.

The failure of language qua reconciling medium, however, not only means man's alienation from self or non-self; beyond such alienation—and this brings me to the second important aspect to be discussed in this context—the spirally expansive developmental and adaptive processes will either be cut short or forced into dead-end streets. In this sense, alienation from self is bound to promote alienation from non-self, and vice versa. Excessive amounts of energies will stay bogged down in the maintenance of unviable adaptive solutions. The individual remains headed for eventual adaptational calamity.

In sum: Language, on a more intricate and observable level than was discussed earlier, mirrors and promotes the ego's capacity to absorb and reconcile adaptational discrepancies and hence solve conflicts. But also, given certain vicissitudes, it mirrors and promotes the ego's failure to do so. Language, therefore, appears strategically important for understanding the individual's dynamic, spirally expansive interplay between structuring and cathecting processes, as this appears to be at the root of all successful adaptation and development.

THE DAWN OF KNOWING INDIVIDUATION: AN OVERVIEW

The dawn of knowing individuation, as here understood, approximately comprises the first three years of the infant's life. We can distinguish a *preverbal* and a *verbal* dawn. During the preverbal dawn, the nuclear ego comes to its own; during the verbal dawn it is put to its great first test.

Thus, during this first crucial life phase, two pivots emerge which maintain the child's spirally expansive development and adaptation: The nuclear ego is the first pivot, and language, building on this nuclear ego and reflecting its proper installation, is the other.

In line with the distinction of a preverbal and a verbal dawn, the infant's developmental and adaptive tasks appear in different lights depending on these subphases. We may say that during the earlier, preverbal, ego-organizing phase, the accent is on *individuation,* and that during the second, verbal phase, it is on *knowing.* Along with such differences in developmental accents, the infant's developmental quest during these two phases must have a different quality.

During the first phase, the infant essentially appears embarked on a quest *to be one and the same;* in the second phase, on a quest *to be one and different.* The *quest to be one and the same* thus is the quest for *preverbal* individuation. It spans Piaget's phase of sensorimotor development and of Spitz's two first psychic organizers. In choosing the above name, I was inspired by a formulation of Lyman Wynne. The infant must remain one and the same, while countless influences hit him. He must remain one and the same despite and because of the tremendous learning and adaptive efforts which are required from him during this first phase. Such a quest to be one and the same essentially seems to denote what Winnicott called the finding of the true self. It is a quest which, even under the best of circumstances, appears to require heavy sacrifices and efforts. The vicissitudes of early denial and repression, as described earlier, reflect some of these sacrifices and efforts.

The *quest to be one and different,* spanning the *verbal* dawn of knowing individuation, requires that the infant has first learned that he can trustingly remain one and the same. On such a basis, he can hope to *"know" via language,* that is, he can hope to understand and integrate sameness and difference on high levels of intricacy.

He will realize he is a person in his own right, with an orientation toward the world which sets him apart from the rest of human beings. His sense of uniqueness implies his awareness of being different from all others—though different in various forms and different to various degrees. In order to recognize such difference he must create those essential patterns of language which sustain and permeate all later linguistic complexity. He must learn to reconcile private needs and culture's contractual requirements, to steer his precarious path between alienation from self and alienation from non-self (others and culture). Thus, his spontaneous needfulness will be able to meet with those ordering and structuring principles which are supplied by the culture.

Both—and this is most crucial—fundamental quests of the infant during this early phase of life are fatefully related to his mother's presence and actions. It will greatly depend on her how the infant succeeds in becoming one and the same and one and different.

For the mother-child relationship has been placed at the crossroads where a given culture and its new member meet for the first time, where the nuclear ego structures itself and where, along therewith, the basic patterns of the cloth of language are woven. This first drama of relatedness therefore becomes decisive for all later possibilities of relatedness and for the individual's ongoing quest for meaning and identity. It sets the stage for the spirally

expansive developmental and adaptive processes that
are bound to come. It is the cradle of his knowing individuation.

Can we further penetrate the dawn of knowing individuation? Can we grasp more clearly the essential de-
terminants and constellations in this relationship?

It is with this question in mind that I, in the following,
shall deal with the relationship of the mother and child.
I shall do so by examining it in the light of those viewpoints which I used earlier to illuminate the psychoanalytic
situation.

IV
THE MOTHER-CHILD RELATIONSHIP

MOMENT VS. DURATION

The mother-child relationship, like the analytic relationship, becomes effective in time. Like an analyst, the mother must make the moment count, and must recognize the importance of timing. She must time her contributions in the sense that she must sensitively gear them to the child's needs and given faculties.

To understand the importance of the mother's timing, it must be seen in the light of the child's extreme early helplessness and plasticity. Both factors work together to make the mother's impact deeper and more far-reaching than can be the case in any other relationship. This constellation of maximal dependency and plastic openness, as now exists for the child, will never be repeated. Therefore, nothing can ever have the same fateful consequences as what is done (or not done) during this phase of the mother-child interaction.

The infant's plasticity and dependence on the mother are not only strong, they also last unusually long. This is a result of man's biologic condition. The biologist A. Portmann, among others, has thrown light on this condition. Portmann compared thoroughly the length of pregnancy and degree of neurophysiologic differentiation which all mammals show at birth. He concludes: "Man achieves at the age of one year that degree of organization which a real mammal, comparable to Man in all other respects, would achieve at the time of his birth. In order to realize this state in the fashion of all other real animals, Man's pregnancy would have to last one year longer than it lasts actually; it would have to last about 21 months." Therefore, Portmann speaks of man's physiologic—meaning normal—premature birth (*physiologische Frühgeburt*). He also speaks of man's extra-uterine early year (*Frühjahr*, which, in German, also means "spring"). The features deriving from man's premature birth both reflect and support man's instinct-openness and hence his need to learn through an enduring exposure to his mother.

It is the long time of this exposure which permits a learning unparalleled in scope and subtlety. It allows a rich interplay of needs and influences between mother and child. It allows the relationship to become unusually deep and meaningful to both partners. It provides the conditioning for the deepest and most lasting identifications which seem possible.

It is through this depth and meaningfulness, made possible by the long time committed to mothering, that the sensitivity described above, can ensue. We thus find in the mother-child relationship a similar balance of moment vs. duration as was found characteristic for the analytic relationship. Just as, in analysis, the concept of timing implies the unfolding of the analytic process over a longer period of time, so the mother's crucial timing of her contributions is made possible by her being committed to, and involved in, a long process of mothering.

In the mother-child relationship, however, the balance of moment vs. duration as a rule operates on a deeper level of intensity and meaningfulness. Instead of being staked out by a contract, the time balance in the mother-child relationship almost exclusively is regulated by biologic and interpersonal needs of the two partners. And these needs are hardly available for distinct delineation and validation as is the case in analysis. For one partner in the relationship—the child—still lacks the necessary tools and requirements for such validation. This fact points to an essential aspect of the mother-child relationship that will be illuminated in the following dichotomy.

DIFFERENCE VS. SAMENESS

The weight of this balance seems to rest heavily on the side of difference, that is, divergence of needs and contributions. It is, chiefly, this dimension of difference that makes the mother-child relationship unique and helps to explain many of its features.

I shall, in elaborating this difference, begin with the needs of the child. In many respects they can be described more easily than those of the mother, at least during the first phase of the relationship.

For these needs of the child, in a sense, are both simple and absolute—such as the need for food, warmth, protection from environmental vicissitudes. They have to be fulfilled lest the child die. They reflect the infant's total dependence on the person who has the means and power to fulfill these needs: the mother (or mothering one). Accordingly, the child's "need-position" at this early stage is marked by two facts—first, the biological and elementary nature of his needs and second, the totality of his dependence on his mother.

The need position of the mother is less simply determined, hence it is more difficult to describe. Also the mother can be seen as being dependent on her child. But this dependence is not absolute in the sense that the infant is dependent on her. And further, though motherhood activates and gratifies biological and elementary needs, these needs, in central respects, must be seen differently than those of the child. I shall try to make this clearer through the following considerations.

The mother has a history which the child has not. The many experiences of her life have left their traces in her character, her ways of feeling, thinking, and relating. Compared to the child, the complexity of her personality is staggering. She has far progressed in her knowledge of individuation. She has become participant in a symbolic world. Whatever there was in terms of biologic drives and needs has thus been run through the mill of her endopsychic machinery: it has become tied to symbols and, along with this, to the symbolic world—a similar set of transformed derivatives from originally more primitive and elementary drives and needs—of other people. Remembrance and anticipation, the development of a fantasy life and world, of language, as earlier described, have all had their impact on those original biological drives and needs.

The mother, thus, may be considered a citizen of two worlds. She is a member in a world of culture, as mediated through language, a world of symbols, meanings, values. And this world she has to transmit to the child. But at the same time, she is the child's biological matrix, the nurturing animal. These two positions of the mother, in turn, interrelate complexly and dialectically.

As a citizen in the world of culture—that is, as a person who has internalized values and expectations and made these at least partly the subject of reflection and anticipation—the mother is able to relate to the child before he enters our world. Before the infant's birth she can make her own image of him, and into this image she can project various joyful or troubling expectations. Her needs, which she will direct onto the child, have been shaped and telescoped through this image. The manner in which her own needs are going to meet with those of the child is thus complexly mediated. Whatever immediate maternal drives and needs will come to the fore in her, they are no longer elementary as are those of the infant.

Thus, the difference in the positions of the two relating partners, at the beginning of the relationship, could hardly be more extreme. Here the mother: adult, differentiated, with a prefabricated image of the child, a transmitter of culture and a nurturing biologic matrix. There the child: without history, undifferentiated (without clear-cut image of the mother, and thus without the means for complex communication, self-presentation, and self-reflection), greatly receptive to whatever will be instilled in him, and totally dependent on his nurturant and protective matrix. This difference of positions, above all, reflects an unequal distribution of the weights of dependency and ability. The mother, in many respects, is dominant. It is from her relative position of strength that she must take on the role of leader. She is both pacesetter and enabler of the evolving bond. Hence the singular character of her position and contribution.

Yet, extreme as this difference may appear, there must, for the relationship to unfold, exist a sameness which matches it. The mother, with all the differences outlined above, must meet the infant on his level. Therefore, she must be able to *be like him*.

It is difficult to conceptualize this sameness linking mother to child. Conventionally, we speak of mother's empathy, her capacity to identify with the world of the child, and so on. But these faculties of mother—to be investigated more fully later—rather presuppose than explain such sameness.

Parenthood allows the adult to reawake the child in himself. It permits the mother to be once more a child herself. Once more she goes through a developmental phase which logically and chronologically she has passed. Once more, childish ways find a place in her adult world. She can again be elementary in her needs, immediate in her expression of them. And in thus becoming a child herself, she gets another chance at her own growth—more deeply emerging out of the core of her personality than could be the case in any other relationship.

Thus, difference and sameness, in this relationship, must be reconciled. The mother's leadership must be matched by solidarity with the child, her adult responsibility by her freedom to relive her own childishness. Only when this balance exists, can the mother be expected to sensitively gear herself to the child's needs. This balance, thus, is required in order that she, as earlier described, can correctly time her contributions. Given this balance, constructive growth and further change can, round by round, occur in both partners.

This balance, as was the case in the analytic situation, is bound to change. It will often be threatened and often, in a sense, lag behind the child's developmental requirements. But then it must catch up with them. It must reconstitute itself on ever-new levels. Indicating a matching of growth processes in both partners, this reconstitution of the balance, inevitably, cannot always be smooth. It can occur under signs of stress and temporary disorganization in both mother and child. But reconstitute itself, it must, lest the developmental dynamic be arrested.

The balance of sameness-difference thus is central to the mother-child relationship as it is central to the analytic situation. The essential difference between these two relationships, as regards this balance, is again partly a matter of intensity and width, and hence of constitutive impact, and partly a matter of lesser conscious manipulability of the mother-child relationship. Thus, as much as this balance allows a matching of needs and growth processes in mother and child, this matching must occur in the naïveté of unreflection. One partner of the relationship, the child, is as yet unable to cooperate meaningfully in that reflective validation which characterizes the analytic situation.

GRATIFICATION VS. FRUSTRATION

The weight in this balance rests on gratification. This gratification seems all-important. But its quality—even more than is the case in other early processes—is difficult to conceptualize. Traditionally, this gratification has become associated with the maternal, nurturant breast. The breast has come to embody that feeling of bliss and goodness, of satisfied, trusting relaxation, of "well-being" which is subjective paradise. It is necessary to experience this paradise once in order that it can be refound later. This subjective paradise, therefore, provides that goal and hope for our later life—obscure as this may be to us—which drives us to seek it by means of our adult projects and relations. But, also, it lays that foundation which permits such re-creation. It supplies the budding ego with the richness and substance required for such a task. This Lewis

simultaneously. (At this stage, Spitz indicates, even crying is confused with laughing by the observer.) The infant's greed, aroused by the seeming good breast, within seconds can become painfully intense. Instead of indicating to the infant his own stirring vitality, the anticipation of desires to be gratified, this greed then threatens to explode his organism. It threatens to engulf him and the breast in a torrent of irredeemable destructiveness. There exists thus a precarious balance, depending on quickly shifting physiologic undertows, between what is felt as manageable or unmanageable, pleasurable and discomforting, between what is good and what is bad.

These considerations illuminate the mother's position in the balance of gratification vs. frustration: Mother cannot help being gratifying *and* frustrating. But she must—and this is central—reconcile these two aspects in a manner which lets gratification win. The good and gratifying breast must outweigh and contain the frustrating and bad one. It is thus for the mother not a question of either gratifying or frustrating her infant—both being inherent in human mothering—but of so tipping the balance in favor of gratification that frustrations, necessarily forthcoming, can be absorbed and managed. The impact of the good experience must translate itself into those personality traits and structures which, now and later, allow the individual to cope successfully with frustration. These frustrations must be accepted as a debit that is well balanced by the stock of good experiences accumulated earlier. Woe to the child who has no such stock of good experiences, for whom—during the decisive symbiotic phase—frustrations overshadowed gratifications!

This point becomes more meaningful in the light of earlier reflections. We must see the co-existing impact of the balances of moment vs. duration and difference vs. sameness. When viewed against the balance of moment-duration, the good experience appears as the central feature of the symbiotic phase. It signifies a deeply meaningful tie existing between mother and child at a time when this is needed most. Good experiences thus are the moments reconciled with anticipated duration. They denote both the chance and necessity for a kind of primordial sharing which, once this developmental stage has passed, can nevermore be.

When viewed against the balance of difference-sameness, another aspect of the good experience comes into focus. This balance, we saw, structures that flexible tuned-in sensitivity of the mother which gears her to the infant's changing needs and evolving capacities. This balance, therefore, chiefly facilitates and safeguards what Sullivan has called tenderness: Mother's genuine *tending* to the needs of the child. Given such tenderness during the symbiotic phase, the mother will fortify the good experience. She will allow the infant to enjoy it fully. She will become its caring guardian. She will not cut it short too often.

Also this third balance of gratification-frustration, like the foregoing balances, is subject to shifts and reconstellations. These reconstellations will have to reflect the child's growing relative autonomy and mental individuation. To the degree that the child separates himself from his mother, he has to anchor himself in the world which society has cut out for him. In order to comply with society's demands, he has to forfeit primitive pleasures. The vicissitudes of the anal stage, such as toilet training, among many others, are bound to clash fiercely with the requirements for socialization.

However, as fierce as these clashes may be, they must have a method to them. They must make sense in the light of the child's future social adaptation. They must not simply be the offshoot of a power struggle: they must be inflicted in conscious anticipation of the child's future within his society. This element of strategic and deliberate imposure of frustrations will become more marked as the relationship and, hence, the balance of frustration-gratification progresses. It marks a certain change in this balance and in the maternal attitude which is required. It is chiefly this aspect which establishes a link between the psychoanalytic and the mother-child relationship in regard to the balance of gratification-frustration.

In the analytic situation, the weight for analytic leverage originally appeared to rest on the side of frustration. It was mainly through its frustrating features—signified, above all, in the crucial role of abstinence—that this situation seemed to become properly analytic. However, at further reflection, this frustration came to be seen as upheld and balanced by characteristic gratifications. Of these, the analyst's understanding, non-moralizing attitude appeared as perhaps most important.

This analytic balance, we now realize, compares to later stages of the mother-child balance: in both instances we find a more or less strategic imposure of frustrations, balanced by certain gratifications. But—and this is central—in order that, in each case, such balance can become operational, a working capital of earlier good experiences is required. Both the analytic relationship and the later phases of the mother-child relationship must take such capital for granted. There remains only this difference: in analysis this working capital derives from a relationship other than that of analyst and analysand. In the later mother-child relationship, in contrast, the available working capital accumulated *in this very same relationship*.

STIMULATION VS. STABILIZATION

Early in the mother-child relationship the weight of this balance is on stability. Stability results from those contributions and features of the mother which convey to the child regularity and predictability. The mother, in caring for the child, lets certain rhythms and expectations establish themselves. She institutes rhythms of feeding, of cleaning the child, of being available to him. She supports and entrenches sequences of wake and sleep. Also, in her behavior and emotional expressions, she reflects sequences and patterns with which the child becomes familiar.

The child thus develops his first notions of the order and

reliability of the world. His very instinct-openness and
dependence, mentioned earlier, make him particularly receptive to his mother's ordering impact. As yet this order
is transmitted to him through his quasi physiologic, unreflected interlocking with his mother. Responding to the
order which his mother represents and structures, he finds
himself ordered.

The early order he thus develops in himself is still crude
and it is hardly tinged by awareness. It is an order of organismic and affective patterns, of motor coordinations, of
instinct-like orientations toward gratifying objects and situations. But this order becomes the basis for the ordered
complexity which is to come. It provides that organismic
foundation out of which the nuclear ego, out of which
self-polarization and self-demarcation can grow.

The regularity and predictability of mother's care for
her child can be considered her attempt at extending into
the child's extra-uterine existence some of the structuring
protection he received during his intra-uterine life. In this
sense her stability is part of her continuing service as a
protective matrix, of her being a *"Reizschutz."* Shielded
by this stability, the child can go on feeling safe. He
learns to trust that the "open" world will be as well ordered and good as was the closed world of the uterus.

Yet stability alone is not enough. In order to become
humanized, to achieve his knowing individuation, the child
also needs stimulation. The concept of stimulation is am-
biguous: It may denote gratification as well as frustration.
It thus overlaps with certain features of the foregoing balance yet also sheds new light on them.

Stimulation is tied to gratification in that any nourish-
ment, any new dealing with the child implies stimulation:
The child is stimulated to respond, to integrate, to assimilate. This applies to food as well as to caresses, lullabies,
and instructions. Stimulation is thus implicit in the caring
efforts of mothering, in the mother's myriad ways of making the child's world rich, human, meaningful. In this
sense, stimulation is a crucial part of the good experience.
But stimulation also can mean frustration: When it re-

quires efforts at response, assimilation, and integration which the child cannot manage. Stimulation, in order to be wholesome, thus must be geared to the stability and order the child has achieved. It must come in doses. Such dosage must be inbuilt into the mother's gratification of her child. It must become part of her tenderness. Thus she can allow the infant to enjoy the good experience fully. She will not cut it short too often. She will be unhurried in her management of him. She will not unduly interfere with his experiencing the rhythms of wake and sleep, of hunger and satiety. She will, therefore, not unnecessarily intensify his greed and excitement, but neither will she subdue and squelch it. She will acknowledge it as part of his vitality but also be aware of how closely it may bring the infant to that threshold where the good experience turns into the bad experience.

Failure to reconcile stability and stimulation turns tenderness into impingement (Winnicott). Such impingement —the untimely interference with the infant's natural rhythms, the spoiling of the good experience—means that stimulation has become over-stimulation and false stimulation.

A mother, for example, eager to show off her small infant, tries to excite him. She rubs and cuddles him energetically. The infant—long overdue for his crib—begins to cry. Not being tuned to the infant's inner state and needs, the mother defines her infant's crying as a "cute anger." Excitedly she asks other guests to touch and stimulate him. "Let him cry," she says. "Crying is healthy." We can surmise the infant's despair when this happens again and again. For such overstimulation and false stimulation will now negate mother qua protective matrix. This outstanding quality of the mother for the child now changes into its opposite: Instead of embodying a safe haven, mother comes to denote mortal danger, the threat of an engulfing destructiveness, of annihilation and terror. To the bad experience is added a dimension of all-pervasive, disintegrative anxiety. This anxiety, inevitably, will include the fear of death to the degree that the infant becomes an anticipating animal, that his knowing individuation emerges.

The balance of stimulation versus stabilization, also, must evolve and change in time. There occurs a shift in weights in that stimulation, like frustration, becomes more important as the child grows up and is humanized. In being stimulated, the child gets the material for learning the complex skills of surviving in a highly symbolic, man-made world. And this material has to accumulate as he grows older. But this stimulation must find an established home base of stability if it is not to turn into over-stimulation and become too disruptive. In order to be fruitfully assimilated, it must hit a receptacle that has been solidly molded by a lot of earlier non-interfering protection; by a safe letting-grow, the child grows at his own pace. In brief, in order to make use of increasingly incisive stimulation, the child must have incorporated a basic stability. Only with such incorporated stability can he trust his inner organization will not irreversibly be thrown out of joint. Only thus can he hope to succeed in his crucial quest for sameness.

In the analytic situation, we must remember, stimulation and stabilization had to be reconciled so as to make possible "controlled regression." Such controlled regression denoted a loosening of the patient's mental organization and hence a heightened receptivity to stimulation. Regression, in being "controlled," was kept reversible. Also, in the mother-child relationship stimulation taxes the child's capacity at assimilation and integration. A temporary loosening of the mental organization will be the result and reflection of the individual's attempt at coping with stimulation. This state, also, may be termed controlled regression.

In both situations, a dependent partner learns by being exposed to stimulations. In both situations stimulation must *not* become impingement. In both situations stabilizing forces are pitched against the disorganizing impact of stimulation. And in both situations it must be taken for granted that the dependent partner's own stabilizing resources will be strong enough to cope successfully with such disorganizing impact of stimulations. We may speak of a working capital of stability which is required in analysis as well as in the later stages of the mother-child relationship. In the mother-child relationship this working capital has—as was the case with gratification in the foregoing dichotomy—been accumulated in the transactions between the same two people. In the analytic situation, in contrast, much of this capital derives from another relationship than that existing between analyst and analysand.

CLOSENESS VS. DISTANCE

The weight of this balance at first reflection seems to rest on the side of closeness. Without such closeness, all the other balances could not become operational. Thus, neither gratification and frustration nor stimulation and stabilization can have an impact on the child, unless the mother is closely available.

Hospitalism, as first described by René Spitz, reflects a complete lack of maternal closeness during the child's crucial early phase of life. Spitz defined "hospitalism" as total emotional deprivation. He made his relevant observations in a foundling home situated outside the United States. Here the children were breast-fed by their own mothers (or by one of the other mothers when the child's own mother was not available) during the first three months. During these three months they appeared normal.

After the third month mother and child were separated. The infants remained in the foundling home. They obtained adequate food, hygiene, and medical care. But as one single nurse had to care for eight children, they were emotionally starved. After separation from their mothers, these children progressively deteriorated. They appeared seriously depressed; later they became completely passive; they lay supine on their cots. "They did not," writes Spitz, "achieve the stage of motor control necessary to turn into the prone position. The face became vacuous, eye coordination defective, the expression often imbecile." In Spitz's films we see these children, withered away in apathy and depression, play with their own bodies in a ghost-like manner. Completely deprived, there is nothing else for them to play with than this only and last source and vestige of self-ness.

Since man is capable of inner distancing, bodily presence and availability may belie the lack of emotional closeness. Then the mother, although bodily close, still remains operationally distant. We speak of the inept, insensitive, self-absorbed mother. Her distancing apparatus vis-à-vis her child has become frozen, rigid, unselective. Her contributions, her psychic nutriment therefore miss the child or hit him inappropriately. The child will remain deprived even though the mother may go through the movements of mothering.

But the mother's closeness, vital as it is during the symbiotic phase, must not become excessive. Hence it must be balanced by distance. Without a balancing, buffering, distancing counter-force, closeness will lead to all-out impingement. The child will be emotionally overpowered, engulfed and intruded upon. This phenomenon has been described by a number of authors under a variety of terms, such as the "too good mother," the "over-identified mother," the "symbiotically enmeshed mother," and others. They all denote an excess of closeness which interferes with the child's differentiation and integration and, hence, with his knowing individuation.

Excessive distance and excessive closeness can thus be seen as reflecting disturbances in the mother's selective distancing: In one case this distancing appears too rigid; in the other case, too loose. However, these extremes seldom seem safely entrenched. Both excessive distance and closeness appear as besieged by forces which aim at their overthrow. However, these forces need not necessarily lead to a genuine and wholesome reconciliation of closeness-distance, but instead to an unwholesome, erratic vacillation between these two elements. This result can be explained as follows:

Beneath the armor of rigid distance strong longings for closeness and intimacy almost inevitably will breed in either partner. Excessive closeness, similarly, will be experienced as squelching. A push toward equilibration, toward a correction of these extreme states seems inevitable. In all intense and meaningful relationships, we may assume such a push to exist. When unfulfilled, this push will reflect and breed strain, tension, dissatisfaction. Because of the unbalance of closeness-distance, powerful needs remain unrealized in and dissociated from the existing relationship and they adamantly demand their entrance into it.

They often succeed in this demand. The strain and tension which build up in the partners become too strong. But—and this is important—the disturbance in the balance of closeness-distance will not necessarily be resolved. There occurs an explosive breakthrough of so far unrealized longings and strivings, but no reconciliation occurs. Instead, one extreme simply overpowers the other. We witness erratic swings from excessive distance to excessive closeness and vice versa. There occurs a turnabout in a revolving stage, but no workable equilibration of the balance of closeness-distance. The swing is too explosive, abrupt, erratic. The balance continues to be disturbed. It remains jerky and lacks modulation and evenness. The mother, in this situation, appears at the mercy of forces which, at one time, keep her too far away and, at another time, pull her too near to her child, but which never allow her to find a secure and proper middle position.

To sum this up: In the mother-child relationship there is, first, an early primacy on closeness and second, a particular need for a balance of distance-closeness which avoids abrupt swings between extremes. The mother-child balance, during the symbiotic phase appears both "closer" and more precariously installed than is typical of this balance in the analytic situation. This intense and precarious balance, in order to be maintained and dynamically developed, greatly requires the mother to be able to moderate and control her "distancing."

However, to the degree that the initial symbiosis loosens,

also this mother-child balance will come to resemble more closely the one existing and developing in analysis. Gradually, a closeness can and must develop between mother and child that is more like closeness of adult partners, capable of inner distancing. We may speak of a *"secondary"* balance of closeness-distance, as compared to the primary, more symbiotic balance outlined above.

In the secondary balance of closeness-distance the child has succeeded in becoming one and different, as earlier described: He can increasingly separate his own viewpoint from his mother's, his own needs and feelings from hers. He can rely on a subtle inner delineating apparatus and on his reconciling ego. This secondary balance closeness-distance is the rule in adult life. But it may break down and then come to resemble the primary balance—at least in some respects. This may occur in a mob situation, or in hypnosis. But also, it may occur in encounters with certain persons, who—unable to maintain proper emotional distance—imperceptibly get under our emotional skin. A casual acquaintance may suddenly make a remark which implies an inappropriate intimacy, for example, "You like all those girls with defects." This is different from a relationship when intimacy evolves "appropriately," and the partners both know that the conditions suitable for intimacy are right. Relying on their ability to reestablish inner separation, they can safely tap intimacy's regenerative reservoir. The analytic situation, we saw, sustains and turns to profit such secondary balance—making combined use of the patient's relatively strong ego, the balancing feature of the analytic situation itself, and the analyst's own reconciling power.

Also in the analytic situation, however, features of the primary balance may intrude, either suddenly or gradually: As the analytic balance develops there may occur a shift (or breakdown) in the patient's (and possibly also the analyst's) distancing apparatus. Important elements of the primary, symbiotic balance now seem reactivated. The climate of the analytic relationship changes. The patient comes uncomfortably close to the analyst's own unconscious. Balint, in a paper *"Die drei seelischen Bereiche,"* in 1957, has described this phenomenon and indicated that during certain phases of psychoanalysis its quality might change suddenly or gradually: "In such periods (of psychoanalysis) any tiniest remark, gesture or movement of the analyst can signify something which goes far beyond anything which he could have intended realistically.

"The patient, further, seems . . . somehow capable of 'unmasking' the analyst. He begins to know far too much about the latter. This knowledge does not derive from some extraneous source of information, but evidently from the uncanny capacity to 'understand' the analyst's motives and to 'interpret' his behavior. One almost is prone to think of telepathy or clairvoyance. . . ."

Such shifts in the balance of closeness-distance in the direction of a primary, symbiotic balance may put the analytic relationship to a test. There may be enough adaptive strength (including working capital of gratification and stability) in the analytic alliance to muster it. Or the analytic situation may become grossly unanalytical: the new closeness and heightened participation can be no more safely absorbed. The two participants become anxiously entangled with each other and the analytic situation sooner or later will break. We shall be better able to understand the developmental dynamic (including shifts and breakdowns) in this and the other of the child-mother balances when we turn next to the remaining linkage points between the psychoanalytic and the mother-child relationship.

TRANSFERENCE IN THE MOTHER-CHILD RELATIONSHIP

Is it—to extend our comparison with the analytic relationship—meaningful to speak of transference in the mother-child relationship? The answer, at first reflection, is "no." The term transference implies that something is trans-ferred, carried over. This something, we saw, is earlier patterns of relatedness, including patterns of perception, of self-reference, of social action. These patterns, having become ingrained, turn out to be inappropriate. They result in conflict, isolation, and arrest of growth. The analytic situation was seen as an optimal setup to break these inappropriate, self-defeating patterns, to undo the partial collapse of relatedness.

The mother-child relationship has no forerunners. The mother becomes a differentiated object for the child only as this relationship evolves. Instead of being the receptacle for transference, the mother-child relationship, in contrast, is *the cradle* of transferences. This relationship above all others, shapes those patterns which later are transferred. This primordial relationship is the soil out of which the fruit of transference grows. If this fruit turns out to be warped or poisoned, the soil later is bound to attract our attention. Reexperiencing, discussing, and illuminating the mother-child relationship therefore, in the course of a psychoanalysis, often becomes an important part in understanding (and thus correcting) the transference aspect of neurotic behavior. But the mother-child relationship in itself cannot be an arena where transference may be experienced.

However, we must at once qualify this conclusion: it is *only to the early* mother-child relationship that this statement applies fully. Later the situation becomes different. To the degree that the relationship evolves in time, it leads to more durable relational patterns in the child. These patterns, when entrenched, may become inappropriate also when seen in the light of later stages and contingencies within the very same relationship. Then this mother-child relationship can be seen as being squelched and restricted by its own past. We may now speak of a transference burden which is inappropriately *carried over not from one relationship to another*, but which inappropriately *is carried over*, within the same relationship, *from one stage to another*. We may thus differentiate between "hetero-transference"—patterns inappropriately carried over to other relationships—and "auto-transference"—

patterns inappropriately carried over to later stages of the same relationship.

In Chapter 1 I gave an example of a transference which now can be defined as hetero-transference: A secretary became ambivalently over-protective toward an older woman in her office. She thereby reenacted a relationship she once had with an older aunt who had replaced her mother. In this case a relational pattern which had originated with a mother-substitute was inappropriately carried over to another relationship.

Let us, on the other hand, consider the case of a young man. This man related to his by then elderly mother in a manner as if the latter were an evil, exciting seductress. He blushed in her presence and became anxiously tense when his mother began to talk. This young man was seriously neurotic and much of his neurosis was due to the fact that his mother had once acted seductively toward him. But his mother had changed in the meantime. She had undergone psychoanalysis and, in growing older, had found new interests and more satisfactory relationships than those she had when her son was young. Within the same mother-son relationship the son had therefore carried over a relational pattern which once served to protect him against mother's seductive intrusion. At this later stage of the mother-son relationship, though, this pattern had become inappropriate. This would be a case of auto-transference in the meaning here intended.

In applying the same meaning, an element of auto-transference can be discerned also in the mother's early seductiveness toward her son. Some of the mother's eroticism seemed appropriate as long as this son was a young infant. This eroticism then appeared a natural aspect of her caring tenderness for him. But this eroticism became inappropriate when her son approached the age of three to four years, that is, when he entered the Oedipal period. It was at this point when her eroticism seemed to turn into seductive impingement.

Both "hetero-transference" and "auto-transference" conceivably can be resolved: Inappropriateness of the implied patterns can be recognized, worked through and outgrown. However, the resolution of hetero-transference seems easier than that of auto-transference. In hetero-transference new perspectives are almost forcibly introduced. It is against the leverage of these new perspectives, it is in the often brutal clash between transferred patterns and the experienced interpersonal reality that the spark of corrective insight can ignite.

Auto-transference, in contrast, seems difficult to recognize. Auto-transference tends to be hidden under a smooth collusion of matching needs, perceptions, and expectations of the two partners. The transference burden of the past, though causing ill feeling and vague malaise, goes unnoticed. The needed new perspectives cannot, it appears, come from within the relationship itself. They require some reconstellating exposure to or intervention by outside forces. Auto-transference, blind and self-perpetuating, therefore often must first be transformed into hetero-transference before it successfully can be resolved. The psychoanalytic situation can be seen as creating and utilizing that form of "hetero-transference" which maximally facilitates corrective self-understanding.

RESISTANCE IN THE MOTHER-CHILD RELATIONSHIP

Resistance in psychoanalysis I described as the patient's power and strategy through which he keeps entrenched specific transferences. The analyst is needed to make palpable this resistance and to finally overcome it. He provides both an object for the resistance to bump against as well as a point of clarifying reference.

In the mother-child relationship, the intermeshing of needs between mother and child and the symbiotic burdens of the past tend to prevent such resistance from coming into being. This must be the more so, the more the mother-child relationship becomes a closed system of interlocking needs and expectations. There is then lacking that leverage of a clarifying opposition which deliberately is brought into play in analysis.

However, some sort of leverage and hence some kind of resistance must be structured also in the mother-child relationship. And this must be so in all its phases. Otherwise, there would be no incentive to change. Nothing would spur the child's knowing individuation.

Such leverage is built into the workings of the five balances described above. These balances operate within the pervasive, regression-spurring relational framework of what Parsons has described as early oral eroticism. Against the child's ever present regressive needs, he must be induced to build a "positive set of motivational capacities" for the performance of non-familial roles without which no society could operate. As the relationship develops, the leverage inherent in the five balances must change in the sense that it increasingly edges the child toward a knowing individuation and, along therewith, to a workable acculturation. The child then can be seen as resisting this individuation and acculturation. He encounters demands he does not like and which entail, for him, change and sacrifice. The mother, the prime agent of this acculturation, besides becoming an object against which resistance is felt, also may increasingly become a point of clarifying reference: to a degree, she illuminates the demanded change and sacrifice in the light of the child's necessary acculturation and future adjustment. In this sense her role, during later stages of relationship, may become similar to that of an analyst.

THE MOTHER'S SPECIAL POSITION

In order to understand the analyst's special position, we need to take into account the wider analytical situation. In order to understand the mother's special position, we must turn to the framework in which she operates. This framework is shaped through the culture in which she lives. This framework must fit central demands: each time and culture must provide an institution that allows a mother to reconcile biologic necessities, the quest for self-worth, the search for gratification, and the requirements for the child's acculturation. This institution I call the *institution of mothering*.

In parallel with the wider analytic situation, this institution of mothering contains three elements, all interdependent. We first distinguish the mother-child relationship as spanning the dialectic of the five balances. In this dialectic, there operate safety devices and feedback mechanisms which—to a degree—keep the relationship going out of its own momentum. But additional factors come to bear on this dialectic. These factors I now conceptualize within the "wider framework of mothering." They comprise, paralleling the wider analytic situation, the non-mothering aspects of the mother's life-situation and her personal qualifications. These elements interrelate as did those which were dealt with in the wider analytic situation:[1] The mother's personal qualifications sustain and complement the support she draws from her total, non-mothering life. And vice versa. I shall, at first, deal with her total life-situation. How does it affect the five balances?

In order to successfully maintain the balance of moment vs. duration, the mother, to a degree, must be able to project herself into the future. Society must confirm her in a project that matches the child's long dependence. Thus society supplements the biologic necessity. It safeguards the long time span required for mothering. Being safely oriented toward the future, the mother can fully immerse herself in the tasks of the moment.

To uphold the balance of sameness-difference, it is crucial that the mother has tasks and a life apart from her tie to the child. In attending to adult matters, she finds the proper vantage point for relating to the latter.

Society, in delineating differing roles according to sex, age, and professional status, provides both buffer and leverage for the mother's dealing with her infant. This de-

[1] Cf. p. 12.

lineation of roles in particular establishes difference while allowing sameness. The mother thus is confirmed and sustained in having one life with and one without her child.

The same applies to the balance of gratification-frustration: in order to be, vis-à-vis the child, gratifying when it counts and frustrating when it is necessary, the mother must find essential gratifications outside the child relationship. Thus, many of her needs for sex, affection, and intimacy must be fulfilled elsewhere. She must not be too starved in these respects and, out of such starvation, hungrily channel her unfulfilled desires and expectations onto the child.

As regards the balance of stimulation-stabilization, the mother must be held in a stable life-situation so as to be able to transmit some of this stability to the child. At the same time, she must find for herself outside sources of enrichment and stimulation so that she can pass on part of this stimulation to her offspring.

The mother, finally, must be rooted in an interpersonal network which permits adequate distance and closeness. Being "held" through this network, the mother is helped to steer the right balance of distance-closeness in her relationship with her own child.

These considerations throw light on the function of the family. The institution of the family essentially is built around the institution of mothering. It is culture's approved agency for rearing and acculturating children. The family, in most of our Western culture, thus crucially structures those aspects of the mother's total life-situation which are of greatest moment to her mothering. It is within the family that the mother has to be the guardian of the five balances. The family either provides or does not provide the needed wider framework of mothering. Therein, the mother's relationship with her husband is central. It is through this relationship that the mother can find essential needs for sex, intimacy, financial support, and a secure anchorage in the social arena fulfilled. A satisfying, supporting relationship with her husband thus exerts a pull toward desymbiotizing her relationship with her child. Her need-pressure, as directed onto the latter, is toned down. She can afford to let become "intransitive" her relationship with the child. She can let the five balances properly unfold.

Other relationships inside and outside the family—such as she may have with her own parents and in-laws, with other children, with siblings, with friends—will, in a complex interplay of forces and balances, come to bear on her relationship with her infant. They all must be seen as forming part of her total life and, hence, of the wider framework of mothering.

I shall, finally, take up the mother's personal qualifications. What is essential about them? In analogy to the qualifications of an analyst, I conceptualize these qualifications as the *mother's reconciling power*. This concept focuses on what the mother needs to have in her personality to be both participant *to* and pacesetter *of* a relationship with a "weaker" partner. What conventionally is called maturity, the capacity for object-love, the observing and synthetic function of the ego, etc., constitute this reconciling power just as this was found to hold true for an analyst.

What, then, differentiates her reconciling power from that of an adequate analyst? What are its special features? The mother, I believe, must be reconciling in a more instinct-like, "physiologic" manner. Most of her reconciliation must occur before the advent of reflective awareness. This *pre-reflective reconciliation* corresponds to the young infant's unique physiologic and affective susceptibility. It matches a need-constellation in the child where "affective integration" has priority. It is to this affective integration that the mother's contributions, above anything else, must be geared.

Reflectivity and self-awareness, therefore, for the mother are not as essential as they are for the analyst. She has, along therewith, less need for that radicalizing insight which requires and fosters "related loneliness" as described above. She must endure a different form of related loneliness. Also she must be able to lessen her biologic resonance with her child and thus accept becoming lonely. Related loneliness also for her is an inevitable aspect of being involved in the dialectic of the five balances. But radical (Oedipal) curiosity, as pitted against the life-lines of one's relatedness—this awesome fruit of a self-understanding reflectivity—need not play a prominent role in it.

As the analyst's reconciling power is best reflected in high moments of free floating attention, that of the mother shines forth in the smooth workings of her empathy (as Sullivan defined the term).[2] In empathically relating to

[2] Sullivan says this about empathy: "Empathy is the term that we use to refer to the peculiar emotional linkage that subtends the relationship of the infant with other significant people —the mother or nurse. Long before there are signs of any understanding of emotional expression, there is evidence of this emotional contagion or communication. . . . We do not know much about the fate of empathy in the developmental history of people in general. There are indications that it endures throughout life, at least in some people. There are few unmistakable instances of its functions in most of us, however, in our later years; I find it convenient to assume that the time of its great importance is later infancy and early childhood—perhaps age six to twenty-seven months." (*Conceptions of Modern Psychiatry*, 2nd edition. New York: Norton, 1953, p. 17.) At other times Sullivan used the concept empathy to explain how a mother may induce anxiety in her infant. Sullivan was aware that many people found it difficult to comprehend empathy. "I have had," he writes, "a good deal of trouble at times with people of a certain type of educational history; since they cannot refer empathy to vision, hearing, or some other special sense receptor, and since they do not know whether it is transmitted by the ether waves or air waves or what not, they find it hard to accept the idea of empathy." But humorously he adds: "So although empathy may sound mysterious, remember that there is much that sounds mysterious in the universe, only you have got used to it; and perhaps you will get used to empathy." (*The Interpersonal Theory of Psychiatry*. New York: Norton, 1955, pp. 41–42.) Empathy, as understood by Sullivan, can be seen as underlying the primary balance closeness-distance mentioned earlier.

her infant she is tender without being engulfing, warm without being intrusive, stable without being detached. She does feel and do the right things at the right moment without having to ask herself why this should be so.

THE CHILD'S SPECIAL POSITION

In what sense, in sum, does the child's position compare with that of the analytic patient? The difference, at first sight, is striking and follows from the earlier considerations. The child can never be viewed a partner in a contract to which he consents and reliably contributes. His total dependence on his mother and his immaturity preclude this. He can never be expected to live up to his part of the bargain (if this expression is applicable at all—compared to the analysand's paying his fees, his attending regular sessions, his obeying the rules of the analytic game).

But—and this seems important—while the child cannot be expected to cooperate in a context of adult rules, he must be expected to cooperate in the context of mutual growth and need fulfillment. In this sense also the child must live up to his part of the bargain, unknowing as he may be about it. Also the child, in many important aspects, must be seen as an active partner, who initiates action and who powerfully goads his mother to respond to him. Hilde Bruch, in particular, has stressed this point.

We may speak of many a baby's successful attempt at seducing his mother to love him. A mother's expectations, her "inner set"—I mentioned this earlier—may negatively predispose her toward a certain baby. This baby then can be seen as undoing the mother's negative attitude.

A forty-two-year-old woman and mother of three children may serve as a case in point. She became unexpectedly pregnant while her three children were reaching or outgrowing adolescence. She had resumed playing and teaching the violin which had been her passion before she had children. She looked forward to a new life devoted largely to her art. The pregnancy jolted this prospect. She became depressed and considered an abortion. Mainly due to her depressive lethargy, she missed the time when the abortion would have been feasible. Gloomily she berated her as yet unborn child. She became negatively set against this infant. But when he appeared he managed to foil any sinister predictions. Through his charm he seduced his mother into loving him.

A child's smile plays a central role in winning a mother's loving response. Many a child in an orphanage virtually saved his life through smiling. Through this smile he caught some special attention from a nurse or a prospective adopting parent and thus he, in a sense, still won in the lottery of finding a good parent—after seeming at first to be a sure loser. This smile appears as the crucial active contribution of the child which triggers the ensuing spiraling positive interchange.[3]

With the growth of the child's ego, his active part in

[3] Observations such as these have led Spitz to speculate on the possible survival value of the smiling response (the first of his three organizers), as discovered by him. This smiling response has many features of an instinct (or innate behavior coordinator). It appears normally around the age of three months and disappears after five to six months, although great individual variations exist. Before the age of three months a child's smile has a random, reflex-like quality. After the age of five months, the smile forms part of an increasingly elaborate and varied interaction with others. The smile of the smiling response, in contrast, can be reliably elicited by any human face or a dummy thereof which makes a nodding movement. Instincts, as defined by K. Lorenz and other ethologists, equally require certain "releasers" in order to be triggered. These releasers can also be presented as dummies and they, too, are often only effective during certain developmental periods. Seen from this vantage point, the baby's body proportions (relatively large head, big eyes, round cheeks, short extremities, combined with clumsy, "cute" movements) can be considered the releaser for the mother's instinctive tenderness-response. K. Lorenz speaks of the *"Kindchenschema."* We observe its effectiveness not only in human babies but also in all kinds of "cute" puppies and animals, teddy bears and dolls.

relating to his mother becomes more varied. In a real sense, he can become his mother's teacher. His greatest teaching tools are the freshness and sincerity of his observations and statements. This cuts through a lot of the more or less intellectual and hypocritical cliché-world which has become second nature to adults. In particular, children can impress their mothers anew with the honest down-to-earth character of human needs and strivings. Many a mother may resent the daily diapering, but she cannot help being grateful for having to communicate on such an immediate and simple basis as is implied in changing diapers. Therefore—on the level that counts—she will love her child for it.

At each new developmental level, the child's teaching role will have to change—just as will the mother's.

POSITIVE MUTUALITY

In the good mother-child relationship we find thus a spiraling dialectic of mutual growth and fulfillment of needs. This dialectic seems difficult to conceptualize. To a great degree it reflects an unwitting logic of the heart, that is, of deeply unconscious and quasi physiological processes which appear at odds with the logic of reason. Still, this logic exists and its laws cannot be broken without punishment.

The process of spiraling mutual growth and need fulfillment, as here described, I shall call a *positive mutuality*. All satisfying human relationships, I believe, reflect such positive mutuality. The mother-child relationship, however, seems most suited to study its crucial features.

Hegel, in his section on the "master and servant" of his *Phenomenology of the Spirit*, offers a conceptual model which allows us to grasp important elements of positive mutuality as here intended. Hegel speaks here of a movement of mutual affirmation. I affirm myself in the other and the other is affirmed in me. This occurs in a complex doubling process of one's self-consciousness. (The word "self-consciousness," "*Selbstbewusstsein*," for Hegel has a rather broad meaning. In some respects it seems to encompass what we nowadays might call a sense of identity, or sense of self.) By doubling my self-consciousness, I lose myself in the other. But in so losing myself, I gain myself. When I retrieve the doubled (or projected) part of me onto myself, that is, when I return into myself, I am changed. The other experiences the same in regard to me. In this manner, our relationship, again and again, will win a new basis.

This description of a positive mutuality is quite abstract. Spitz has elaborated in greater detail those features of the spiraling give and take which, I believe, are crucial in any good mother-child relationship. René Spitz speaks of the dialogue between mother and child. "Such dialogue," he writes, "is not a verbal dialogue. It is a dialogue of action and response which goes on in the form of a circular process within the dyad, as a continuous mutually stimulating feedback circuit." Emotion is a central element in this dialogue: "The action can be and mostly will be invested with emotion, but the same applies, of course, to the response. The action may involve a minimum of emotion; the response may be emotion alone, as easily as emotion-charged action. The action may be directed or nondirected, and so may the response . . ." This is not a repetitive process. On the contrary, the reverberations provoked in the mother by the child's initiative and those in the child by the mother's resulting behavior (and vice versa) produce ever new constellations of increased complexity. It should be added that these are constellations and structures resulting from energy displacement. Each of these circular processes will achieve some sort of gratification, or frustration, and then subside. Traces will be left in their wake in the psyche and the memory systems of each of the two partners. These traces will modify the next circular process in its inception, or in the form it takes, or in its unrolling, or in the way it achieves its goal, thus adding to the increasing complexity of the dialogue.

In Chapter III I described the infant's knowing individuation as a process through which the nuclear ego is established and his personality develops according to the principles differentiation-integration and adaptive reconciliation. This involves an intra-psychic as well as an interpersonal dimension. I submit that it is *through a positive mutuality, unfolding in the ongoing reconciliation of the five relational balances that knowing individuation is achieved.*

My approach does not establish causal relationships. Instead, we trace a complex and changing transactional field. If we focus on specific phase-constellations within this field, it is in the awareness that these phase-constellations represent important but transitional aspects of one process.

We must also keep this in mind: While steadily developing, these balances must have their phase-specific placement of weights. The reconciliation must be such as to give, during certain phases, priority to a particular side of the balance. And second: These balances operate interdependently. Thus, within the total interpersonal constellation the impact of specific balances can be either *reinforced or weakened* depending on how certain relational balances "cluster together."

In accord with this approach, we should keep in mind the subdivision of the dawn of knowing individuation outlined earlier, that is, we should distinguish between the child's quest to become one and the same, spanning the first eighteen months, and his quest to become one and different. (Still, this division of phases in many respects remains crude. It will be necessary to subdivide further the symbiotic period into phases which have strategic relational significance. However, in the present context the above division will suffice to show how the concept of relational balances can be integrated with the concept of a positive mutuality.)

Let us, with these points in mind, consider how a positive mutuality bears on some crucial aspects of early ego development. The *quest to become one and the same* during the first eighteen months of life can be seen as providing the leitmotiv for the strategic constellation of balances which is necessary: All these balances must be so tipped as to serve the child's quest to become one and the same and to find his true self.

In this quest, primary gratification appears crucial. It imparts to the child his early sense of self-worth: "The child has no way of knowing that he is valuable unless he observes someone who thinks so. This is very plain. Demonstration of love is proof of love" (Becker). And gratification, in the sense here outlined, is the currency of love the child can use. In being nourished, fondled, and admired, his self-esteem is kindled, maintained, and strengthened.

Also, stability is all important in this quest. Without his mother's stabilization and reliably anticipated presence the child's quest to be one and the same will be doomed to failure. This stabilization, more than anything else, appears to be at the root of what Erikson has called "basic trust." It seems to underlie the "object constancy" of Piaget. The mother's enduring commitment underpins such stabilization.

Further—and this seems most important—early gratification, stability, and closeness must combine to make for a phase-constellation which optimally fosters the neutralization of instinctual energies. We may speak of a *neutralizing mutuality* which, in the interplay of structure and cathexis, as earlier described, will allow for an optimally smooth ego efficiency and ego growth.

Early gratification, we saw, provides the expanding mutuality with its main working capital. It ensures a warm libidinal circuit in which frustrations are toned down. Thus aggressions are kept to a level which still can be absorbed by the nuclear ego and by the "positivity" of the mutuality. The developing psyche will not be overtaxed with the problem of how to contain and how to detoxify this aggression. It will not be exposed to strong regressive, deneutralizing pulls at a time when its pivotal nuclear structures are being precariously installed.

Early stability contributes to this toning down and subtle modulation of instinctive and erotic energies. (Hartmann expressly ventured the thesis that early object constancy promotes neutralization.) But so does early closeness. The primordial sharing during this phase, never to be equalled in later phases, its all important gratification and stability, imply the perhaps "closest closeness" possible between humans. A quasi physiologic resonance, requiring mother to empathize unreflectively with the child's needs and moods, is central. The language of love, in order that it reaches the child, requires this kind of closeness. This must be an "even," relaxed, modulated closeness. The rhythms of tender affection must constantly and gently touch the child, but they must not engulf him.

The quest to be one and different, in order to succeed, requires a positive mutuality, wherein difference of the mother, frustration, stimulation, and distance gain more weight in the evolving relational balances. Thus the symbiotic band is loosened, self-polarization and self-demarcation are promoted. The child can learn to experience himself as a focus of manipulatory causality which differs from other human foci. Positive mutuality now implies increasingly that the partners relate to each in the awareness of the other's complexity and difference.

Like physical health, a positive mutuality during the dawn of knowing individuation seems not in need of demonstration by examples. We enjoy it, we take it for granted; but we are not concerned as to how it comes about. In a good early relationship between mother and child, enjoyment, accordingly, grows out of the operation of the five relational balances. The child, on the whole, is happy. He thrives; he enjoys the exploration of the world around him. The mother, in seeing her child thriving, is confirmed in her motherliness. She also, on the whole, is happy. This happiness begets happiness and—despite and because of all the labors and problems involved in mothering—the positive mutuality unfolds without much ado.

Happiness implies a lack of fear in human relationships, and this requires in the child the capacity of *fearless attention*. I shall conclude this chapter by briefly elaborating this concept which, like no other concept, seems suited to integrate important propositions of this essay.

FEARLESS ATTENTION

Attentional processes, we found earlier, provide a link between the principles differentiation-integration and adaptive reconciliation. They mirror and propel the expanding interplay between cathexis and structure, as they put the emerging mutuality on the right track. They crucially contribute to make positive this mutuality. This attention is the window through which the child reaches the matrix of his survival, of the interpersonal reality which for him counts most: His mother.

Already in the pre-verbal dawn of knowing individuation this attention must gain features of a structured independence: It must soon achieve and reflect a secondary autonomy (in the sense indicated by Hartmann) vis-à-vis pressing instinctual urges and bodily states. It must become resistive to internal (somatic) and external distraction. Given such secondary autonomy, attention can be expected to reconcile doing (gearing the child actively to mother's contribution) and undergoing (allowing himself to be influenced), closure and openness.

But further: This early relative autonomy of attention-fostering structures must cost little in terms of energy. For energy, after having served to cathect an attentional structure, must quickly be made reexpandable. It will be badly needed to keep going the developmental, adaptive dynamic and, interdependent therewith, the dialogue. This means: The energy which builds and cathects the infant's incipient attentional structures must be mainly *neutralized* or neutral[4] energy. Given this neutralization, attention can

[4] R. W. White had made a strong case for our postulating independent ego energies which would make understandable various forms of exploratory and "effectance" or competence behavior—behavior which cannot easily be conceptualized as

become intent and yet smooth, focused and yet flexible. It can have an ordering purposefulness and also adaptive agility.

Such attention, above everything else, will have a fearless, trusting quality. The mother trustingly is experienced as the guardian of the infant's quest to become one and same. But the child knows also she will let him become one and different. She can be approached and explored with joy and minimal anxiety. This, therefore, appears the key to what makes neutralizing and positive the incipient mutuality: The mother, tenderly tending to the infant, allows the latter to attend fearlessly to her—and vice versa.

---

resulting from the neutralization of conflicting drive energies. Clearly, also attentional processes, as were described, reflect much of such exploratory and "effectance" behavior. Therefore, also in these attentional processes it may seem more appropriate to think in terms of "neutral" rather than in terms of "neutralized" energies.

V
NEGATIVE MUTUALITY

Just as illness illuminates the conditions of health, so does negative mutuality throw light on positive mutuality. Negative mutuality implies that vicious circles operate in a relationship. These vicious circles interfere with its spiral expansion and differentiation. Hence, they interfere with the differentiation and growth of the partners. Instead of mutual growth there is mutual stagnation and impairment; instead of mutual affirmation there is mutual negation.

In this chapter I shall deal chiefly with those forms of negative mutuality which illuminate the plight of schizophrenic patients. These patients—I shall elaborate this later—confront us with extreme human potentialities: They reveal in stark contours what could have been (or still can be) our own fate. These patients, also, teach us about extreme human relationships. They give a special meaning to the concept negative mutuality and, in particular, to that negative mutuality which may develop in the early relationship between mother and child.

This chapter will consist of two parts. In the first part I shall deal with the negative mutuality which affects mainly the child's quest to be one and the same. This covers the first phase of knowing individuation. In the second part, I shall deal with negative mutuality as it bears on the quest to be one and different.

THE QUEST TO BECOME ONE AND THE SAME

A negative mutuality during the first phase of knowing individuation (from birth to approximately eighteen months) implies that the relational balances are not properly reconciled. Some balances may be more affected than others.

If moment and duration remain unreconciled, the mother may fail to impart to the incipient dialogue a necessary dimension of depth and meaning. The mother remains uncommitted, the relationship an ad hoc affair. The infant will be less motivated in engaging himself, in rallying his vital forces in the service of an expanding, moving alliance.

The balance sameness-difference may be so disturbed as to not allow a primary physiologic resonance. The differences built into the relationship then become too overpowering. Incorporation of and identification with the mother thus must become fragmented, jerky, and "unphysiologic." The two partners do not meet through primordial sharing.

Without a predominance of gratification there will not be enough working capital for future neutralizations. Regressive pulls will have dangerous leeway. In particular, frustration-born aggression will quickly tend to reach forms and levels which can no more be safely mustered by the reconciling potential inherent in the immature psyche and in the evolving relationship. And further: Without demonstration (and hence proof) of love during this crucial first phase, all later demonstration of love will not convince. There will have to be a constant struggle (tremendously unnerving and costly) in order that love can be utilized.

In a disturbed balance between stimulation-stabilization, the child may become over-stimulated or "overstabilized." Object-constancy may turn into object-inconstancy. There will then be lacking in mother's care and presence that smooth, reinforcing, predictable quality which seems so central, both to the building of workable identifications and to successful neutralization; a quality which, during this first phase, must pervasively enter into all the other relational balances.

Lastly, an unreconciled balance between closeness and

distance—be this in the form of excessive distance, or of erratic swings between distance and closeness—equally will interfere with the proper reconciliation of all the other balances and hence, with the child's adaptive and maturational efforts.

In sum: The child's quest to become one and same will be betrayed. The incipient mutuality will be negative instead of positive. There will be little chance that neutralization exerts its expansive developmental thrust.

This incipient *negative* mutuality can greatly vary in form and intensity, depending on the quantity, constellation, and timing of relevant factors. Certain balances can so cluster together as to reinforce their deneutralizing impact. Others can mitigate it. And all-important remains the phase during which negative constellations become operative.

STRATEGIES FOR INTERPERSONAL SURVIVAL

We are in a position to trace important implications of a negative mutuality during the early dawn of knowing individuation. During this time, a betrayal of the quest for sameness will reverberate into all layers and aspects of the evolving nuclear ego. This ego will be impaired. Yet along with thus being impaired—and this is crucial—it will be taxed with adaptational tasks far beyond its age and reconciling powers.

This is the dilemma to which the child is exposed: His adaptational apparatus, while still most immature, will come under fire and yet he has to carry a heavier than normal adaptational load. What can he do? This much is plain: Whatever he does, he remains tied to the defensive and reconciling arsenal available to him at this early period. He cannot reach beyond his immature nuclear ego.

In this dilemma, I submit, the infant can adopt certain alternate strategies. These I call *strategies for interpersonal survival*. None of these strategies, we shall see, can save the child from the above dilemma. Yet each strategy, in a sense, promises a way out. What are these strategies?

In most general terms, the infant can either try to re-move himself (and his adaptational apparatus) from the threatening mother; he can psychologically flee or fight his mother and thus find for himself some sort of moratorium or respite from her. Or he can make what is, in a sense, a heroic effort of trying to detoxify mother psychologically. Thus he can try to contain her badness. In so doing, he will make use of whatever weapons he might find.

His main strategies for coping with the above dilemma, therefore, appear first, *flight-fight* and, second, *"control"* of mother. Both these strategies must bear the imprint of the child's early level of differentiation-integration. To a degree, I believe, these two strategies can be traced in all human relationships. But it is the negative mutuality of the early mother-child relation where these strategies, from the vantage point of the child, truly become strate-gies for survival. Let us consider them.

It was Sullivan who suggested a mode of psychological flight which seems consonant with the infant's early nu-clear immaturity. He called it "somnolent detachment." The infant, exposed to massive frustration and anxiety, tries to numb out all feelings. He retreats into a kind of stupor which is a sort of self-inflicted emotional deep freeze. Through this stupor mother becomes removed, hazy, and quasi non-existent. We may speak of a primitive all-out denial of mother.

It is mainly certain catatonic patients—adolescents or adults—who give us an inkling of this early and primitive flight of an infant from his mother. These patients are stuporous; they appear stricken with terror. Their vegeta-tive systems seem in turmoil. Not seldom their heart rate is more than twice the normal rate, while their blood pres-sure is dangerously high. All the tension and energy mo-bilized in the body seems used up in creating a psycho-logical state of dazed insensibility. Everything appears blurred. Neither a feeling from the inside nor a suggestion from the outside, it appears, can touch the person.

Sometimes this all-out denial of and flight from the

nother may have less of an escapist tinge and gain more
f a structured and actively rejecting quality. Then psy-
hologic flight seems to merge into fight. In the extreme
ase, the child seems to erect a massive paranoid barrier.
We can observe such barriers in certain children who are
diagnosed as autistic. Sometimes these children appear
utterly unreachable. Their faces and their bodies convey
a forbidding "no" to their environment. The paranoid bar-
ier may become so tightly entrenched that love's later
abors, even when coming from well-meaning and compe-
ent mothering persons, appear lost. These early escape
trategies, when seen in the light of the principle of
eeded adaptational reconciliation, reflect constellations of
xcessive closure which occur on quite primitive levels
f personality organization.

The second strategy—the attempt to control the mother
psychologically—implies more complex adaptational proc-
sses than is the case in the first (flight-fight) strategy. *In
his second strategy, the nuclear ego must be molded for
ymbiotic survival.* This requires, essentially, two things:
he still existing unstructuredness and immaturity of the
uclear ego must be turned into an adaptational asset in
he sense that it facilitates a sensitive, immediate empathic
esonance with the mother. At the same time, a certain
ifferentiation of the nuclear ego is prematurely pushed.
elf-polarization and self-demarcation seem to develop
precociously.

Certain schizophrenic patients suggested to me the
uality and meaning of this second controlling strategy.
One of these patients was Mary K., a young mother of
wo children. She had become hospitalized with a diagno-
is of acute paranoid schizophrenia. I saw her as a psycho-
herapist shortly after her acute state had subsided. Mary
eemed to have a subtle ability to tune herself to my
noods. With a glance, it appeared, she could take in how
I had slept, whether I was grouchy or preoccupied; even
ny fantasies, I felt at times, were laid open to her. In a
vay, I found this appealing and yet most troubling. A
trange emotional radar, it seemed, was scrutinizing me

and I could not help becoming hyperalert and over-sensitive myself. Many sessions left me exhausted.

Mary's emotions could change quickly and so could my reactions to her. Within a short period, for example, I could feel myself becoming annoyed (often without knowing why), slightly sexually aroused, preoccupied with death and destruction, and then feel a sad tenderness. Not seldom I found it difficult to establish whether these changing feelings of mine were indicating what Mary had projected on to me, or whether in some quasi-magical way, Mary had succeeded in amplifying my own feelings for me. I was often made anxious by so much seemingly empathic, and yet erratic and questionable communication between us. Much of the time I felt cornered, underhandedly pushed and made defensive. I realized, though, that Mary was much more anxious than I was. It was as if she, while transacting, was constantly treading on dynamite. She seemed immensely sensitive to being rejected.

Mary did not care about (or was not capable of) expressing herself clearly in language. She used to talk in the evocative mode. Equivocal and hidden meanings seemed to abound in her speech. When she talked about the warm sun outside she meant, I felt, the warmth of some person. But frequently I could not be sure about my interpretation. (Did she perhaps, I might wonder, in talking about the warm sun, refer to what she saw as coldness in her therapist? And so on.)

Mary's style of relating to me, as just described, indicates transference. In important respects Mary related to me in the manner in which she had learned to relate to her mother.[1] In puzzling about my own feelings and reactions toward Mary, I began to ponder how this relation-

[1] Not only her mother, of course, was brought into the transference; so were her father, a sibling, and other important figures of her past. For simplicity's sake, however, I shall focus on such attitudes and behavior of hers which I had reason to attribute to her early relationship to her mother. (Cf. also what Harold Searles has to say on this subject. He writes, ". . . I consider it valid to conceive of the patient's transference to the therapist as being in the nature, basically, of a relatedness to

ship might have felt during its earliest stages. I tried to visualize her powerful, threatening mother. In so doing, I began to understand some implications of the child's attempt to mold his nuclear ego in striving for symbiotic survival. S. Ferenczi, Melanie Klein, Harold Searles, Hanna Segal, and other authors have helped me in such understanding.

These authors point to many a schizophrenic's splitting and fragmentizing processes which are characterized by a certain looseness and magic-like agility. Melanie Klein and some of her pupils speak of the "bad breast," "bad mother," or "bad me," which the later schizophrenic learned to split away as an infant. These concepts are difficult to explain. They are largely metaphors and are derived from what transpired in the analysis of children and psychotics. The terms imply that the infant, while relating to the mother, can be aware of global feeling states and, along therewith, of certain fantasies. (This assumption, though, is questioned by many analysts: Here we run into the problem of trying to make visualizable something which seems to precede and to defy our adult conceptual modes.) These global feeling-states and fantasies stand for parts of the self, for the symbiotic twosome, as experienced by the child.[2] Ego splitting is then seen as a way of coping with conflict at this early level of psychic

the therapist as a mother figure from whom the patient has never, as yet, become deeply differentiated. Furthermore, I believe that this 'sickest'—least differentiated—aspect of the patient's ego functioning becomes called into play in any relationship which develops anything like the intensity that the therapeutic relationship develops." "Transference Psychosis in the Psychotherapy of Chronic Schizophrenia," in *Collected Papers on Schizophrenia and Related Subjects*, (New York, International Universities Press, 1965), IV, 662.

[2] H. S. Sullivan, in *The Interpersonal Theory of Psychiatry*, analyzes the nursing situation wherein the concept of the mother as one separate person develops only after complex processes comparable to those mentioned above, have unfolded. He emphasizes, in particular, "good mother" and "bad mother" personifications. (New York: Norton, 1953, pp. 66–73, 80–91, 110–22.)

differentiation and integration. This goes as follows: The child tries to preserve the image of the good mother (or breast) since only on a good mother can he dare to depend. His bad feeling-states, however, contradict such an image of motherly goodness. Therefore, he splits away what is not good about himself or his mother—this may include his own and mother's destructive impulses and fantasies. But this implies a splitting of his budding psychophysiological organization.

Besides precocious nuclear splitting, empathic resonance—the immediate tuning-in to the mother's unconscious needs and fears—becomes the main survival asset. Such empathic resonance, we saw, can be assumed to form part of the primary balance of distance and closeness as found, at least to some degree, in any ordinary early mother-child relationship. However, when the nuclear ego is molded for symbiotic survival, empathic resonance is unduly fostered. The child is made over-empathic.

My patient Mary, as earlier described, presents evidence of both heightened empathic resonance and ego splitting in the sense here intended. She appeared hypersensitive to and aware of fantasies and feelings of mine of which I myself was only dimly or not aware. But also, in order to ensure that I remained a good and dependable matrix (or mother), she had to split away, and hence negate, much of the knowledge she had gained through her empathy. For her the knowledge about my unconscious was a dangerous, unsettling knowledge. For example, she would not accept that I might be tired, preoccupied, or angry since it was necessary for her to see me as loving, unperturbed, and all-out dependable. She showed herself split about what she knew about me. She thus could not properly digest this knowledge, see it in perspective, and hence make it usable so as to enrich her transactions. Both her ego and this knowledge, we might say, became fragmented. Intra-psychically, she worked at cross purposes. Some of this knowledge she projected onto me—remaking me in her own (unconscious) image and, insofar as she projected her own bad impulses on me, achieving the very thing she tried to avoid: Turning me into somebody unreliable and bad. Some of this knowledge she precariously dissociated. In thus relating to me she tried to control me; she tried to fit me into her own confused and confusing psychic framework and anticipatory set. In this process she exhausted herself and (to a degree) also me.

I have elsewhere elaborated important aspects of this early controlling strategy. I spoke of the infant's adaptation to the "stronger" person's reality. By molding his nuclear ego for symbiotic survival an infant might learn to cope with even a highly unstable, overstimulating, erratic mother who is, in short, dangerous. He so employs his adaptational arsenal that he skillfully learns to spot and "control" any dangerous psychological move in the all-powerful mother. A similar strategy is employed by many persons placed in positions of dangerous dependency, such as women in paternalistic households, slaves or concentration camp inmates. They all tend to perfect certain psychologic skills at controlling and manipulating the more powerful partner. And these skills seem to rely heavily on the above described combination of empathic resonance and precocious splitting (though naturally, in adults, this combination will operate on much higher—and therefore partly different—levels of differentiation-integration than is here implicated).

In psychotherapy I tried to be unlike Mary's unstable, overstimulating, and erratic mother. Yet, in many respects, she related to me as if I were such a mother. This was the transference aspect in her behavior. But what from one angle could be considered as transference, from another could be seen as a way of life. Her adult ego functioned now as if symbiotic survival were still the crucial issue, as if any person to whom she related more closely were still, in one way or another, a replica of her dangerous mother. To be sure, what once served interpersonal survival, did so no longer. On the contrary. Still, her present behavior allowed a glimpse into what her early struggle for survival might have been like.

Compared with the first described strategy of flight-fight, this second "controlling" strategy avoids excessive closure. There is more of an effort to reconcile doing-undergoing and closure-openness. Both strategies, however, only help to a point. They cannot lastingly resolve the infant's dilemma. In either strategy he can succeed only by paying an enormous price: He must mortgage his future chances of development and relatedness. In succeeding in these strategies he ensures that the negative mutuality will remain negative, the betrayal of the quest to become one and same will remain unredeemed.

In the case of flight-fight the disastrous consequences are immediately evident. In fleeing or fighting his mother the infant flees and also fights his supporting matrix, bad and dangerous as she may be. Yet it is the only matrix he has. Therefore, he can only flee or fight halfway. In order to survive at all, he must reach a compromise. This compromise usually takes the following form: In rigidly shielding himself psychologically, the infant allows only the barest minimum of mother's sustenance to reach him. Mother's nutriment must only come in trickles. His lot will be *premature (relative) self-sufficiency and restriction.* There will only be a minimal chance for growth and expansion. Not unjustifiably have these children been compared to automatons, robots, and dummies. Their premature, restricted self-sufficiency stigmatizes them.

In the course of time, I have come to see many people as suffering from a premature self-sufficiency and restriction even though these persons may never be called autistic or be placed in institutions. Yesterday I saw a salesgirl who, I think, will probably not hold her job for long. Though she was appropriately dressed and had nothing conspicuous about her, she made people avoid her. Her smile had a drab, mechanical quality. A kind of resigned, dull bitterness in her seemed to kill all joy and life around her (like a person who sprays mildew wherever she goes, I thought). I wondered what early relationships she might have had.

In the second strategy the disastrous consequences are not so immediately apparent. However, they are also inevitable. In molding his nuclear ego for symbiotic survival the infant jeopardizes his chances at later unsymbiotic survival. In order to live successfully beyond a symbiosis he needs, we saw, an operational and ordered complexity within. Only thus can he hope to cope with increasing outside complexities. He must establish a solidly cathected repressive barrier and a solidly cathected, "embodied" body image. In brief: Self-polarization and self-demarcation must be so constituted as to allow tolerance and reconciliation of conflicts deeply and on a large scale.

But this will be difficult or impossible if the nuclear ego is pressured into a precocious differentiation. The infant's attempts at splitting away the bad breast, the bad mother, and the bad me, etc., must achieve too early and too precariously what later, more effectively and solidly, should be achieved through repression. This precocious splitting seems to have an unorganized, eerie quality, indicating quick but uninvested energy displacements. It seems out of step with the infant's age-adequate adaptive capacities. It reflects not an ordered, but a jumbled complexity within. It goes together with a body image not solidly embodied. This fragile, precociously differentiated nuclear ego, in brief, is over-specialized for symbiotic survival. But therefore, like any over-specialized structure, it has very little range for change, expansion, and for adaptation to interpersonal cultures other than the symbiotic culture.

A child who adopts the second strategy—control of mother by molding his nuclear ego for interpersonal survival—will not be restricted in the aforementioned sense. He avoids such restriction while exposing himself to over-stimulation, conflict, and unpredictability. He dares to share in the life of his bad and difficult matrix. He opens himself to becoming confused. Therefore, his lot will not be self-sufficient restriction but *conflictual entanglement*.

However, coming as it does at the dawn of knowing individuation, his encounter with human confusion and conflictfulness will be too great a challenge. In too early and too exclusively specializing himself for symbiotic survival, he fails to be what, in the words of Konrad Lorenz, is required of any human being: To be a specialist in non-specialization. He loses his flexible, future-oriented, adaptive openness.

Self-sufficient restriction and conflictful entanglement appear to be basic interpersonal alternatives which present themselves anew at all developmental crossroads. They will be basic concepts throughout the following part of this essay. The quality and intensity of restriction or entanglement will depend on the given interpersonal context and on the kind of differentiation-integration already achieved. Both conditions will tend to endanger any evolving mutuality. But they will endanger it differently.

Self-sufficient restriction (with, in extreme cases, the building of a paranoid wall) will tend to create quickly an interpersonal climate of silent despair, frustration, and autistic unconcern. It results in a living parallel to, but not with, one another. Emotional feedback, always painfully negative, will tend to peter out. What first could be described as negative mutuality may turn into no mutuality at all. There remains *only* parallel living.

In this first stage of knowing individuation self-sufficient restriction in the child may have a doubly malignant impact on the evolving dialogue (or more correctly: lacking dialogue). The child is cut off from his vital nutriment when he needs it most. But also the mother, in such primordial estrangement from her child, will receive a devastating blow. She will lose trust in her own motherliness. She will become anxious, frustrated, guilty. This will radiate back to the child. She will make him the object of hostile attacks. The latter, in self-defense, will entrench himself more in his rejecting solitude. And so the negative mutuality feeds on its negativity.

In conflictful entanglement the negative mutuality is phenomenologically different. It is, in a sense, less severe: There is more meeting of needs, more sharing, and hence more real mutuality. While self-sufficient restriction means the infant has to get along on the barest minimum of maternal nutriment, he now has to get along on the *wrong* nutriment. In the light of his developmental needs he gets too much in some respects and too little in others. As a result, he is pressured into *unequal development*. Within the unequal development the precocious differentiation of his nuclear ego appears the most fateful aspect.

The earlier the development becomes unequal, the more difficult will prove a later reintegration. Therefore, the infant will tend to fear excessively change and further differentiation-integration. Along therewith, he will need to cling to the relational status quo. But also the mother, in turn, will tend to need the unequally developed infant. She cannot tolerate his becoming different. She needs him as a specialist in symbiotic survival. Therefore, she also will excessively fear changes and expansions in the relationship.

Conflictual entanglement, in the sense here described, thus robs the relationship of its forward thrust. It tends to promote symbiotic modes of relating, it entrenches early developmental fixations. The other is too much needed as he is and too little as he could be. Proportionally to the decrease in hope for a spirally expansive future there is an increase in a mutually needful, anxious, clinging dependency: the present drowns the future.

FEARFUL ATTENTION

Fearful attention contrasts with fearless attention. The one marks a positive, the other a negative incipient mutuality. In the light of my previous considerations such fearful attention, during this earliest stage, can manifest itself differently, depending on whether the infant embarks on a course of self-sufficient restriction or on one of conflictful entanglement.

If the infant is driven to flee-fight his mother and to seek his salvation in premature, restricted self-sufficiency his attention will tend toward global closure. It will be put into the service of all-out distrust. The infant tries to make himself a fortified, forbidding island. This global closure may have—when a fleeing tendency prevails—a more stuporous, escapist flair, or it may have a more actively rejective tinge. In any case, this attention will greatly lack in differentiating and reconciling capacity. At the same time, it will maximally tend to tie up attentional cathexis. Neutralization of instinctual energies thus is minimal. Such attentional constellation, therefore, both mirrors and promotes a negative mutuality of the kind first described—a negative mutuality approaching non-mutuality. It reflects an interpersonal climate of silent despair.

In conflictful entanglement the attentional constellation is more complex. Now the attentional processes reflect more of a differentiating and reconciling capacity and endeavor. Specifically, undergoing and openness have a greater share in the adaptational panorama. This enables the infant, among other things, to synchronize himself with his mother's fantasies, expectations, and needs even when these are not in her awareness. In being open and undergoing, he sensitizes himself to the cues coming from his mother, relying on very primitive mechanisms of free floating identification and empathic resonance.

At the same time, by precociously straining and differentiating his nuclear ego, he tries to cope with maternal deficits, impingements, and inconsistencies as well as he can. In this sense, he attempts to build into his attentional processes a secondary autonomy as described above. But such autonomy appears precocious as does the nuclear ego. It appears very unsuited to serve as an early crucial springboard and relay station for that smooth, expanding interplay between cathexis and structure which is the hallmark of successful neutralization. The lacking neutralization seems reflected in the fact that these attentional structures are both over- and under-cathected. They are over-cathected in the sense that they consume and tie up too much energy which should be made available for new, due learning processes. (A tremendous amount of energy appears needed to mold and engage the nuclear ego for the task of symbiotic survival.) They are under-cathected in the sense that energy displacements seem too loose, too undirected. They seem to be lacking a necessary balancing element of disciplined containment.

In such primary deadlock of neutralization the forward thrust of both development and relatedness appears endangered. The nature of the danger will become even clearer when we turn to the second phase in the dawn of knowing individuation.

BETRAYAL OF THE QUEST TO BE ONE AND DIFFERENT

The Ego at the Verbal Dawn of Knowing Individuation

In order to succeed in the quest to become one and different, posed during the second phase of knowing individuation, the infant must have succeeded in becoming one and same. The positive mutuality required now builds on the positive mutuality achieved earlier. Previous neutralizations of instinctive energies begin to bear their first important developmental fruits. Let us review what this implies.

Externalized conflict becomes an essential element in the interpersonal panorama. The nuclear ego having been solidly installed, the infant can more forcefully assert himself than was possible before. Freud, Abraham, Erikson, René Spitz, and others have described how maturational and developmental achievements on the one side, the vicissitudes of toilet training on the other, stake out the arena on which the drama of the anal period can unfold. The child can become directly aggressive. He can retain his feces or deliver them inappropriately with a flash of hostility. He can resist his mother in anal stubbornness. But also, with self-polarization and self-demarcation thoroughly grounded, he can absorb and detoxify a good deal of his aggression by, so to speak, processing it. He can repress it and turn it against himself. He can create himself an inner battle ground. Out of such inner battles can arise important and not necessarily pathologic defense mechanisms and character traits which comprise or back up the secondary autonomy of the ego described by Hartmann.

In this sense, the ego's neutralizing potential appears intimately tied to what happens during this period. Further, along with such possible forceful internalization of aggression and conflict, guilt can become highly influential. The superego begins to take shape while the dawn of knowing individuation approaches its end.

The quest to become one and different comprises all these aspects of the anal period. However, in the context of this study, two aspects stand out: first, conflict and self-assertion essentially are experienced with and against the same one person: the mother. And second, speech, the third psychic organizer in the sense indicated by Spitz, is being born. The child not only can act out "yes" and "no" through his body, he also can put "yes" and "no" into words. The quest to become one and different can be executed through and be reflected in language.

These two facts—the mother's becoming more of a counterpart to conflict and aggression, and the emergence of language as a reconciling medium—most clearly highlight what a positive mutuality in the second half of the symbiotic period must be like. They make us understand which shifts must occur in the relational balances: now, in order to remain neutralizing, these balances must be so tipped as to leave room for and promote self-assertion, separation, and "knowing differentiation" of the child. This does not mean—and this point is most important—that the child's quest to be one and different differs radically from his quest to be one and the same. On the contrary, both these quests have one common denominator: *to be one*, that is, to be one who is whole and who, in his wholeness, is constantly confirmed by his mother. The gradual shifting of relational weights which is now due indicates that the "whole one" also must become a differing one—vis-à-vis his mother and the other important persons in his environment. This means the positive mutuality has to become more complex, more mediated, more separate, though not necessarily less deep and meaningful. It becomes more of a meeting of two distinct individuals. How does this show up in each relational balance?

Moment-Duration

The relationship now has its history. The enduring bond both testifies and reaffirms that mother and child have become and will remain meaningful to each other. The child, for the mother, has become a living reality around which memories and well-founded expectations begin to cluster. The mother, for the child, has become an object —clearly recognized and differentiated from other objects and immensely cathected. The intensity of his separation and stranger anxiety (emerging at about eight months but remaining an all-important aspect throughout this second period) gives negative proof of the depth and meaningfulness of his attachment to his mother. However, this attachment, evidence of the successful reconciliation of moment-duration, now must become less instinct- and need-tainted and more emotional. Its depth must be maintained through a more mediated vitality: The emotions must find vehicles of differentiated expressive potency. It is through these more complex vehicles that the meaningfulness of the relationship must be conveyed. Of these vehicles, language from now on will be paramount.

Sameness-Difference

The primary sameness in the "physiologic *Weltanschauung*," so central during the first phase, gradually must recede in importance and must allow the differences, which are built into the relationship, to assert themselves. Thus, for the child, the mother must begin to emerge as a person with roles, responsibilities, feelings, and motivations different from his own. In the recognition of such differences he learns to define himself. Specifically, he must learn to distinguish (and on account of such distinction to assert) his own bodily feelings and needs. Hilde Bruch has demonstrated how central such recognition and differentiation of bodily needs and feelings (such as hunger, sleepiness, but also of bodily discomfort) are to later successful interpersonal survival. Based on such primary recognition of what he himself feels, fears, and wants, the child can develop the motivational language that fits his true self. This requires that his mother, on her part, now more clearly delineate and confirm—because of and despite the still existing and deepening solidarity between them—their individual differences. For this task she needs language as much as does the child.

Gratification-Frustration

Early gratification, we saw, provided the expanding mutuality with its main working capital. Thus, this early gratification has strategic neutralizing significance. It must, during the first phase, tone down frustration and aggression to manageable proportions so as to avoid an erosion of nuclear structures at a most critical period. This working capital must continue to accumulate during this second phase. But also, it must be put to greater use. It must now serve to make bearable a necessarily greater share and intensity of frustration. For the balance of gratification-frustration must now be more tipped in favor of frustration. This frustration provides the sting, painful as it may be, which propels the ego toward greater autonomy and efficiency. It reflects, in the words of Hegel, *"den Ernst des Negativen,"* the "seriousness of the negative," which is indispensable to any human growth. Certain frustrations mother must inflict in deliberate anticipation of the requirements of acculturation and in the interests of safety. The child, for example, cannot be allowed to play near a busy street, even though this street may appear as his natural playground. He cannot be allowed to destroy valuable property. Again and again the adults must set limits which make sense. Insofar as these limits interfere with the child's immediate needs and concerns, frustrations will be experienced. Yet most frustrations, it seems, simply derive from a greater assertion of differences as described above: In tending to the various tasks implied in her adult role such as doing household chores, caring for other children, leading an intellectual life of her own, etc., the mother automatically will have to curtail her attention to and investment in the growing child. She frustrates him unwittingly and in so doing puts him more on his feet.

The birth of younger siblings—often occurring during the second phase of knowing individuation—brings in its wake dramatic and intense frustrations for the older child. Mother cannot help shifting her major attention away from him, at least temporarily. This older child may react with a sullen depression. Or he might say innocently: "Baby too small, stork must take it back," or he might actually try to hurt his baby sibling. Even if he does not react overtly at the time being, a later psychoanalysis may uncover rage and rivalrous feelings of murderous intensity.

Stimulation-Stabilization

Stabilization and hence object constancy continue to be most important during this second phase. After all, the child's quest to be and remain one and the same still goes on. But along therewith, the quest to be different gains momentum. Stimulation must have a greater share in this balance. And because of the relatively solid installment of the nuclear ego and hence of a repressive barrier, achieved during the first phase, more stimulation can be safely digested. Therefore, the evolving positive mutuality must encompass more of an active cross-stimulation to and fro. In such cross-stimulation, ever new terrain is gained for shared experiences. Both partners as well as the relationship become richer. Increasingly, language becomes the main tool and mirror of such mutually enriching cross-stimulation.

For example, in order that a child may learn nursery rhymes and baby songs, he must be exposed to such rhymes and songs. He must be stimulated. In some way mother must take care to make songs and rhymes available and meaningful to him. Thus she helps him to build a base from which imagination, artistic sensitivity, and a subtly modulative intelligence may branch out. Children in institutions such as foundling homes, hospitals, and orphanages miss out on this base and their intellectual development, among other things, remains crippled. Provence and Lipton have demonstrated this convincingly by thoroughly comparing institutionalized children with those living in natural homes.

Closeness-Distance

The immediate, unreflected, instinct-tainted closeness of the first phase, this home base of primordial sharing, must slowly give way to a slightly more "distant closeness." The increasing importance of difference, frustration, and stimulation, as reflected in the preceding balances, translates itself into growing distance between mother and child. Again, it is essential that this greater "distancing" be organic, that it is not too abrupt or erratic. The earlier closeness must be outgrown, not abandoned.

SHARED, FLEXIBLE ATTENTION

Fearless attention, as mentioned earlier, must develop into a *shared, flexible attention.* This crucial, complex achievement during the late dawn of knowing individuation sustains as well as mirrors a positive mutuality between mother and child. But also, insofar as a shared attention fails to develop, we become able to pinpoint what may be wrong in the relationship. It is mainly the emergence of language which now adds a new dimension of complexity to the attentional processes which reflect and propel the expanding interplay of cathexis and structure. Those features which make language the reconciling medium par excellence—such as space- and time-binding, abstraction, the integration of evocative and propositional elements, etc.—also make attention more intricate and potentially more reconciling.

The concept of shared flexible attention, as here intended, builds on the works of E. Schachtel and of L. Wynne and M. Singer.

E. Schachtel introduced the concept focal attention and differentiated five structural features. Acts of focal attention are, first, *directional;* they are not global as are most primitive forms of experience. They are, second, *directed at a particular object;* this may be an external object such as a chair, a rock, or human face, or this may be an internal object such as a thought, or feeling. They, third, take hold of the object; they aim at its active mental grasp. Each focal act, fourth, usually consists not only of one sustained, but several renewed approaches to the object. "These approaches explore different aspects and relations of the object." They are made from different angles. But also, they often start repeatedly from the same angle. The same aspect of the object will thus be assimilated more thoroughly. "They also usually—probably always—alternate or oscillate between a more passive, receptive, reactive phase and a more active, taking-hold, structuring, integrating phase." Acts of focal attention, fifth, exclude the rest of the field (environmental or internal).

It is only gradually that attention can become focal, complex, and flexible, as here described. E. Schachtel has traced important developmental steps. The very young infant, Schachtel notes, is not yet able to look at anything or to listen to anything in the sense we employ these terms. He experiences light or noises as coming from a vaguely perceived, general direction. At four weeks, he stares vacuously and diffusely at the world. A few weeks later he stares in a certain direction and occasionally he focuses his eyes at people and objects in his environment. From approximately ten weeks on he focuses on the same object for a prolonged period. A little later he starts to follow a moving object with his eyes, to hold onto it and keep it in focus. From the seventh or eighth month he likes to focus on small objects—little buttons, tiny toys, etc. In general, his attention becomes more energetic, more active, more selective.

During the later dawn of knowing individuation, the child—first vaguely, then more and more sharply—not only focuses his attention via the senses on an object seen, touched, and so on, but also on the idea of an object. Later not only objects, "but also their relationships, real or fancied, to the child and to each other, become the objects of focal attention in thought." It is at this point that the reconciling mastery of a differentiated language becomes crucial.

The sharing of a common focus—which L. Wynne has described and elaborated—implies that each partner in the relationship can focus his attention flexibly and imaginatively on what the other conveys or wants to convey. This, we can say, puts focal attention, as outlined above, to its maximal test.

Each partner must now focus on the other as a focusing subject in his own right. This implies that he must not approach the other's proposition in the light of his own unreflected preferences. He must not only address himself to the concrete or seemingly logical meaning of the other's message. Instead, he must make an effort to comprehend what the other really wants to get across: He must put himself into the other's shoes, adopt the other's viewpoint. Second, he must make an effort to present his own proposition clearly so as to help the other in his (the other's) focusing task. Third, he must strive to make sure he and the other are in accord as to what they communicate about. Where such sharing of a common focus fails, the ground is prepared for a negative mutuality.

Since I grew acquainted with the work of L. Wynne and M. Singer, I became aware of the varied phenomenology and implications of what we might call the negative mutuality of everyday life. The failure to share a common focus of attention is always at the core of this negative mutuality. For example, we notice those persons who seem so over-invested and over-focused in their own ideas that they never seem to care to comprehend what the other has to say. There are others who present their own viewpoints so vaguely that any ordinary partner would be over-taxed if the latter, in an honest and serious manner, tried to make sense out of it. There are other people who never seem concerned about clarifying and assessing what seemingly they established between themselves.

Patients and families with psychiatric and—in particular, psychotic—problems thus only mirror and exaggerate what, in minor ways, seems everpresent. Take, for example, this brief interchange between a daughter, mother, and father, as reported by L. Wynne and M. Singer (This discussion was tape-recorded and transcribed while the family members were waiting for an interview):

Daughter, (*complainingly*): Nobody will listen to me. Everybody is trying to still me.
Mother: Nobody wants to kill you.
Father: If you're going to associate with intellectual people, you're going to have to remember that still is a noun and not a verb.

Or this conversation between a father and mother:

F: Well those . . .
M: One minute it's . . .
F: . . . shoes are . . .
M: . . . rainin', and the next . . .

These could as well be excerpts from a play of the modern theater. They represent gross failures in sharing a common focus of attention. We may become aware of these gross failures only after we have learned to watch out for them.[3]

To sum this up: The term "shared flexible attention" denotes a positive mutuality. It indicates the individual can undergo—that he can suffer and integrate changes within himself which respond to the changes in the other, and vice versa. Shared, flexible attention, this means, operates from a constantly altered home base. In the ongoing relationship, active attention can be reconciled with passive detention, closure with openness. The relationship can be lasting and, at the same time, can be experienced as new. It can be stabilizing *and* stimulating. The dialogue can go on and the mutuality remain positive.

A flexibly sharing attention, we must now remind our-

[3] I shall introduce further examples for failures in the sharing of a common focus in the following chapter on schizophrenia.

selves, grows out of fearless attention, described earlier
It was in a climate of fearlessness and basic trust that
attentional processes could find their first reconciling mold
which now, with the advent of language, becomes more
differentiated and, in a sense, more visible.

However, in order that fearless attention can give rise
to flexibly sharing attention, the child must succeed in his
quest to be one and different. And to succeed in this quest
he must be supported by that neutralizing constellation
of relational balances which now is due: A constellation
which leaves increasing (though still moderate) room for
difference, separation, frustration, and stimulation.

What will happen when such a neutralizing constella
tion does not come forth? How does a negative mutuality
during the verbal dawn of knowing individuation show
up? With this question I shall deal next.

NEGATIVE MUTUALITY DURING THE VERBAL DAWN OF KNOWING INDIVIDUATION

Depending on what happened earlier, the negative mu
tuality during the verbal dawn of knowing individuation
will be different. Such difference is crucial. If there exist
a working capital of good experiences, a solidly installed
nuclear ego, if fearless attention preceded the advent of
language, the impact of disturbed relational balances will
be less shattering than if all this were missing.

I shall, at this point, leave aside this first possibility
that is, I shall not systematically analyze disturbed rela
tional balances and hence a negative mutuality which suc
ceeds a successful quest to become one and the same
The principle of such systematic analysis is clear. It de
rives from the preceding considerations and would have
to integrate the findings of Freud, Abraham, Erikson
about the vicissitudes of the anal period, of Piaget, Heinz
Werner, Charlotte and Karl Bühler, etc., about the growth
of language, as well as many other well-known contribu
tions about child development during this phase.

Instead, I shall focus on the second possibility: on a negative mutuality during the second phase of knowing individuation *which has to cope with the consequences of preceding negative mutuality.* This means disturbed relational balances will hit a child who has little or no working capital of good experiences, who has no solidly installed nuclear ego, and who did not enjoy fearless attention. This child, we saw, was forced to adopt certain strategies of survival—such as fight-flight or "control" of his mother—leading him to either self-sufficient restriction or conflictual entanglement. In each case he mortgaged his future chances of development and relatedness.

Now—during this later phase of knowing individuation—the time has come where the first mortgage becomes due. And along therewith, the dilemma of the child becomes more complicated and difficult to resolve.

Let us turn back to the dilemma which earlier forced the child to adopt the above survival strategies and which hence drove him either into self-sufficient restriction or conflictual entanglement. The dilemma was this: His adaptional apparatus, while still immature, was being impaired and yet it had to carry a heavier than normal adaptional load.

In choosing either one of the above survival strategies, the child, now and later, created for himself the following situation: In addition to the current developmental and adaptive tasks, he has to cope with the backlog of his grim relational past. Specifically, he has to cope with the consequences of an unequal development as outlined earlier. There are now developmental blanks on the one side, precocious and unharmonious exaggerations on the other. His differentiation-integration has been thrown off the track. In brief, his earlier dilemma has transformed itself into his new dilemma: He must struggle with a difficult present *and* correct a bad past.

In the light of this new dilemma, the child's interpersonal orientation from now on can be expected to reflect two general tendencies. The one is the tendency to correct the bad past. This tendency can be seen as serving the child's long-term adaptive interests. It aims at an over-all reequilibration. This reequilibration, in order to be thorough, requires a kind of *reintegration at the base,* a correction of developmental imbalances at their point of genetic and organic fixation.

The other general tendency, in contrast, serves the child's short-term adaptive interests. It operates according to the principle: A bird in the hand is worth two in the bush. Immediate survival comes first. The child will cling to the status quo and hold on to whatever gains he has made. In line with such a policy, he will try to turn into adaptive assets his developmental imbalances. Exactly this, we saw, was the case in the two survival strategies described above. The building of the paranoid wall and the employment of precocious splitting, among other maneuvers, reflect attempts at turning an unequal development into an adaptive asset.

Clearly, these two general tendencies work at cross purposes. Short-term and long-term interest do not go together; they are in conflict.[4] This means specifically: The more successfully an individual turns his developmental imbalances into adaptive assets, the less likely will he seek and endure a reintegration at the base. He would, as he sees it, only jeopardize his painfully won adjustment while exposing himself to severest disintegrative turmoil and anxiety.

[4] Analogous conflicts may be found in many areas of modern life. In the sphere of economics, for example, immediate survival interests may drive people to exploit land resources—such as timber or pastures—ruthlessly. This leads to soil erosion which interferes with their long-term interests. The needed reintegration at the base might later imply a recultivation of the land—a staggeringly difficult task. Likewise, many persons encourage a baby boom as a means to mobilize the economy via building, increased consumption of baby products, etc. The long-term economic and psychological consequences in terms of air and water pollution, suburban sprawl, interpersonal aggression due to overcrowding, mass unemployment, etc., may pose similarly forbidding problems for the needed reintegration of the economic and human base.

The coexistence and antagonism of these two general tendencies give the key for evaluating the extent and quality of a negative mutuality once a relationship has acquired a history. Thus they also give the key to a better understanding of a negative mutuality as it may exist during the verbal dawn of knowing individuation.

This means that the principles of "differentiation-integration" and "adaptive reconciliation," now have to be applied with a new perspective in mind. We must, in any phase-constellation, evaluate these two general tendencies described above. Thus, an added dynamic aspect is introduced. We get some indication of the strength of self-corrective tendencies and potentials which operate within a given "adaptational set" and within a given relationship, even when a negative mutuality existed and still exists. Each moment, these self-corrective tendencies and potentials are seen as either compromising or fighting with short-term adaptive interests. For example, a manifest severe disturbance in some particular phase-constellation will have to be evaluated quite differently depending on whether it is viewed as an attempted reintegration at the base or as a relatively permanent adaptive solution. In other words: We take into account how far, in any developmental and adaptive constellation, disturbance and regression are or are not serving a reactivation of a spiral developmental and relational expansion. This comprises what Kris has described as regression in the service of the ego, or what Wynne has called "adaptive regression."

A THIRD GENERAL PRINCIPLE OF DEVELOPMENT AND ADAPTATION

These considerations lead us to introduce a third general principle of development and adaptation. I would like to call it the *"principle of adaptive antagonism."* In each phase-constellation, this principle must be applied conjointly with the earlier principles of "differentiation-integration" and "adaptive reconciliation." It forces us to take into account how far each individual, each moment, does or does not allow for a reintegration at the base in what might be called an adaptive upheaval, that is, how much he is able and willing to liquidate developmental imbalances at the price of momentary adaptational difficulties and failures. It forces us to gauge carefully the possible restitutive aspect of any disintegration and regression.

In order to illuminate this third principle, let me turn to David O., a thirty-two-year-old scientist. David's problems fall into that "ordinary" range of troubles which may steer a person into psychoanalysis. He was not psychotic. I choose him because he himself could give an adaptational assessment of his development which highlights the above principle.

David sought analysis because he was a homosexual. Also, he found it increasingly difficult to work. This difficulty he saw partly as a result of his homosexuality: Sexual thoughts and fantasies kept him preoccupied much of the day and night. Often, he said, he felt depressed. In addition, he suffered from certain compulsions. For example, he was unduly concerned with such questions as "Who should salute whom first."

David knew he was a homosexual before he had heard the word homosexuality. "It was like a natural, instinctual force. It took hold of me and that was it." However, it was not before the age of nineteen that he began to succumb to this force. While serving as a camp counselor, he got entangled with another counselor. Since then he had had many homosexual affairs. All were fleeting and all were unhappy. After first feverishly idolizing his friends, he tended to become quickly disappointed. The sexual act, exciting as it was, left him greedy and drained. Solitary masturbation he found, on the whole, more satisfying than sexual activity with other men. Such masturbation, though, left him guilt-ridden and lonely.

David felt drawn to the gay world; he formed part of it, yet he criticized it: "It's all a gigantic vanity fair, a cozy hothouse, heated up by jealousy and sadism." He wished to have children, though he was afraid of the bodily closeness with "such helpless, fresh-skinned creatures." Women, for the most part, left him cold. Having to go through the motions of a date was a dull, unnerving nuisance. He noticed, however, that certain aspects in certain women appealed to him in a sexual way; buttocks, for example, or soft, round legs aroused him. Aggressive women attracted him more than the "soft, shy types." (Female breasts and genitalia he detested.)

David was the oldest of three boys, who all had homosexual problems. He was the most intelligent and reflective of the brothers. He realized that his mother had spoiled him in many ways, while teaching him to despise his philandering father. David's high intelligence and psychological knowledge made him (unlike the vast majority of homosexuals) realize that his "homosexuality"—which felt to him so natural, so innately self-evident—was after all, learned. This homosexuality, in its varied psychological and quasi-instinctual ramifications, was, he concluded, his response to relational vicissitudes of his early life.[5] His mother's binding erotic over-stimulation—combined with the relative psychological absence and her denigration of his father—was therein a major force. This he could acknowledge as a scientist who lets the facts speak even when these facts speak against "your dearest beliefs."

With this respect for scientific facts strong in him, David could formulate his dilemma as follows:

"Each day I live longer in the gay world, I shall get more entrenched as a homosexual. This means I shall get more lonely, more caught up in the mess I am in. And yet the gay world keeps me going. That is where

[5] These vicissitudes partly overlap with, or are similar to, those elaborated in this essay. They would also lend themselves to a description within the conceptual framework here presented. However, since my main—though somewhat arbitrary—focus is on schizophrenia, I shall not systematically deal with the origins of homosexuality at this point. The reader is referred to the extensive psychoanalytical literature on this subject.

I can feel some warmth, and can have a drink with what, for me, is honest human company. Unfortunately, I am a scientist and not a magician. Therefore I cannot fool myself about what change must mean for me: It means tearing up what's holding me now together. Though I once learned my homosexuality, now I *live* it. My homosexual fantasies now form a short-circuit to my bloodstream. I feel terrified about that and I cannot conceive how I can become a heterosexual."

As just described, David had made adaptive his homosexuality, at least to a degree. He had turned it into a way of life whereby he, besides mere sexual satisfaction, could find some warmth and seemingly honest human company. At the same time—and this is important—he realized that this adaptation was *antagonistic* to his long-range wishes and needs. He realized that only a reorganization at the base could resolve his dilemma. Yet the prospect and implications of such reorganization at the base terrified him. He knew this could involve regression and disintegration for an open-ended period. The question was: Was it worth it and could he endure it?

The third principle of adaptive antagonism therefore helps us to arrive at an over-all adaptational assessment. Therefore, it must build on the two foregoing principles. It now allows us to gauge how far an individual's adaptive future has been mortgaged on behalf of past and present survival. It brings into focus how, in the final analysis, conflict, through being accepted but not being fought out, can win out over reconciliation.

This leads to some general considerations: The concepts of conflict and reconciliation, in a most general sense, require each other in order to make understandable any developmental dynamic. They dialectically are interdependent. Reconciliation presupposes conflict and conflict aims toward reconciliation. Hegel, in his history of philosophy, most systematically and comprehensively has developed this dialectic. Yet this dialectic is also central to Freud's psychoanalytic theory. For Freud, his two basic principles of mental development, pleasure principle and reality principle, are *conflicting* principles. This conflict returns in ever new constellations, most of which can be conceptualized as a conflict between id and ego. The resolution of the conflict—that is, the reconciliation of the conflicting forces—leads to some altered and, as a rule, more complex constellation. For example, the pleasure principle, in early trying to win out over a recalcitrant reality, has to submit to a postponement of gratifications, and thus has to give rise to an apparatus which makes possible such postponement: The ego. Now the conflict resumes and the ego is further modified while, at the same time, the arena is staked out for new and partly different conflicts. And so on and on. In this process the intra-psychic scenery becomes most complexly structured, each structural layer reflecting a particular phase and kind of conflict-solution. Each such conflict solution then further reflects a dialectical balance of cathexis-counter-cathexis—with so much energy being tied up in costly defensive structures and symptoms and so much energy being expendable for new conflict solutions and reconciliations. And so forth.

Given such ongoing dialectic between conflict and reconciliation, it seems imperative to attempt, at one point, an over-all assessment in regard to the strength of either conflict or reconciliation in a given person. This requires a long-range perspective on this person's life struggle. It requires some idea of what he could have achieved and still may achieve. And this is the point where the above described third principle of adaptive antagonism must be considered.

To a degree, each such assessment must remain open-ended. We are directed to the question: What gives value and meaning to a human life? What do we mean by successful adjustment or self-realization?

Hegel, we may note, while attempting an over-all assessment of mankind's struggle up to Hegel's time and while "reconciling" in a most comprehensive manner, still acknowledges and describes unsuccessful reconciliations. Thus, in his philosophy of history, he does not justify and hence reconcile *all* human suffering. He introduces the concept of the *"schlechte Unendlichkeit,"* the "bad infinity." And there remains the *"unglückliche Bewusstsein,"* "the unhappy consciousness," a state of deep inner conflict which, it appears, can never be fully overcome.

Freud also, we know, was pessimistic about the possibilities of final satisfactory over-all reconciliations for any given individual. Although conceiving an ideal state of successful adjustment, characterized by genital primacy and relative lack of neurotic conflict, this state still indicated an instable equilibrium. For one thing, he conceived of our sexual needs in a way which made them appear incapable of lasting gratification; for another, he saw also seemingly successful human adjustments as being founded on illusions (e.g. of a religious nature) which would have to give way, should the demands of reality ever become harsher.

LANGUAGE AND RELATIONAL STYLES

Language, as emerging during the verbal dawn of knowing individuation, affects in various ways an existing negative mutuality: It can lead to greater self-awareness as well as confusion—it can, in facilitating and enforcing greater developmental and relational complexity, promote successful reconciliation and self-correction as well as mire the child in despair and dead ends. But further, language, in making the child complexly expressive, now allows him to differentiate more clearly his adaptive strategies and constellations. It allows him to distinguish certain cognitive and relational styles and structures and to evaluate their dynamic implications. Specifically, it allows him to gauge reconciling and corrective potentials within these structures and styles. It allows him to apply the principles of "differentiation-integration" and "adaptive reconciliation" with the dynamic leverage now provided by the third principle of "adaptional antagonism."

In the following, I shall briefly sketch several such relational and cognitive styles in the child, as these reflect a negative mutuality during the verbal dawn of knowing individuation. In so doing, I shall build on the concepts developed earlier; that is, I shall view these styles in the light of his (the child's) embarking, during this second phase, either on self-sufficient restriction or on conflictual entanglement, assuming that these are basic alternatives which present themselves again and again at relational and developmental crossroads. However, I shall now make a distinction within these two relational modes with regard to their time of principal emergence, and hence of their relative rootedness in a strong nuclear ego, as defined earlier. This means that I shall distinguish four such relational modes: First, a self-sufficient restriction which essentially establishes itself during the preverbal dawn of knowing individuation and which, during the verbal dawn, is little altered but reinforced; second, a self-sufficient restriction which "more successfully" can build on a preceding positive mutuality and which appears highly tainted by the vicissitudes of the anal period; third, a conflictual entanglement which continues, during this second phase, to bear strongly the imprint of an earlier negative mutuality; and fourth, a conflictual entanglement in which the negative mutuality chiefly operates during the verbal dawn. What do these four relational modes reveal in the light of the above considerations?

VICISSITUDES OF SELF-SUFFICIENT RESTRICTION AND CONFLICTUAL ENTANGLEMENT

(1) *Self-sufficient restriction as chiefly instigated and shaped during the preverbal dawn of knowing individuation.* The need for closure, in this relational mode, remains over-powering. At the same time, neutralization of instinctual energies is minimal. Due to the strong incipient negative mutuality, the neutralizing interplay between cathexis and structure, as described earlier, gets deadlocked at the beginning. Alienation from self as well as from others is

and remains extreme. Corrective movements may occur during the verbal dawn of knowing individuation but—with the same mother remaining—the vicious relational circle is likely to spin on. The child may acquire some basic language but this language will have little modulated differentiation. It will be minimally effective as a reconciling medium. Chiefly, in some primitive and inflexible manner, it will be made to serve the needs of closure.

But such closure, though excessively slanting all adaptive efforts, remains precarious: Once the shield of closure cracks, an amorphous dedifferentiation on a very low level of energy investment must be feared. And this amorphous disintegration is not likely to herald a reintegration at the base. For this first relational mode has very little reintegrative resiliency. Thus, with the advent of greater developmental and adaptive stress, closure may change into amorphous dedifferentiation and the latter may become the enduring adaptive solution.

Kerstin D. was a patient who suggested this relational mode.[6] She was twenty-four years old when I saw her the first time. This was at the occasion of her fourth admission to a mental hospital. She was then a tall, blond, and slightly overweight girl. Her healthy color and attractively shaped face made her appear a Nordic beauty. But this picture of a beautiful young woman faded at closer sight: One noticed that her hair was not well kept and that her lipstick was smeared. There was something tiring and sullen about her. She did not ask any questions relating to her prospective stay in the hospital and she gave the impression of being under tranquilizing drugs. But this was not the case when I first saw her, although in the past she had repeatedly received such medication.

Kerstin could not be considered cooperative. But neither did she belong to the group of notoriously difficult patients. The nurses' chief complaint was that she slept long into the day and that they had to make a big fuss to get her going. But once she was dressed she participated in

[6] Cf. see case history on Ernest, M., p. 156.

the routine patient activities, though in a glum, passive manner.

I saw Kerstin in individual sessions and in a group therapy which took place twice a week. In the group therapy she never initiated a question; and only at rare occasions did she participate in an ongoing conversation. Immediately after she had become a member of the group, various patients attempted to draw her into a discussion. But such attempts became rarer and rarer as time went on. For there was something forbidding about Kerstin, something that paralyzed people who wanted to reach out to her. She was not negative or rejective in the more common sense of the term. She just seemed to create a kind of emotional no-man's land between her and the rest of the human world. It was mainly when other patients in the group angrily decried some aspect of the hospital or the staff—which was frequent enough—that one could notice a gleeful, participating smile on her face.

Also in her individual sessions Kerstin was silent much of the time. However, there were occasions when she talked. She talked then in a manner which appeared both monotonous and abrupt. She would blurt out a number of sentences such as, "Why cannot I leave this hospital?" "Why cannot I lead a normal life?" "Why have other girls boyfriends and I not?" "I want to leave this hospital." These seeming questions, however, were not intonated as questions. She did not seem to expect an answer and did not seem to listen when I tried to offer one.

Most of what I got to know about Kerstin's life I learned from sources other than herself. My main informant was Kerstin's mother, who, perhaps less through what she said and more through how she said it, gave me an idea of what their early relationship might have been like. This mother, by now in her late forties, was still a beauty. In her outer appearance she conveyed impeccable taste. There was a pressured quality in her talk which revealed undertones of bitterness and frustration. Kerstin, she told me, was her youngest child. Her oldest son, five years Kerstin's senior, had recently married and settled in a foreign country. She had one other daughter who, still un-married, studied medicine.

Her marriage to a successful industrialist, a manufac-turer of electrical tools, had been stormy and difficult. She never enjoyed sexual relations with him. There were at-tempts at reconciliation and these attempts were usually accompanied by a resumption of sexual intercourse; but these reconciliations were short-lived.

She had married to get away from her own mother whose nagging criticism drove her to distraction. When, at the age of nineteen, she met the man who later became her husband, she decided to get him to marry her, "since he looked like the best catch around." She virtually se-duced him and intimated she was pregnant. This did not turn out to be the case but the marriage was nonetheless arranged. A bitter running feud developed wherein each partner tried to hurt the other in his or her most vulnerable spots. However, it was only around the time of Kerstin's birth that this feud led to a divorce.

Kerstin could not have arrived at a more inconvenient time. This pregnancy, for the most part, was a torture and an embarrassment to her mother. However, with great will power and circumspection she managed to carry through with the divorce while she was tied down with the infant. The divorce became final when Kerstin was ap-proximately a year and a half old.

Kerstin's delivery was difficult. She was born a month prematurely and was a cry-baby. Colic was a major problem until she was about seven months old. Kerstin then became much easier to handle. In fact, according to her mother, Kerstin in some way turned from an extreme troublemaker into a good baby. "I finally got things or-ganized. I arranged for a college student to take care of the evening feedings while I did them in the mornings." When Kerstin was a little older than one year she became quite fat. But this problem, her mother said, "was cor-rected by our paying more attention to her food intake. We just cut down on the food." Apart from this, her mother could not remember anything extraordinary about

Kerstin's early upbringing. Kerstin, her mother rep ....,
learned to walk and to talk at the normal age and went
to kindergarten when she was five years old. Neither in
kindergarten nor in grammar school, according to her
mother, were there any major problems. "Kerstin was just
a good, normal child."

The data here presented do not seem to tell much. Still,
we get a glimpse of her mother's bad relationship to her
own mother, whom she describes as cold and nagging and
from whom she tried to get away at all cost. Her marriage
to an unloved husband was essentially a means to achieve
this goal. In telling about her life, Mrs. D. gave evidence
that she rejected her young daughter not only unconsciously but also consciously. This was understandable
when one considers her earlier life-situation and the fact
that she was herself rejected by her own mother.

We might wonder what happened when Kerstin, not
yet a year old, changed from a troublemaker into a "good"
baby. This question is difficult to answer after more than
twenty years have passed. However, the expression, "Kerstin was such a good baby," should make us suspicious.
Again and again we hear formulations such as this one
from mothers who are alienated from and insensitive to
their babies' needs. When such a baby becomes "good"
for these mothers, he has, it appears, found a way to make
operational his self-sufficient restriction. Such a baby stops
being demanding and annoying since he has resigned
himself to get along on minimal rations of emotional sustenance. He has given up clamoring for feedback which,
he has come to realize, only worsens things. His passive
"good" compliance becomes his strategy to hold down the
intensity as well as frequency of any meaningful interchange between him and his mother. These mothers—to
use a term employed by Theodore Lidz—can often be
characterized as impervious. They are impervious to the
complex needs of the child and, in particular, they are impervious to any signs in the child which demand a respect
for his beginning relative autonomy.

We might, with this perspective in mind, also wonder about the meaning of Kerstin's fatness at the approximate age of one year. This fatness, it seems, resulted from over-feeding, which, in turn, reflects a disregard on the part of the mother and of the care-taking college student for the fine signs of saturation or resistance in the baby. Both these women, we might assume, virtually stuffed the food down the baby's throat. They seemed little concerned as to whether Kerstin had enough food or not, whether she showed pleasure or displeasure. Notice also the seeming mechanical fashion in which her feeding problem is later corrected. This mother, preoccupied, overworked, and in-wardly resentful, seemed to have had neither the time nor the ability to gear herself to Kerstin's needs as expressed by Kerstin herself. Instead, she could only satisfy these needs as these were learned from the textbook.

Later, it was Kerstin's seeming "goodness," that is, her lack of self-assertion and inventive imagination, which caused a teacher in early high school to suspect something was wrong with her. Kerstin apparently tried hard in school and elsewhere to comply with what she was told to do, but seemed quickly overtaxed. She proved particu-larly inept in the perhaps most important task of adoles-cence: To stake out a satisfying sexual identity and part-nership. She appeared pathetic in her attempts to attract boys by flaunting herself as a dumb blonde. Kerstin could never comprehend that sexual satisfaction and partnership are not just a matter of waiting for the boys to show up, but that they imply a subtle and complex mutuality. Kerstin's passivity therefore was not of that kind which might attract certain boys and which might be fun to over-come; it was more the passivity of a piece of wood. Already during adolescence we might assume that Kerstin dis-played some of the same qualities which caused people in the hospital to shy away from her. Her seeming compli-ance betrayed a self-sufficient restriction which was deeply entrenched in her personality.

Kerstin's first admission to a mental hospital at the age

of seventeen appeared more like the inevitable outgrowth of a relational course, embarked on early in life, than as a dramatic foreseeable event.

(2) *Self-sufficient restriction as chiefly instigated and shaped during the verbal dawn of knowing individuation.* Neutralization of instinctual energies, in this second relational mode, serves more successfully the needs of closure than in the foregoing instance. Profiting from a better preceding mutuality and hence from a sounder nuclear ego, the child can give his restriction a more solid obsessive underpinning. His "no" vis-à-vis the mother and the world gets more systematic force and profile. This greater forcefulness also leaves its imprint on language, as it emerges during the verbal dawn. Given a fair amount of linguistic stimulation, his language will become a more differentiated adaptive and defensive tool than is the case in the preceding situation. Equipped with such language, he can, among other things, more successfully hold off anxiety and conflictual impulses through isolating and intellectualizing techniques. At the same time, he may achieve a certain systematized logical stringency of language.

However, such logical stringency and obsessionalized restriction will exert its toll: His alienation from self and others, as described above, will be deep. Language, thus streamlined and prematurely (though energetically) closed, will be ill equipped to absorb many important data of the child's inner as well as outer reality, such as motives, moods, and needs in himself and others. Undergoing and openness have too little place in his adaptive panorama. The child will lack interpersonal depth: His imaginative span with regard to the complexity of human motives, feelings, and confusions will remain narrow. Thus, in a very important sense, restriction means impoverishment. The chances for future growth are severely limited.

The cases of Catherine L. and Spencer F., as described on pages 74 and 76, can be seen as representing a relational mode of this second kind. Catherine L. was meant to illustrate an alienation of ego from self; Spencer F., to exemplify the ego's alienation from non-self. These two types of alienation, I indicated, usually occur in the same person, although one type tends to be more marked than the other. I emphasized then the failure of language as a reconciling medium. Language in these two cases became, in a sense, prematurely closing and it became also, particularly in Spencer F., aggressively invested. Such premature closure and aggressiveness in investment of language appear as a central element in the self-sufficient restriction of the second type here presented.

Let us now consider the case of Ernest M., a sixteen-year-old adolescent who, in my opinion, reflects important features of this second relational mode. (No one person, it may be added, will ever fit these modes neatly. Life and the vicissitudes of human relationships are just too complex for that. Still, a relational typology, as here suggested, may bring into light important features of developmental failure which otherwise may be difficult to notice.)

Ernest was recommended for intensive psychotherapy because, approximately from the age of twelve years on, he developed a number of disturbing habits. Some of these habits seemed to disappear after a while; others remained, although they varied in preponderance. For example, Ernest ate his food exceedingly slowly. He would chew every bite three times as long as his brothers and sisters did. Also, he refused to eat with a fork. He was an excellent athlete but his workouts seemed over-done. Every morning, regardless of the season, he would run in his shorts around the block, raising many eyebrows. But most disturbing was his manner of talking. When he talked, he halted often and he constantly seemed to grope for words. In this way, any conversation with him became a long, drawn-out affair which taxed his partner's patience. Also, he liked to coin new words. Sometimes these words had a creative flair to them, for example, when he described as "daymares" certain unsettling daytime experiences which he wanted to distinguish from nightmares. But most of the time his new concepts appeared just odd and stilted. He would say, for example, "The manipulati-

bility of one's life creates problems insofar as the manipula-
tibility of others is concerned. The mechanics of the
organization of life are too overflawed." With similar sentences he filled the letters which he wrote to me or to his
parents. He tried to learn as many abstract (and unfamiliar) words as possible. The two books in his possession
were two huge dictionaries.

In his last year before being admitted to the hospital,
his schoolwork (in a private institution) had deteriorated
disastrously. His slow, over-elaborate way of formulating
sentences had driven his teachers to distraction; but also,
much of the time he seemed just unconcerned about what
he was supposed to learn. He appeared then totally self-
absorbed. The parents consulted several psychiatrists who
diagnosed Ernest as "borderline schizophrenic," "severe
obsessive compulsive neurosis," and "childhood autism."
All agreed, however, that psychotherapy was needed.

When I saw Ernest for the first time I felt it difficult to
reconcile these rather sinister diagnoses with the picture of
the lanky, amiable fellow he presented. Ernest was an
expert Ping-pong player, skier, and swimmer. However,
even in these sports wherein he excelled, certain rigid
mannerisms and habits made him vulnerable. When playing Ping-pong, for example, he seemed fixated on serving
the ball in a certain over-elaborate manner. Once a partner
caught on to this manner, Ernest was in trouble. Even in
these sports, one could therefore notice how he failed in
sustaining a flexible sharing mutuality.

These failures became highlighted when this mutuality
was required to become verbal, as this was expected in
our therapeutic sessions. In these sessions I found it difficult and tedious to share a common focus with Ernest.[7]
These aspects of his personality, among others, seemed
significant: Ernest was a boy with a high energy level.
(This high energy level distinguishes him from Kerstin,
described earlier.) Further, from his infancy on he seems

[7] For external reasons his therapy had to be terminated after a relatively short period of time.

to have had an unusual problem in controlling his aggression. As a small boy he hit other children and animals ruthlessly and impulsively. His aggression was fueled when a younger brother, Eric, was born. Ernest was then about two years old. It was at this time that he began to display what others described as a rugged stubbornness. Also, it was at this time that he began munching food for hours. This is the time, we must now remember, when Ernest molded his language to serve as his reconciling medium. His language, it appears now, far from installing itself as a relatively smooth reconciling instrument, became highly and prematurely over-invested and over-exploited. Ernest needed it unduly for the discharge of his aggressive drives but, also, he transformed it into a special stage whereon he could carry out his inner battles.

In line with this viewpoint it made sense to regard his libidinal over-investment in language as a substitute for and means of coping with masturbation—his conflicts, guilt, and pleasures connected therewith. Even in our psychotherapeutic sessions Ernest seemed to process and manipulate his cumbersome sentences with an orgastic, though conflict-ridden intensity. On a later level of psychic organization his peculiar language imitated as well as competitively mimicked his father who liked to use high-sounding and pompous words.

Ernest, like Kerstin in the previous example, was born into a tangled family situation. His father, son of a wealthy family, had been an indomitable pilot of sports planes until he suffered a crash which left him permanently injured. Although he held a rather high-titled office in the family-owned company, his contributions to this firm were practically nil. Most of his time he spent attending various sports and social events. Ernest's mother was a beautiful woman and in her early twenties was an excellent tennis player. When I met her—after repeatedly trying in vain for an interview—she impressed me as cold and hurried. She could remember few details from Ernest's early life. She emphasized, however, that Ernest had always been more troublesome than his younger brother Eric. She admitted she had never felt very close to Ernest. Also, from early on she had been afraid Ernest could do something rash and mean. Her apprehensions were borne out when one day she found Ernest beating his infant brother with toy bricks. Similar incidents followed. She became confirmed in her belief that Ernest had an evil streak in him. Ernest's later relationship to his father was much warmer than the one he had with his mother. With his father he would often attend soccer games and other sports competitions. It appeared that quite early his father had taken on some mothering functions toward Ernest although his father's mothering lacked consistency. When I saw his father he struck me as easygoing, good-natured, and immature. He mentioned that around the time of Ernest's birth he had an affair with another woman. A number of such affairs followed. He and his wife, he said, had long learned to go their own ways.

I shall, at this point, not attempt to elaborate on the complex psychodynamic aspects of this case. Instead, I shall focus on one episode which occurred during our psychotherapeutic sessions. This episode illustrates some of the meaning of self-sufficient restriction.

We happened to talk about "learning things." Ernest, in his clumsy, circumstantial way, tried to describe to me how he had learned certain techniques of skiing. Shortly thereafter we came to talk about his lack of friends. It was true, he admitted, he had no friends. And this was borne out by the facts. His partners for Ping-pong and tennis were the only persons with whom he had some enduring mutuality. If he was not occupied with his sports, he would either lounge around or study in his dictionaries. Ernest realized all of a sudden that he was very lonely. He left the session extremely upset. In the next session he asked me to become his teacher and teach him friendship. He asked: "How do you find a friend? What do you say to him? What do you do when he asks you a question?" and so forth. I was struck by the naïveté and yet appropriateness of these questions. It revealed to me what a price, in terms of the most simple interpersonal know-how,

Ernest had had to pay for becoming the self-sufficiently restricted boy he was.

The more such restriction becomes built into the character structure, the less the chances for a reintegration at the base. It seems unlikely, though, that a self-sufficient restriction of this second kind (with its principal roots in the *verbal* dawn of knowing individuation) can turn into more or less permanent amorphousness.

(3) *Conflictual entanglement as chiefly constituted during the preverbal dawn of knowing individuation.* The child, in early molding his nuclear ego for interpersonal survival, dangerously weakens his repressive barrier and hence his ability to endure instinctual conflicts and to channel energies directedly and forcefully. His capacities for neutralizations, both impeded and unduly strained during the preverbal dawn, may, during the verbal dawn, be precariously upheld or they may be drawn into a disastrous whirl of regressive dedifferentiation. Such a child, in a sense, remains less alienated from himself and from his mother, with whom he is symbiotically enmeshed, than would be true for the prematurely and excessively enclosed child mentioned above. However, the final result of both these early survival strategies can be very similar: Under the stress of developmental and adaptive expansions this conflictually enmeshed child sooner or later may become reduced to a state of amorphous dedifferentiation which then remains his enduring adaptive solution.

A conflictual entanglement, as here suggested, appears often associated with that type of mother who, in the psychiatric literature, has come to be labeled as "schizophrenogenic." This is a bad term since it suggests a simple and straight causation of schizophrenia. Such causation does not exist. Theodore Lidz, in writing about the mothers of schizophrenics, distinguishes several types. He describes cold mothers who seem to fit the description I tried to give of the mothers of Kerstin and Ernest. But he also mentions a type of mother—and this is the mother usually labeled as schizophrenogenic—who, in a confusing and erratic manner, seems over-invested in her young child. These mothers conceive of themselves as most well-meaning and loving but, as it turns out, all their investment in their child seems to contribute to the latter's detriment.

Mrs. Elaine K. impressed me as such a mother. Mickey, nineteen years old when I met him the first time, was her only son. Immediately upon seeing mother and son I could not help becoming struck by the intensity and quality of their entanglement.

Mrs. K. looked like the caricature of a faded Hollywood beauty. She was high strung and there was an immensely pleading, pressuring quality in her talk, which was difficult to follow. She spoke several European languages fluently and slipped repeatedly from one language into another without being aware, it seemed, that she created a problem for the listener. Overtly the exclusive topic of her talk seemed to be Mickey, her son. But in her many digressions and jumps from one sub-topic to another, she really seemed to talk about herself—about her own loneliness and frustration, about her mistreatment by her divorced husband, about her own unrequited loves. At times I sensed seductive undertones in her attitude toward me.

Mrs. K. broke with her German parents when, during the first stages of the Second World War, she married a diplomat from a neutral country. Mickey was born approximately one year after her wedding. "Mickey," she said, "was then the one who kept me alive. I felt terribly lonely. There was this language problem." She could never feel warm with her parents-in-law.

She had wanted a girl. "With girls you can have a woman to woman talk. Men can be such brutes." When her baby turned out to be a boy she was disappointed. She decided on the name Mickey since, "Mickey could mean a boy as well as a girl." Also, she let Mickey's hair grow long like the hair of a girl until Mickey was about five years old. Mickey's delicate and pale features and his tendency to become ill easily suggested to her that in his boy's body he had also some female fragility. She let

Mickey sleep in bed with her until he reached the age of seven or eight. Mickey developed asthma when he was four years old and this asthma has remained one of her chief worries since. (When he came to the hospital, Mickey's pockets were stuffed with inhalators and asthma tablets, which he used frequently, even when there was no noticeable asthma attack.) Her husband did not effectively interfere with her ways of bringing up Mickey, although he often disapproved of them. It was as if he had soon decided not to consider Mickey as his but as Elaine's child with whom she could do what she pleased as long as she did not bother him too much. Mrs. K. hinted her husband might have been a covered-up homosexual.

It became clear from Mrs. K's description that she could not help developing possessive erotic interests in Mickey. But these erotic interests she did not clearly acknowledge. They were expressed diffusely and underhandedly. For example, there was a glow in her eyes when she described her enjoyment in bathing Mickey's delicate body. When Mickey reached adolescence she became very concerned about his relationship to girls. By this time her divorce from her husband had become final and she had moved to a city in Western Europe where she established herself as a painter. She became interested in a young art student, a girl from South America, whom she persuaded to live in their household. She would have liked for Mickey to fall in love with this girl who was just "a darling." Mickey, though, seemed too passive to fall in love. Despite the fact that he suffered from asthma he took to chain smoking cigarettes. His mother considered this harmful but permissible since she herself smoked a lot. In addition to smoking many cigarettes, she relied heavily on tranquilizing tablets. She encouraged Mickey to take them also whenever she felt he was upset. Occasionally, she also took Mickey's asthma tablets herself when there were no tranquilizing tablets at hand. "When I am too excited or nervous, I just have to have something and, after all, there's not so much difference between these tablets."

Mickey looked younger than his stated age and wore

his hair in "mod" style. When I saw him first, he was either smoking or sniffing at an asthma inhalator. There was an appealing, babyish quality about him. When he smoked, his hands trembled lightly and there seemed to be an anxious alertness in what otherwise was a bland though appealing smile. Repeatedly he stated that he was "fine, just fine." At closer acquaintance he revealed various kinds of strange sensations. For example, he felt his body had become a piano on which somebody was playing. He could sense the strings vibrating in him. He was concerned that the one who was playing on his body-piano was also playing on his genitals. He heard voices. Some of these voices, sounding harsh and punitive, made him anxious and sleepless.

Mickey became a well-liked and docile patient. Cheerfully he seemed to accept his hospitalization and appeared unworried about his future, about where the money was to come from, etc.—as long as his mother thought this was all right. He offered himself as a kind of plaything for two aggressive female patients who sent him on errands and at times encouraged him to snuggle up with them. They called him "Mickey Mouse" or "Doggie." Unlike Mickey, his mother could not get on a good footing with the nurses and other members of the hospital staff. She would harass them with inquiries and unsolicited advice. After a few months she removed Mickey from the hospital. She just could not live without him although she knew that living with him would be hell.

(4) *Conflictual entanglement as chiefly constituted during the verbal dawn of knowing individuation.* This child has also to cope with developmental imbalances, but his nuclear ego, on the whole, is stronger than that of the preverbally entangled child. Neutralization got off to a better start. There is more differentiated relatedness. Language can be used more successfully to understand oneself and the other. Hence, of all the four relational modes here described, the alienation from the self and the important other seems least marked. In the early exposure to complex

and contradictory human emotions and motives, there is more place for the experience of depth, for the development of interpersonal sensitivity, and for the creative, imaginative mastery of one's relational plight.

The relative weakness of self-polarization and self-demarcation continues to be a great challenge and vulnerability. The adaptive balance remains unfavorably tipped on the sides of too much undergoing and openness. Thus, an individual will be in danger of entrapping himself in a dedifferentiating and deneutralizing circle if additional demands are made on his adaptational apparatus —as when phases of biologic and social expansion and reorganization coincide with intensifying relationships. However, dedifferentiation under stress now may give way to a reintegration at the base. And further, such dedifferentiation will be less amorphous in quality than it was in the above instances. There will be more of a creative collision of primary and relatively well-circumscribed secondary processes.

In the three examples of relational moods so far described, the individual's alienation from self and others seriously crippled and impoverished his life. As an example for the fourth relational mode, where such alienation seems least marked and where we may find an unusual interpersonal sensitivity and a creative imagination which feeds on inner conflict, I choose that author who has given us probably the richest and most insightful description of the schizophrenic experience: August Strindberg.

At this point I cannot even sketch how Strindberg illuminated schizophrenia by means of his works. In all his writings Strindberg gives form to his own complex and contradictory emotions and experiences. He does this in a manner which transcends his personal plight. His eight autobiographical volumes are particularly revealing. The novel *Inferno* is perhaps the best description of a schizophrenic experience to be found in literature. Among the many books and articles which have been written on Strindberg, two stand out from a psychiatric and psychoanalytic point of view. These are Alfred Storch's monograph on Strindberg, and Theodore Lidz's study on Strindberg's creativity and schizophrenia.

In the present context I shall limit myself to pointing out how Strindberg's characteristic relational mode—reflected in his capacity to experience depth and to endure conflict, in his extraordinary sensitivity, in his ability to exploit the collision between his primary and secondary processes creatively, in his relative weakness of self-polarization and self-demarcation, etc.—seems related to the characteristic conflictual entanglement he had with his mother.

Unfortunately, we know little as to how Strindberg related to his mother during the dawn of his knowing individuation. Strindberg, like all of us, had an amnesia for his early childhood experiences. However, in his autobiographical novel *Son of a Servant,* he gives us an inkling of what this relationship might have been like. But more importantly: We can use his description of that relationship wherein he, in his own words, rediscovered features of his early relationship with his mother. This was his relationship to Siri von Essen, who became his first wife and who bore him four children. It was the most fateful and tangled relationship he ever had as an adult. He describes it in his autobiographical novel *Confessions of a Fool.*

Strindberg had a wet nurse and a number of nurse-maids, who, we must assume, fulfilled an important mothering function for him. When Strindberg later meets his wet nurse, by now a white-haired old woman with a shrunken bosom and shaking arms, he becomes conscious "of a debt, a misplayed debt which can only be paid by eternal gratitude." Strindberg gives us some idea of the conflicting feelings he had toward his own mother. "The mother," he writes, "had a nervous temperament. Flared up quickly but quieted down soon enough." He points out that "to the children she was Providence itself. She cut overgrown nails, bandaged injured fingers, always comforted, calmed, and soothed after the father had punished, although she was also the official accuser. The children thought she was small-minded and mean when she 'squealed' on them to Papa, so she did not win their respect. She could be unjust and violent and could administer punishment unreservedly on the bare accusation of a servant. But since the children received food and comfort from her they loved her."

Strindberg reports an early episode where he experienced his mother as assisting in his execution. This episode provides an example of what, in the literature on schizophrenia, has come to be known as a double-bind. Since Gregory Bateson introduced this term, we understand thereby an interpersonal situation wherein a person is exposed to conflicting messages which are conveyed through different expressive channels. While this happens an escape route is closed. A person under the spell of such a double-bind cannot help becoming confused.

The double-bind to which young Strindberg became subjected was as follows: His father once at dinner discovered a half empty wine flask. Father asked who had drunk from the bottle but nobody responded. At this point, young Strindberg blushed. "So it's you," was his father's reply. His son, who had never noticed where the wine flask was hidden, burst into tears and sobbed, "I didn't drink the wine." Thereupon his father responded: "And now you are lying also."

When he was about to be punished his mother asked him to plead his father's forgiveness. "His father," we read, "had brought out the whip from behind the mirror." "Please, dear Papa. Please forgive me," bawled the innocent child. "But now it was too late. Asking forgiveness was tantamount to confession." Young Strindberg was thus asked to justify himself and to confess, but he was also made to understand that any attempt at justification would be regarded as implicit confession and as a trick to wiggle himself away from his deserved punishment. There was no way out for him.

Strindberg's relationship to Siri von Essen, while re-enacting important aspects of his relationship to his mother, flung him into a turmoil of dedifferentiation and deneutralization as described earlier. His many conflicting emotions and needs, brought to unbearable intensity, overwhelmed his capacity to appraise realistically his inner and outer reality. This reality—his own feelings, needs, and motives as well as those of his important others—became distorted, over-blown, and fragmented. He became, at least temporarily, split in regard to these inner and outer realities, that is, he became schizophrenic.

Still, he went a far way in facing these conflicting experiences honestly and—for reasons which perhaps never can be fully comprehended—he forged out of them his plays and novels. We may doubt whether Strindberg, in becoming schizophrenic, achieved a reintegration at the base. After recovering from his psychosis of the midforties—the time of his *Inferno*—he continued to lead a restricted life. But he continued to be deeply creative. He wrote his dream plays. "The dream plays," writes Theodore Lidz, "even as dreams could condense the timeless, the contradictory, the unresolvable ambivalences and multiplicity of interrelated primitive conflicts with which he had become preoccupied. Only through these symbolic dream plays could the complexity of the tragedy of Strindberg's life be expressed other than through psychosis."

Strindberg found in Siri von Essen the idealized perfect mother whom he, the unwanted child, soon to be replaced by younger siblings, never had. "I was shaken," we read, "utterly confused, as if I were gazing at a vision. The instinct of worship, latent in my heart, awoke and with it the desire to proclaim my adoration. The void which once had been filled by religion ached no longer; the yearning to adore had reappeared under a new form. God was deposed, but His place was taken by woman, woman who was both virgin and mother. . . ."

He describes the ensuing symbiotic unification: "From that day I no longer belonged to myself. She had inoculated me with her blood; our nerves were in a state of high tension; the unborn lives within her yearned for the quickening fiat which would call them into existence; her soul craved for union with my spirit, and my spirit longed to pour itself into this vessel." He describes the explosive, dedifferentiating force of feelings thus aroused: "I was almost delirious with want of sleep; my pent-up feelings overflowed; this womanly tenderness, the secret of which none but a motherly woman knows, was a new experience to me." He describes his agony, his hallucinations, and his wish to destroy her. "My soul was lacerated, sick to death. The influence of that little female brain, so different from the brain of man, disturbed and disordered the mechanism of my thoughts." We learn of his sudden separation from her, as this separation grows out of an unendurable closeness, a separation which then becomes equally unendurable. He could not escape her. "Her personality was grafted on mine and was dominating it. I existed only through her; I, the mother-root, led an underground life, nourishing this tree which was growing sunwards and promising wonderful blossoms." He feels devoured by her and yet wants to be devoured. He wants to enslave her and yet be her slave. We see him nourishing a deadly hate which feeds on an hyper-alertness of his partner's failings. He coldly analyzes her frigidity, her lack of culture and manners, her prostitute-like behavior. (In his play *Miss Julie*, he has given dramatic expression to this part of his relationship to Siri.) He becomes aware of her homosexual tendencies. At the same time, he tortures himself for being so hateful and coldly analytical. And again and again he seeks his rescue in his writings.

These are only a few of the many aspects of Strindberg's conflictual entanglement.

SHARING ATTENTION IMPAIRED

Sharing attention grows out of fearless attention which is brought under the spell of language. Language makes attention more intricate and potentially more reconciling, but also serves as a window through which one can more subtly spot its pathology. I shall now summarize such pathology of attentional processes; a pathology which reflects and sustains a negative mutuality, as this exists during the verbal dawn of knowing individuation.

Any of the four preceding relational modes, this means, will result in a kind of attentional disturbance which is characteristic and specific for each relational mode.

Self-sufficient restriction arising out of the preverbal dawn of knowing individuation will result in attention which is both furtive and rigid. Since the child is ridden by fear and distrust, he will avoid sharing a focus with his mother. Such sharing for him would mean defenselessness and surrender. Still, while only minimally sharing a focus, his attention can be focal in a sense; that is, reflect some directedness and investment of attentional cathexis. But this focality will be "rejective" instead of "receptive." Its shielding and closing function will be predominant. It will be badly defective as to openness and undergoing and hence will have very little adaptive flexibility in the sense indicated earlier. Either gradually or acutely, we saw, such defensive, rigid focality may give way to an amorphous drifting existence as in the case of Kerstin D. In this new attentional constellation, undergoing and openness will have a greater share than before. Now the individual, in a sense, can let himself be influenced easier. But, because of the general amorphousness and low and undirected investment of energies, a meaningful sharing of a focus with the mother (and any others) cannot be expected either.

A self-sufficient restriction with strong obsessive underpinnings—the second relational mode described above—is equally slanted toward defensive closure. But it represents, as a rule, a more viable adaptive solution. The individual more successfully can hold onto an attentional focus, although he hardly can share it for a longer period. In order to be able to "share" an attentional focus, he would have to be less rigid and more open and undergoing. The evolving mutuality will depend on how much he can afford to loosen up and make use of the reconciling potential of language.

A conflictual entanglement of mainly preverbal origin

will greatly prevent any build-up of attentional structures. The elements of doing and closure will be badly missing. The child may try to share in whatever focus the mother may offer by way of passively going along with it and by cultivating a sort of free-floating, agile empathic resonance. Such emphatic resonance to a degree seems to thrive on preverbal undergoing and openness. Language can be expected to make such resonance more difficult, that is, to make for more confusion. The sharing of a focus, through language, instead of being consolidated and verified, becomes a painfully complicated and frustrating affair.

This holds partly true for the fourth relational mode and attentional constellation: For a conflictual entanglement mainly constituted during the verbal dawn. Closure, structure, and directedness will be lacking or in jeopardy also in this constellation, but not so badly. The attentional panorama is more varied. In general, more energy and affective color will enter into the child's attentional efforts. To a degree, in this case also language seems to interfere with an empathic resonance. But language also is exploited. It will play an adaptive role of some sort. Language as reconciling medium may become "creatively" idiosyncratic: It seems to serve more to disguise, to qualify, to relativize than to confirm and to validate consensually. Hence, there will often be an idiosyncratic, slanted sharing of a focus—but still more real sharing than would be the case in the preceding constellation.

VI
BEYOND THE DYAD

When the child reaches three, the dawn of knowing individuation approaches its end. This also concludes the symbiotic phase in the mother-child relationship with which this study chiefly is concerned. However, in order to understand better the singular importance of this early phase and relationship, a glance beyond seems necessary.

The child's individuation will go on. In a very important sense, this individuation must never stop. In each new developmental phase the individual will have the alternative of either further growth or deterioration. A halfway solution does not exist.

In line with my previous considerations, such ongoing individuation must be conceived as a spirally expanding adaptive and developmental process. This means new rounds of differentiation-integration must emerge, doing-undergoing and closure-openness must be adaptively reconciled, and the consequences of an earlier unequal development and negative mutuality must be corrected.

As the child learns and as his psychic organization grows more complex, his relational tasks also become more varied. His relationship with his mother will continue for a long time to come, and its dialectic of relational balances will further unfold. But other relationships will superimpose themselves. The child will also meaningfully relate to the father, the siblings, the members of the extended family, peers, and many others.

Each new relational diversification will affect the primary dyad, and vice versa. With any new meaningful relationship of the child, the dyadic relationship will have to change. In a sense, it must become less exclusive. It must be rearranged so as to accommodate the new relationship. In relating to more than one person, the ego's reconciling task will become more difficult. More neutralized energy will be required. The child now must differentiate which feelings and which reactions belong to which person and he must integrate all these constellations into consistent relational strategies and workable identifications. He must increasingly cope with mixed feelings and, as a rule, with stronger ambivalence. He must understand and take into account varying interpersonal alignments.

But all these added relational tasks, though in one sense reflecting a loosening of the dyadic tie, in another sense build on the latter. In embarking on his new relations, the child must use the working capital accumulated in this relationship. His earlier positive mutuality will have to spill over into the new mutuality.

Specifically, he will enter into any new relationship with a set of expectations and attitudes that have been shaped by the earlier relationship: He will establish transferences. That is, he will transfer processed elements from the primary to the latter ties. The fate of such transferences will hinge on his capacities for imaginative adaptive reconciliations and these, again, are greatly a matter of early neutralizing relational balances. Therefore, such transferences will either successfully be absorbed into a new positive mutuality, or they will impede this mutuality because of their rigid, defensive quality.

The fate of these transferences is reflected in the attentional processes transacted vis-à-vis the partners of the new relationships. For example, any excessively closing and furtive attentional style will reflect the transference of earlier, "shielding" survival strategies unto a new relation, etc.

The Oedipal period spanning the child's fifth and sixth years marks relational crossroads of crucial significance. It dramatically enforces and highlights the first fateful relational diversifications beyond the mother-child dyad. Freud has described, for the first time, its important features. The child now meaningfully must relate to two persons in a manner which allows him to retain and reconcile important elements of each. And this, at a time of a first forceful erotic awakening. The son must, while experiencing the father as a frustrating rival, nevertheless learn to identify with his assertive manliness. He must "process" his hate in a manner which leads to a (not too strong) idealization of his father, importantly constituting in this very process his superego. He must "give up" his mother and yet so store her image that it will later—at the prime of his post-adolescent genitality—impel him to find a suitable partner.

The daughter also must complexly solidify her identity and, at the same time, diversify her relationships. Unlike the son, she need not shift relational gears as much as must the boy who, after a close, symbiotic tie with his mother, must learn to model himself after a person of a sex different from his mother's. The daughter's task, one might say, is less the transformation than the revision of an existing relationship. This fact, among other things, makes the Oedipal experience different for boys and girls.[1] But the daughter, like the son, must learn to tolerate and process the conflictual feelings which inevitably arise in this triangular situation.

Clearly, this crucial Oedipal phase-constellation must build strongly on a positive mutuality during the dawn of knowing individuation. The quest to become "one and same" and "one and different" must have successfully been

[1] Girls, for example, while ordinarily remaining more closely identified with their mothers, also seem to have fewer delineating mechanisms at their disposal whereby they might fight a regressive reactivation of the early symbiotic bond. Thus, a woman's orgasm appears as a rule more "regressively open-ended" than that of the man, and female schizophrenics seem more easily pulled into a "clinging, diffusely dependent condition" than do their male counterparts. Also, many girls in adolescence seem to be much closer to the archaic-devouring mother than do boys. They might try to fight the frightening regressive pull by dashing into promiscuity. (Peter Blos has written extensively on this subject.)

resolved in order that the challenges of the Oedipal period can be met.

Adolescence can be compared to the Oedipal period. It, too, marks a period of critical biologic, psychic, and social expansion and reintegration. It, too, poses the challenge of new relational diversification. How this challenge is met will depend on how the earlier relational tasks were solved. For example, too strong fixations or missed and slanted identifications with either parent during the Oedipal period will now exert their toll: The individual will not succeed in finding a heterosexual partner who signifies both liberation from and successful identification with the Oedipal parent.

But adolescence, also, crucially will bear the impact of the early mother-child relationship. The two most important achievements during the dawn of knowing individuation—the installment of a solid nuclear ego and of language as a reconciling medium—now are put to what is, in a sense, their most critical test. They are needed to successfully master these reintegrations and upheavals which now are due and which have been described by Anna Freud, E. H. Erikson, P. Blos, E. Jacobson, and many others.

In between the Oedipal and adolescent period and including both, stretches the life in the family. The importance of the family culture (or better, in the definition of Parsons and Bales: subculture) for shaping the growing child's relational styles, for determining his relational successes and downfalls has only recently been fully recognized. The studies of Lyman Wynne and Margaret Singer, of Theodore Lidz and his associates, of Murray Bowen, Gregory Bateson, Don Jackson, Ronald Laing, and many others, have highlighted its importance. Such importance derives from the fact that the family, at least in our Western culture, is the institutionalized, enduring training and testing ground for most relational styles and practices.

The family, therefore, in manifold ways will influence the mother-child relationship: It will influence how it structures itself, how it unfolds, and it will, at the same

Through this handling of analytic time, both analyst and patient create a kind of temporal moratorium. The analytic time, contracted and paid for by the patient and safeguarded through both parties, demarcates a realm in which both moment and duration creatively balance each other.

The second dichotomy, brought about and reconciled in the analytic situation, is DIFFERENCE vs. SAMENESS.

The analytic situation highlights differences in the two partners' roles and expectations. The most crucial difference, implicit in and upheld by the contractual arrangement, is that between patient and doctor. The patient, by definition, suffers and has problems. The doctor is motivated and qualified to relieve such suffering and to assist in solving these problems. It is this primary difference in roles and expectations which provides the main lever to correct what Freud recognized as the neurotic's main dilemma: his tendency to again and again reenact old patterns of relatedness and thereby to avoid new life experiences, insight, and change. In structuring such difference of positions, Freud greatly diminished the chances for these reenactments to occur. Against the patient's powers of turning what is new into what is neurotically familiar, the analyst now upheld the evidence and power of the unfamiliar. Corrective emotional experiences could thus develop.

But such difference of positions, in order to translate itself into insight and eventual change, requires sameness of values and frames of reference. To a degree, both doctor and patient must speak the same language; their cultural backgrounds must not be too disparate. There must be some nuclear agreement as to what goals and conduct are desirable in life.

The difference of roles and expectations, to turn into a lever for insightful change, therefore must be balanced by a sameness of basic orientation. And the more pronounced the difference, the more important become, in the relationship, the linkage-points of sameness. The two forces must be seen as facilitating each other while, at the same time, becoming reconciled.

As the analytic situation unfolds in time, this balance of forces will be tested in various ways. In a sense, it is bound to become upset. For example, the patient's original complaint and problem, against which the doctor's help was evoked, may point to deeper problems. As these enter the analytic arena, new feelings and expectations tend to emerge. For example, feelings of wanting to be cuddled, "loved," and taken care of by the analyst often seem hard to accommodate in a professional relationship. The doctor's position as commonly defined, and the main bastion of difference, will thus come under attack. The analyst, on his side, will notice in himself similar "unprofessional" wishes, fears, and expectations. As the relationship develops this balance thus will be threatened with upheavals, shifts, and loosening. However—and this is important—in order to maintain a creative dialectic, this balance, again and again, will have to be established.

The third dichotomy, crucially structuring the analytic situation, is GRATIFICATION *vs.* FRUSTRATION.

This dichotomy expressly refers to the two partners' needs—to how these needs interact in this relationship. Traditionally the frustrating aspects have been emphasized. The contract between doctor and patient excludes many gratifications inherent in other relationships. In particular, it forbids or greatly limits certain instinctual gratifications. Both partners, in other words, agree to avoid "acting out." Sexual relations and many other indulgences, find no place in this relationship. Hence the stress on abstinence—in both analyst and patient—as that basic requirement which fosters verbalization instead of acting and which, in the long run, makes for a more mature and conscious dealing with one's inner life and problems. The constant frustrating pull of this abstinence thus goads the patient to a greater maturity: where ID was, EGO shall be.

Yet such abstinence and frustration, we recognize at further reflection, is not total. It strategically has to direct

B. Hill, in his book *Psychotherapeutic Intervention in Schizophrenia*, has expressed in a beautiful simile. "The child," according to Hill, "in relating to the mother, incorporates mother's 'goodness' essential for the build-up of his psychic and moral personality just as he takes in and assimilates the minerals in her milk—the constituents of a good body."

Since Freud we speak of orality and the oral phase to delineate the essential occurrences during this stage: the contact between the child's mouth and mother's breast becomes that plane on which organic nurture (e.g. with milk) and affective nurture meet. They both, inseparably, constitute the *"good experience."*

Winnicott has indicated how such good experience, as our primary reservoir of self-worth, trust, and hope, can be seen as propelling the required developmental dynamic. "The baby," he writes, "hates to waste an experience and much prefers to wait and bear frustration of primitive pleasures if waiting adds the warmth of a personal relationship." The original good experience thus makes waiting and frustration bearable and even pleasurable. It goads the baby to find warmth on a new plane of relatedness. This relatedness is more long-drawn, more mediate, more feeling than the foregone primitive pleasures. It now provides a base from which reality can be more easily accepted and mastered. For there is now the promise, upheld by actual experience, that new warmth will come. The primary good experience therefore can be seen as the pivot for all later sublimation and neutralization (in the sense indicated by Hartmann). It is the base for a nuclear relative autonomy which allows the baby to utilize and test new skills and approaches—waiting being one of these—which, almost imperceptibly, will re-create the warmth of self-worth and love on new levels of personality organization and interpersonal discourse.

How does frustration enter this picture? In order to answer this question, we must recall the early interpenetration—the one-package character—of physiologic and affective processes. Thus, just as the "good experience" is a conglomorate of such processes, so is the "bad experience." The good breast therefore has its counterpart in the bad breast. This bad breast denotes "ill-being," displeasure, tension, the lack of relaxation and comfort. There exists, side by side with the subjective paradise, subjective hell.

And nobody at this early stage, we must assume, can avoid getting to know what it is like. The chief reason, again, is the infant's helplessness and lack of maturation. He does not yet have that framework of concepts and habits which, to a degree at least, allow the normal adult to manage his affects, to prevent these affects from overthrowing him. The infant cannot yet "know" about his affects. He cannot yet give them a place in the continuum of his life. He cannot yet relate himself to these feeling states: Recognize them as experiences which now are here but later will fade out. These experiences are not yet embedded in language and, hence, in an awareness of time which "binds" them and tones them down. He cannot yet see them in perspective. Being able to do this would require him to possess already his home base of reconciling faculties and structures: His nuclear ego, as this was described in the previous chapter. But this nuclear ego does not yet exist. The dawn of knowing individuation has just begun. Self-polarization and self-demarcation have not yet been accomplished.

Small children cannot yet tell us about their experiences. Therefore, in a sense we can never really know how they feel—despite our observation and empathy. But certain psychotic patients, in their immense anxiety, may give us an inkling thereof. Some of these patients can—later!—put into words how it feels when all inner structure collapses, when one is overwhelmed by greed and rage which no force in the world seems able to halt.

The infant, more than we can imagine, appears at the mercy of his experiences. And these experiences quickly may change or become intolerable. Good experiences for the infant thus can quickly turn into bad experiences. The infant, Spitz points out, during an important early period, is both uncomfortable and about-to-be-comfortable almost

GRATIFICATION-FRUSTRATION

As in the early mother-child relationship, gratification, in this therapeutic situation, seems all-important. Gratification, we saw, provides the working capital on which any developmental and relational expansion has to draw. And in the schizophrenic patient such working capital is badly lacking. The therapeutic relationship, as much as possible, must make it grow.

Mme. Sechehaye most eloquently has stated this fact. For her, the schizophrenic's road toward improvement must start out from gratification, from pleasure. Other authors such as Hayward have defined schizophrenia as a deficiency syndrome, as comparable to rickets which result from a deficiency of vitamin D. The schizophrenic's main deficiency was in love, in gratification, and this the therapist must now provide. A female patient of Hayward and Taylor tells us how she experienced such remedial gratification. It is a most moving account, strongly suggesting some of the meaning which the primordial gratification must have for a child. The following is an excerpt of the patient's descriptions:

By feeding me you gave me the strength to love or hurt you as much as I wanted, but you didn't mind. This was terribly important. I watched carefully while you nursed me to see if you got thinner. I had to be sure that I wasn't taking too much. I'll never forget the day your suit seemed tight and you agreed you were getting too fat. It made me feel so safe.

You wanted to feed me so you wanted me to live. Mother is dry, like the desert. She loves the desert. She never nursed me. With you it was the first time I ever sucked a breast.

No one seemed to understand that I couldn't go ahead and grow up until all the holes from the past were filled up. I couldn't go ahead until I had a chance to feel safe and happy as a baby. You have to go down before you can come up. When you feel sure you belong to someone, everything else works out all right. If you've once been loved, you never forget it.

You have no idea how the warmth of your body would bring me back from my crazy world. It would change my whole picture of life when you held me. I had been so sure that no one could ever give warmth to me. You made everything look different.

When my violent feelings became too strong, I would have to close down on all my feelings. I would become cold and dead. I would even lose my love for you. At these times the only thing that seemed real about you was the physical warmth of your body when you held me.

Everyone should be able to look back in their memory and be sure he had a mother who loved him, all of him; even his piss and shit. He should be sure his mother loved him just for being himself; not for what he could do. Otherwise he feels he has no right to exist. He feels he should never have been born.

No matter what happens to this person in life, no matter how much he gets hurt, he can always look back to this and feel that he is lovable. He can love himself and he cannot be broken. If he can't fall back on this, he can be broken.

You can only be broken if you're already in pieces. As long as my baby-self had never been loved then I was in pieces. By loving me as a baby, you made me whole.

Such remedial gratification, in order to become possible in the therapeutic relationship, to some extent requires the preverbal symbiotic mother-child relatedness to become reconstituted between therapist and patient. Harold Searles has described many important features of such needed reconstellation of early relational modes: in the relationship there must be a place for a sharing of feelings and anxieties which characterize the symbiotic bond dur-

time, influence the continuing individuation of the child. The family, for one thing, will greatly come to bear on the shifts of the five relational balances in the direction of greater separation of mother and child. It will, further, reinforce and aggravate or undo and mitigate the results of a negative mutuality which existed in the early dyadic relationship. Particularly Lyman Wynne and Margaret Singer, in recent works on "Thought Disorder and Family Relations of Schizophrenics" have tried to conceptualize how differing parental relational styles and cognitive sets may have either an aggravating or mitigating impact on such results of an earlier negative mutuality.

However, it will remain difficult to evaluate aggravating or mitigating relational constellations and transactions. Many factors do interplay. It will be necessary to estimate how the other relationships affect the primary dyad, how they affect the growing child's differentiation-integration, his given adaptive reconciliation and, most importantly, how they either facilitate a reintegration at the base or only further entrench the child in unpromising short-term adaptations.

VII
SCHIZOPHRENIA RECONSIDERED

We shall now pause in order to look anew at schizophrenia. What light is thrown on this disorder by the insights and conclusions that we have reached so far?

BLEULER'S CONCEPT OF SCHIZOPHRENIA

To answer this question, I shall start with the concept of schizophrenia as developed by Eugen Bleuler. Elsewhere I have more lengthily dealt with Bleuler's contribution. At this point I shall only outline some of its crucial features.

Bleuler, in introducing the concept, differentiated the so-called fundamental symptoms, specific to schizophrenia, from accessory symptoms which also could occur elsewhere. The fundamental, specific symptoms he found in a characteristic disturbance of association and affectivity,[1] a predominance of fantasy over reality and a concomitant relative intactness and availability of such functions as perception, memory, and orientation.

Thus Bleuler departed from what Kraepelin and others had considered essential in dementia praecox. Schizophrenia no longer was synonymous with flamboyant mental disturbance, as reflected in hallucinations, delusions, gross mannerisms, etc. For it was exactly these latter "psychotic" symptoms which Bleuler defined as accessory. In this manner Bleuler widened and relativized the con-

[1] The term "affectivity" refers to a person's feeling state. This feeling state can be either appropriate or inappropriate when viewed in a transactional context. Schizophrenics are held to display inappropriate affect; e.g. they may give a shallow laugh when talking about something serious, etc.

cept. The schizophrenic disturbance of thinking and affectivity, in Bleuler's view, differed from normal modes of thinking and experience only in terms of degree and overall constellation, but not in terms of quality. "Even normal persons," he wrote, "show a number of schizophrenic symptoms when they are emotionally preoccupied, particularly inattentive, or when their attention is concentrated on a single subject. Among these symptoms are peculiar associations, incomplete concepts and ideas, displacements, logical blunders and stereotypes." And further: "The individual symptom in itself is less important than its intensity and extensiveness and, above all, its relation to the psychological setting." He introduced the concept of latent schizophrenia: "There is also latent schizophrenia, and I am convinced that this is the most frequent form, although admittedly these people hardly ever come for treatment." Bleuler, in short, in mild and embryonic forms saw schizophrenia as all-pervasive.

But Bleuler—and this is important—not only widened and relativized the concept of schizophrenia, he also unified it. This he did by focusing on the schizophrenic's so-called loosening of associations. The pivot in his theorizing about schizophrenia became this passage:

In the normal thinking process, the numerous actual and latent images combine to determine each association. In schizophrenia, however, single images or whole combinations may be rendered ineffective, in an apparently haphazard fashion. Instead, thinking operates with ideas and concepts which have no, or a completely insufficient, connection with the main idea and therefore should be excluded from the thought process. The result is that thinking becomes confused, bizarre, incorrect, abrupt. Sometimes, all the associative threads fail and the thought chain is totally interrupted; after such "blocking," ideas may emerge which have no recognizable connection with preceding ones (p. 22). (*Dementia Praecox or the Group of Schizophrenias*. New York: International Universities Press, 1950, p. 22.)

The "loosening of associations" thus indicated a breakdown of the purposefulness and hierarchic structuring of our thought processes. It implied further the breakdown of a balance which tends to make thinking communicative and adaptive. In most general terms, this balance can be stated as follows: In order to serve adaptation and communication, our associations must be purposefully and hierarchically integrated and yet retain some of their spontaneous quality. If such integration fails, schizophrenia will result.

Thus focusing on the loosening of associations, Bleuler could first find a common denominator for such diverse schizophrenic symptoms (many for the first time clearly delineated by Bleuler himself) as delusions, hallucinations, mannerisms, autism, (self-centeredness) ambivalence, depersonalization, etc.: all these symptoms could be understood as deriving from such loosening of associations—in reflecting either characteristic variations or secondary counter-measures to control or repair it.

Second, Bleuler could account for other features in the schizophrenic disturbance whose connection with thinking is not immediately apparent, such as disturbances in affectivity, in drive mastery, and, most generally, in relational capacity; features which he and many others have clearly described.

This he did by explaining the loosening of associations (and hence, schizophrenic symptoms) dynamically along psychoanalytic lines. Bleuler's theory of schizophrenia, in this respect, extends and elaborates the psychoanalytic theory developed by Freud. This Bleuler clearly acknowledged in his monograph of 1913.

Certain complexes—that is, conflicting affective constellations—could be seen as causing the breakdown of the above balance, thus loosening up associations and leading to schizophrenic symptomatology. In this symptomatology Bleuler recognized therefore the disjunctive force of such complexes, just as Freud had found these to lie behind many a neurotic symptomatology (here, the central complex being the Oedipus complex). Like Freud, he emphasized the importance of dammed-up and frustrated sexual needs. These needs, so to speak, over-powered and perverted those mechanisms which normally "bind," modulate, and hierarchically organize our associations.

Bleuler, in developing these ideas, clearly noticed the similarities existing between, on the one side, dreams, as illuminated by Freud, and schizophrenic symptomatology on the other. In each instance those laws seem abandoned or perverted which make our thinking communicative and adaptive in a conventional sense. Yet with this central difference: In dreams these laws are cancelled only temporarily. The dreamer will return to waking life. The schizophrenic, in contrast, may abandon them forever. In making idiosyncratic his thinking, he loosens his hold on the conventional world. His nightmare becomes his everyday reality.

In sum, schizophrenia, for Bleuler, represented a widespread disorder of thinking and affectivity, which was recognizable by its symptoms. It could be latent and manifest. Its symptoms, as a rule, appeared during early adulthood. These symptoms, in mild and passing forms, also could occur in normal persons. Therefore, their quantity and relation to the psychological setting were considered important. The "loosening of associations" was seen as the unifying principle, on the one side, in ordering the manifold and seemingly diverse schizophrenic symptoms and, on the other side, in pointing to a common pathogenic factor or constellation of factors.

Schizophrenia, thus conceived, opens the door for further exploration mainly in two directions: first, in the direction of the "psychological setting" and hence of that point where (in terms of Hegel's logic) quantity turns into quality, where schizophrenic symptoms in normals cease to be normal and become evidence of schizophrenia. Second, this concept directs us to explore and delineate further those pathogenic factors or constellations which overthrow the above balance and thus "unbind" associations.

Eugen Bleuler, for a number of reasons, did not follow

up on these explorative tasks staked out by his own pioneering work.[2] He later grew more skeptical about some of Freud's theories. He thus tended to give less weight to dynamic explanations along psychoanalytic principles. This, in turn, led him to postulate—in accord with the prevailing psychiatric tradition—organic causes for schizophrenia in a manner which greatly sidestepped and partly negated the implications of his earlier dynamic formulations. These organic causes now, so to speak, translated themselves more directly—without the interplay of complex psychodynamics—into psychic symptoms, thus seemingly supporting a rather unsophisticated view of "mental symptoms." Thus Bleuler, almost imperceptibly, later again seemed to come closer to the "organic and distant observer position" of a Wernicke, Griesinger, and also a Kraepelin. And along with such, explicit and implicit, shifting of the postulated pathogenic focus in a direction of a "naive organicity," the question of the psychological setting, as indicated above, also becomes less pressing. Until after World War II, it roused little interest in German academic psychiatry.

A FIELD THEORY OF SCHIZOPHRENIA: SCHIZOPHRENIA IN THE LIGHT OF THREE GENERAL PRINCIPLES OF DEVELOPMENT AND ADAPTATION

In the following, I shall address myself specifically to the two main questions left open by Bleuler's earlier work: the question of the "psychological setting," that is, its role in turning quantity into quality, in causing symptoms which also can occur in normal persons to become evidence of schizophrenia; and second, the question of the nature of "schizophrenogenic" factors and constellations. Clearly, these two questions suggest a kind of answer which relates them to each other, which establishes

[2] Some of these reasons I have outlined in "Bleuler's Concept of Schizophrenia: A Confusing Heritage." *Am. J. Psychiat.*, *123*: 996–1001, 1967.

an interdependence, complex as this may be. This means that I shall attempt a formulation which encompasses these questions. Taking, like Bleuler, the loosening of associations as my theoretical pivot, I shall try to offer a field theory of schizophrenia which, in suggesting certain answers to the above questions, coordinates a number of relevant viewpoints.

The field theory of schizophrenia which I suggest builds on the three general principles of human development and adaptation outlined earlier. Thus, I submit this general definition of schizophrenia to be specified in the following: *schizophrenia reflects a disturbance in human development and adaptation whose characteristic features are brought to light by jointly applying three principles: differentiation-integration, adaptive reconciliation, and adaptive antagonism.*

This means, schizophrenia reflects

(1) *A disturbance in differentiation-integration.* This disturbance can either be primary in that it indicates an original, uneven development. From the beginning, certain psychic features and structures become over-developed and differentiated and others less developed and differentiated. Thus, a phase-adequate integration does not come about or is insufficient. Or this disturbance can be secondary in that it results from a *dedifferentiation* of certain structures and functions already differentiated and developed. Such dedifferentiation can be explained as a regressive deneutralization of instinctual energies in the sense indicated by Hartmann. Therefore, the schizophrenic disturbance can be both primary and secondary; and it can represent a mixture of both primary and secondary elements. This, no doubt, is the likeliest constellation.

Such a disturbance in differentiation-integration is clearly suggested in Bleuler's original delineation of schizophrenic symptomatology: in pointing to the schizophrenic's disturbance of associations and affectivity, Bleuler emphasized the *simultaneous* relative intactness of such functions as perception, memory, and orientation. In the light of this classification, the individual's adaptive apparatus, in schizophrenia, reflects, if not uneven development, at least uneven availability of capacities and functions.

Lyman Wynne recently has summarized certain formal core disturbances in schizophrenia which can reflect either un- or dedifferentiation and, at the same time, a failure of integration: (a) the capacity to differentiate self from non-self; (b) the capacity to recognize and distinguish different kinds of feeling states, impulses, and wishes; (c) the delineation of distinctive, specialized skills—motor, cognitive, expressive, linguistic; (d) the capacity to discriminate different parts of the object world, personal and non-personal, and to distinguish abstract and metaphorical representations from their literal and concrete counterparts. He further suggested a temporal dimension in such disturbed differentiation-integration: "Because integration and articulation necessarily bring together percepts and processes which are already partially differentiated, recent and partial disturbances will be apparent primarily as failures of integration; more profound disturbances will involve failures of both differentiation and integration."

The principle of differentiation-integration, we can say, primarily establishes a historic or longitudinal perspective. A disturbance in differentiation-integration brings into focus past developmental vicissitudes. It makes us understand how the past fails the present.

The principle "adaptive reconciliation" makes even more explicit such failure. It, so to speak, complements the above longitudinal with a horizontal perspective. It brings into focus crucial features of the given adaptational context. Disturbances in differentiation-integration inevitably are made transparent in this context.

Schizophrenia, in this sense, also indicates

(2) *An unsuccessful adaptive reconciliation.* Such unsuccessful reconciliation may manifest itself in behavioral extremes of either doing or undergoing, or it may show

up in an unharmonious, "jerky," unmodulated integration of the two elements.

On a general level, extremes of undergoing have been commonly noted in schizophrenia. Many observers consider as pathognomic such traits as extreme passivity, lack of energy, lack of lustful strivings, a tendency to diffuse drifting, a fundamental lack of self-willed, structured, goal-directed action, etc. The classical symptom of catalepsy (*flexibilitas cerea*—waxen flexibility) dramatically highlights an extreme of undergoing.

Extremes of doing seem less conspicuous in schizophrenia, but have also been noted. Cases of intense catatonic excitement would be an example. Eugen Bleuler, in his classic monograph, mentions manic conditions characterized by euphoria, flight of ideas, pressure of activity.

However, most cases of schizophrenia somewhere seem to belong to the in-between-group, that is, they indicate an unharmonious, erratic, unadaptive integration of the elements doing and undergoing. Bleuler and many other authors have emphasized the frequent, seemingly unmotivated and abrupt swings from passive to active forms of behavior, and vice versa. This holds true for behavior which conventionally is designated as hebephrenic, paranoid, or catatonic. The classic description of catatonia includes stupor as well as excitement.

In the present context thinking can also be considered a form of behavior. Freud described it as trial action (*Probehandeln*) with very low energy quantities. In this sense, the thinking of the schizophrenic can be expected to reflect a similarly unsuccessful reconciliation of doing-undergoing such as characterizes his behavior in general. His thinking or cognitive orientation manifests either extremes of undergoing, or doing, or—and this is most likely —an unharmonious mixture of both.

The dichotomy "doing-undergoing" primarily illuminates the *action* aspect of behavior, that is, the modes and intensity of energy investment. The dichotomy closure-openness, while interdependent with the foregoing, chiefly throws light on the structural features of behavior.

Again, on a general level, extremes of openness appear to play a main role in schizophrenia. Such general terms as extreme pliability, conformity, "being like clay," etc., denote this aspect. On the other side, extremes of closure are conveyed by such terms as maximal rigidity, blockage (*Sperrung*), stupor, entrenchment, unreachability, autism, etc. And many observers emphasize the unharmonious and non-adaptive concurrence of extreme openness *and* closure in schizophrenia.

On such a general descriptive level, though, the dichotomy closure-openness seems to add little insight to that which the dichotomy doing-undergoing adduces. Evidently, the terms used to elaborate it are too similar to those of the latter dichotomy.

But such is not the case when we try to specify characteristic structures or styles of thinking which occur in schizophrenia. Then the dichotomy closeness-openness becomes highly meaningful in delineating typical constellations. Corresponding to extremes of undergoing, extremes of openness appear to play a major role in schizophrenic thinking. These extremes can, according to Lyman Wynne, be called instances of *"amorphousness."* The term comprises "global, predominantly undifferentiated forms of functioning" and, specifically, thinking. Wynne speaks of a "woolly, indefinite, impoverished vagueness." Such amorphousness would be typical of many schizophrenics who conventionally are diagnosed as cases of hebephrenia, chronic undifferentiated schizophrenia, and so-called schizophrenia simplex. Richard D., as described earlier, reflects such an amorphous form of schizophrenic thinking.

Extremes of closure, again less frequent and conspicuous than the extremes of openness, reflect a rigid, seemingly self-sufficient isolation. Certain cases which traditionally are diagnosed as paraphrenics or paranoid characters seem to approach such extremes most closely. Their thinking, often highly systematized and obsessionalized, shields these individuals so as to make them impervious to many important data of their inner reality (such as their own feelings, needs, motives) and outer reality (such as feelings, needs, motives in others).

However, it is again the group in between these two extremes which seems to comprise the bulk of schizophrenic patients: in these patients the elements closure-openness are integrated jerkily and unharmoniously. It is this group which seems fittingly described by Bleuler's concept "looseness of associations," as outlined earlier. Lyman Wynne has introduced the term "fragmentation" to define this group. He expressly notes the similarity of this concept to what Bleuler wanted to denote by "looseness of associations." Bleuler himself spoke of loosening as a "fragmentation of the thinking processes." "Schizophrenic thought disorder," Wynne writes, "has classically been regarded as involving fragmentation or loosening in overtly disconnected but well-differentiated percepts and thoughts, for example, in unintentional intrusions of primary process phenomena into ordinary thought."

Lyman Wynne, as is evident from this description, has based his classification of schizophrenic forms of thinking on the principle of differentiation-integration, as earlier defined. This is fully in accord with the present classification. For this classification essentially is that of Lyman Wynne. However, in now tying this classification more clearly to the principle of adaptive reconciliation (and specifically closure-openness), I emphasize the adaptational context more strongly. In other words, by evaluating how schizophrenic thinking reconciles or does not reconcile doing and undergoing, closure and openness, we evaluate how a so far achieved differentiation-integration meets its adaptive test.

At this point Bleuler's concept "looseness of associations" appears in a new light. This concept, as we saw, for Bleuler became the unifying principle or pivot in his theorizing about schizophrenia.

In the scheme here developed the "looseness of associations" or "fragmentation of thinking processes" now marks the center of a developmental-adaptational panorama. No clinician would hesitate to apply the term schizophrenia—split mind—to the cases in the middle of this center. For these are the patients who appear deeply "split" in one way or the other. For example, "they appear to think at cross-purposes," their thinking, in becoming fragmented, seems split from their feeling, their inner life seems split from the concepts which should express it. These patients, in succumbing to a loosening of their associations, reveal their "divided self" blatantly. Looseness of associations, in other words, is the core feature by which schizophrenia can be identified.

However, this "center of schizophrenia," held by the disturbance of association and thinking as just described, dilutes itself in fluid transitions toward the extremes of amorphousness on the one side and of entrenched isolation (or maximal closure) on the other. To the degree that these extreme poles are approached, "looseness of association" ceases to be the core feature and the concept of schizophrenia seems to become problematical. With regard to the extreme of amorphousness, Bleuler himself leaves some doubt as to whether very undifferentiated, amorphous forms of thinking still represent varieties of schizophrenia. Sullivan, among others, seems to have shared such doubts. He suggested that certain forms of insidiously creeping hebephrenia or "process schizophrenia" might not belong to the group of schizophrenias at all. As regards the extremes of closure, they have, in the United States as well as on the European continent, remained a bone of classificatory contention. In the German psychiatric literature, for example, the concepts Paranoia, "Paraphrenie," and "sensitiver Beziehungswahn" (Kretschmer) till today survive as disturbances that are either not at all or only tangentially related to the group of schizophrenias. The same holds true in the United States for such concepts as "paranoid personality" or "paranoid character structure."

The meaning of such new placement of the "looseness of associations" becomes clearer once we apply to the understanding of schizophrenia the third general principle of adaptative antagonism.

This principle, we saw, builds on both foregoing principles. In adding a further dynamic dimension, it allows an over-all assessment of a given state of relatedness and adaptation. It takes into account an individual's presumable future and his past. It sensitizes us to how far he may be engaged in correcting this past. His symptoms, from a broad perspective, are seen as serving or not serving survival. How far, we ask, are they restitutive, how far does their seeming severity reflect an attempt at a reintegration at the base?

In the light of this third principle, schizophrenia, therefore, reflects

(3) *A state of Adaptive Antagonism.* This is in accord with a dynamic, psychoanalytic interpretation of schizophrenic symptoms as originally attempted by Bleuler: Any schizophrenic symptom or constellation of symptoms reflects an adaptational compromise which has a defensive as well as a restitutive aspect. In this sense, schizophrenic symptoms are not different from neurotic symptoms. They reflect a defense against anxiety and the threat of disintegration and an attempt at adaptation despite anxiety and (actual or potential) disintegration. But compared to the neurotic, this adaptational compromise appears more pathetic, since it leads to or accepts a break with reality. Thus it tends to mire more malignantly the schizophrenic in his adaptational dilemma. For one thing, his main defense mechanisms—denial, projection, apathetic withdrawal, "splitting" of the ego, etc.—are of such an order that, in exchange for the break with reality, they provide only little defensive gain. For another, the schizophrenic's very "lability of neutralizations" (Hartmann) makes him excessively vulnerable to more or less normal adaptational (and specifically, interpersonal) stresses: crucial ego functions quickly give way to a regressive pull.

We can—and it is at this point that the third principle becomes important—adequately evaluate a schizophrenic's state of adaptation only when we take into account his present and future adaptational problems as well as the burdens from his past. Thus, in schizophrenia, temporary adaptational failure and upheavals may be necessary to liquidate the burden of the past. What is adaptive and what is restitutive appears in a more complex perspective.

In the light of this third principle, therefore, two phases in the life of the schizophrenic become particularly important: first, the earliest phase, that is, the dawn of knowing individuation; for it is here, where the "burden of the past" is gathered, where the nuclear ego and language qua reconciling medium are marred; and second, the phase of adolescence and early adulthood, for it is here where this burden becomes heaviest and possibly unbearable.

IMPLICATIONS OF THIS FIELD THEORY

I shall begin with the question of nosology.[3] In the nosology of schizophrenia, as in any other psychopathology, the problem is as follows:

In order to delineate meaningfully one form of psychopathology from another we must somehow "freeze" the developmental-adaptational dynamic. We must get hold of relatively enduring patterns or structures which then can be compared. Everything now depends on how we freeze this dynamic and how we get hold of these structures. The problem is this: These structures are always welded to an adaptational context. What they are worth is only revealed in a transactional setting.

It is a tribute to Bleuler's genius that he, in delineating schizophrenia, focused on that "structure-in-action" which appears to give greatest leverage for inference and comparison: the structure of our thought processes. These structures, for each individual, are relatively enduring (and if they are not, this in itself is significant). These structures are so high in the pyramid of differentiation-integration that almost any failures in earlier differentiation-integrations, any lack of skills, any previous adverse

[3] The classification of disease entities.

experience, are bound to show up in them. And further: These structures, to a degree, carry their transactional context with them. The way a person thinks and communicates also indicates how he relates and transacts, how he invites a response from the other; it indicates how he hinders or promotes a spirally expanding adaptation and development.

In thus exploring thinking qua "structure-in-action," Bleuler succeeded in uniquely extending our knowledge about that adaptational disturbance he termed schizophrenia. At the same time, he meaningfully delineated schizophrenia against other psychiatric conditions. Still, as we saw, he exploited his great discovery only halfway: although acknowledging the importance of the "psychological setting," that is, the transactional context, he did not further investigate how this setting is welded to the structure of thinking, which here really means: to the structure of disturbed thinking. In thus omitting the context of the structure, I believe, also the structure of disturbed, schizophrenic thinking remained unexplored in essential respects. Central questions as to its etiology and pathogenesis remained unanswered.

The present theory now attempts both to increase and to clarify the inferential leverage of the concept "structure-in-action" as applied to schizophrenia. It does so by letting it branch out in several dimensions. It directs the searchlight back into the dawn of knowing individuation to the time and to the circumstances which structured the structure; then to the context in which the worth of this structure is revealed; and finally to the challenges that will await it. Let me briefly take up these aspects one after the other. In this manner, the problem of nosology will reflect on the pathogenesis as well as the differential etiology of schizophrenia.

A. *The Structuring of the Structure:* Schizophrenia predicated on what happens during the dawn of knowing individuation.

The structure in question is the structure of the nuclear

ego. This ego can be seen as carrying the main adaptational burden: It must integrate functions and interests on ever new levels of complexity, it must ensure the individual's spirally adaptive expansion.

In this study I have focused on two phase-constellations that indicate that crucial consolidations of this ego have been achieved. I have focused on first, the achievement of self-polarization and self-demarcation and second, on the emergence of language as a reconciling medium.

Many core features of schizophrenia seem directly related to the individual's not successfully achieving these phase-constellations: A faulty or lacking self-polarization makes for a precarious instability of the repressive barrier. There is now lacking "the organized, ego-integrated stability of defenses" (Hartmann), which we find in neurotics and normal persons. There results a characteristic vulnerability to all kinds of stresses. This person easily is over-thrown and he easily begins to slip regressively. His neutralizing capacities seem minimal.

A defective self-demarcation—being interdependent, as we saw, with faulty self-polarization—seems to be at the root of the schizophrenic's well-known boundary problems. Federn, Schultz-Hencke, Laing, and many others have described how precariously these boundaries are cathected —boundaries as to what is me and not me, inside and outside, body and not-body, etc. Thus, such persons easily feel engulfed, encroached, intruded upon, and they must seek distance in ways which adaptationally are expansive.[4]

---

[4] One patient, for example, states that her thoughts are no longer inside herself. She hints they are locked away in the hospital drawers. Also, her body has become part of the chair on which she is sitting. She complains that another patient has gotten under her skin and she seems to mean this literally since she rubs some parts of her body aggressively. An adolescent girl, in an acute panic, has lost all natural body feeling. "I know I still have my body, but it feels void, unreal." Also she mentions that all her thoughts have become mechanical. Some time later she indicates her mother has gotten inside her in order to pull her thought strings. She can no longer differentiate

Language as reconciling medium—the second important nuclear achievement, which builds on the foregoing—also crucially seems to fail in schizophrenia. Language, as welded with propositional thinking, fails "to tame" these associations, to tie them adaptively to the cosmos of conventional meanings. It fails in its time-binding, abstracting, structuring capacities as these were described earlier. It fails to integrate propositional and evocative elements. It fails in gearing the ego to the within, to the needs and moods of the individual as well as to the outside world.

In such failure it exposes the individual to alienation from himself and from the others. Such dual alienation again seems most characteristic of schizophrenia. It is at the root of the break with reality. It accompanies the loosening of associations, but it also is present in the more amorphous, and "closed" types of thought disorder, as classified by Wynne.

Thus, the structuring of the nuclear structure, as occurring during the dawn of knowing individuation, appears central in the genesis of schizophrenia. How then—and this opens the question of the differential etiology—can we differentiate the relevant factors and constellations?

Traditionally, biologic (hereditary) and experiential factors have been adduced and postulated. Rosenthal, recently, gave an over-view of this state of affairs. The question is how much weight have these various factors or sets of factors in the total balance and how do they interrelate? One answer then is bound to illuminate the other.

So much seems clear: The nuclear structures and adaptational functions here described have biologic maturational roots. But these roots, in the ongoing and spirally

---

whether her mother's voice is inside or outside of her, but also, she is not sure whether her own voice has become her mother's. Hayward and Taylor describe how a patient could not distinguish between emotions and their physical components: She accused her doctor of taking away her feelings by wiping away her tears. Not uncommonly schizophrenic patients may cut or otherwise hurt themselves in order to be reassured about their body boundaries.

expanding differentiation-integration, are shaped and modified by interchange with the environment during development. This viewpoint is *epigenetic*.[5] Lyman Wynne has stated it as follows: "The interchange or transactions at each developmental phase builds upon the outcome of earlier transactions. This means that constitutional and experiential influences recombine in each developmental phase to create new biologic and behavioral potentialities which then help determine the next phase. If the transactions at any given developmental phase are distorted or omitted, all the subsequent phases will be altered because they build upon a different substrate."

I shall, in the context of this study, not discuss the possible significance of biologic, constitutional factors in the structuring of the nuclear ego and hence in the pathogenesis and etiology of schizophrenia. This, to a point, Lyman Wynne has done. In accordance with the over-all orientation of this work, I focus instead on one experiential aspect. I approach the structuring of the nuclear ego mainly from a relationship point of view. Specifically, I view the failure of crucial nuclear achievements as being interdependent with a negative mutuality in the early mother-child relationship (which may become reinforced or mitigated in the life of the family). This provides a special conceptual leverage to trace and differentiate how, during a most critical period of biologic maturation, intra-individual psychologic and biologic processes interweave.

The possible origins of schizophrenia, when viewed from such relationship angle, crucially will reflect the time at which characteristic relational balances become effective. In the light of this time factor we can, for a first orientation, differentiate between the first and the second stage in the dawn of knowing individuation. Thus we will ascertain whether the child essentially was betrayed in his "quest to be one and the same" or in his "quest to be one and different."

[5] The word epigenesis, according to Webster, denotes a development which involves the gradual diversification and differentiation of an initially un- or less-differentiated entity.

But in order to do so, we must coordinate this temporal axis with another axis that allows one to take account of the characteristic constellation and movement of relational balances as earlier described.

It is in bringing together these two viewpoints—time factor and dialectic of relational balances—that we may differentiate a number of constellations which are all pathogenic, but not equally schizophrenogenic: All these constellations tangentially seem related to schizophrenia (as defined by Bleuler) but—and this seems important—not all of them induce a schizophrenic way of life. In the following, I shall limit myself to outlining broadly some possible constellations which seem not to lead to schizophrenia in the sense established by Bleuler.

Thus we may delineate constellations which, in having their main impact during the preverbal dawn, lead to excessive deprivation of the child. The mother, in these constellations, may appear highly uncommitted and therefore fails to make positively operative the balance moment-duration as outlined above. The other balances are so tipped that difference, frustration, lack of stability, as well as stimulation and extreme distance prevail. These children may succumb to the syndrome of hospitalism as described by René Spitz. Under a less seriously depriving constellation of relational balances, they may show lesser kinds of developmental defects. Nearly all children growing up in institutions seem to have such defects, as has been recently confirmed by Provence and Lipton.

Roger M., now nineteen years old, may serve as an example. His mother was an unstable waitress who lived promiscuously. Roger was her third child. She handed him to an orphanage shortly after his birth. Roger was one of the very few inmates of this institution who never received a visitor. At the age of seven years he was adopted into a family with a daughter one year his senior. It was the contrast to this new-found sister, a lively, normally developed girl, that brought into full light the damage which had been done to Roger: He knew no nursery rhymes or songs, he could neither read nor write. His imagination was barren. While his sister could draw colorful pictures and embellish them with stories, Roger could merely produce a few awkward scribbles. He could not initiate any games with other children. (However, unlike his sister, he could work in the garden with a certain robot-like diligence; for with such work he had spent much of his days in the orphanage.)

His progress was slow—despite the genuine endeavors of his new parents. When he finally attended a private school, he turned into a troublemaker and terrorizer of other children. At home he became extremely sensitive to rejection. He persecuted his sister with envious rage and frequently broke her toys. This subsided gradually when he became more assured of his parents' love and understanding. Still, the damage caused in his formative years could not be completely undone. Roger studied a craft. He did not excel therein, but learned to work solidly. When meeting with people, he tended to withdraw shyly. Although showing many features of self-sufficient restriction, Roger presented no schizophrenic thought disorder. He could be considered schizoid, but not schizophrenic. Also, his self-sufficient restriction bore more the marks of an interpersonally induced deprivation than those of an early survival strategy of fight-flight.

But it seems that also *within* given families, children can become similarly deprived. These children will also have to adopt survival strategies of self-sufficient restriction, but the later pictures, in all likelihood, will not be typically schizophrenic—at least in the fragmented, middle-of-the-center sense. They may become autistic, developmentally retarded, and possibly, given some sort of minimally sustaining pseudo-relationship, sociopathic. (According to Sullivan, sociopathic individuals have, as children, been exposed to both excessive neglect and hate.)

When I used to provide psychiatric emergency service in the slum area of an American metropolis, I saw many youngsters fitting one of these labels, besides others who showed signs of a fragmented core schizophrenia, as just described. Claude Brown, in his *Manchild in the Promised*

Land (New York: Macmillan Company, 1965), describes movingly the ghetto-world which produces such deprived children. Against the background of this ghetto-world, the case of Tom A. appears in no way extraordinary:

Tom was the third of nine children of whom three died as infants. Tom's mother worked in a white household. This left her with little time for her children, who were first handed over to an alcoholic sister of hers, and later were supposed to watch out for each other. The sister, Tom's aunt, was promiscuous and performed many of her sexual activities in front of the children. The men who came to see her were often brutal and would tease the children. Tom's father, himself an alcoholic, a philanderer, and given to violent tempers, was no stabilizing influence. The whole family was crammed into three rooms. In the living room stood the television set around which the family was gathered when I came to see Tom. Tom, then fifteen years old, played with a knife, but nobody seemed concerned. A short while before, Tom had thrown a baby down a staircase because he had gotten fed up with her crying. The baby had been seriously hurt. Tom had shown no feelings. Also he had no schizophrenic thought disorder in the narrower sense here intended. He appeared cold, impulsive, and permanently hardened.

In contrast to such all-out depriving constellations, we may delineate relational constellations (or balances) which appear more directly "schizophrenogenic." These balances may have their main pathogenic impact during the preverbal as well as during the verbal dawn. However, the situation appears worst when a negative mutuality which started during the preverbal stage gains momentum during the verbal phase. Such was, more or less, the case in the examples for the four relational modes described in Chapter v.

In these constellations there is, as a rule, more quantity of maternal relatedness than in the foregoing instance. In fact, the mother may often seem over-invested in the child. But this quantity does not translate itself into an appropriate phase-adequate, relational dialectic. Instead, this dialectic becomes slanted and erratic. Sameness, in the earlier described sense, may too strongly win out over difference with the result that a seemingly spoiled and symbiotically over-identified child will experience as frustration what should be experienced as age-adequate challenge. Gratifications may too early be made contingent on certain forms of compliance. Stability may be precarious. Closeness and distance may not be reconciled and there may be, instead, abrupt swings from one extreme to the other. And so on. The many varieties of such "schizophrenogenic" relational constellations can be deduced from the scheme which was presented earlier.

Such a slanted relational dialectic—or negative mutuality—in a sense also results in depriving the child. But in another sense it is more appropriate to say it stupefies, confounds him. During a most critical maturational period he is bound to be both over- and under-stimulated. He is pressured into developmental imbalances which jeopardize his future development and relatedness.

But further, such slanted and erratic relational dialectic, involving the child during the dawn of knowing individuation, will inevitably corrupt his confidence in his own emotional reactions and his own perception of reality. He will be put into severest double-binds, as described earlier in the context of young Strindberg's early relationships: He will be subjected to conflicting and inappropriate messages while possible escape routes have been blocked. He cannot but become confused. In sum: He is confounded as well as imbalanced—and this at a time when "learning to learn" and a balanced individuation seem most imperative.

In a negative mutuality of this second kind—in a relational dialectic that is more confounding than depriving—the child very likely will try to mold his nuclear ego for symbiotic survival. Thus, his survival strategy will aim at "control" of his mother. In so doing, he will employ his developmental imbalances precariously. In sum: He will let himself be drawn into conflictual entanglements as earlier described. And it is such conflictual entanglements which, with further contingencies arriving, foremostly seem to give rise to those schizophrenic developments which best fit Bleuler's original description.

I shall, in this context, not deal with the "further contingencies." There can, as is clear from all my foregoing considerations, never be a straight developmental path from a symbiotic conflictual entanglement to a later schizophrenic fragmentation. For interpolated between these two stages in the life cycle is the epigenetic drama. Countless developmental and relational vicissitudes come into play. In the chapter "Beyond the Dyad," I have hinted at some of these vicissitudes. They form, under various angles, the subject matter of the classical works of Freud, Sullivan, Erikson, and others. There is, foremostly, the life in the family with its chances of either—at least to a degree—correcting or aggravating what, in the child, has been structured during the dawn of knowing individuation.

This much though can be said: The child, in adopting a certain survival strategy during the dawn of knowing individuation, will also later tend to employ this strategy whenever possible. This strategy, in a sense, "joins up" with his nuclear ego; and if the strategy changes, also this ego must change. This early strategy thus will enter into all efforts at adaptation and relation. It will mold the individual's cognitive and relational styles. It will tend to elicit the characteristic responses from the other. It will greatly determine the kind of forthcoming mutuality—whether negative or positive, whether deadlocked or spirally expanding—which is possible for him. In this sense, an earlier conflictual entanglement will make its imprint on all later relatedness.

This becomes clearer when we, next, more specifically focus on the context which brings to light "the structure-in-action." How, in other words, is a pre-schizophrenic or schizophrenic structure transactionally revealed?

B. *The Structure in Action:* Schizophrenia revealed in the transactional context.

We can view this "structure-in-action" either from a distant or a close position. In the first case we have a macroscopic field. We can include all persons to whom the individual is meaningfully related. We view, in other words, the whole relational set—with its various alignments, with its potentials for relational and developmental expansion, but also with its characteristic dead-end features and points of blockage. Only such a macroscopic view will reveal an individual's full range of adaptational flexibility. It seems ideally suited to encompass the family as a whole.

If we view this "structure in action" from a close position, we will not get such a broad grasp of the individual's integrative potential. But what we lose in depth of perspective we gain in sharpness: We can study his reconciling powers microscopically. Specifically, we can see how far he is able to initiate and maintain a positive mutuality, how he, in the process of focusing and shifting attention, can reconcile doing and undergoing, closure and openness. We can more distinctly recognize how elements of earlier survival strategies impinge on his present relating. We can observe how he employs language as reconciling medium. We can see "double-binding" situations operating. It is therefore this microscopic approach which will best reveal the kind and severity of any thought disorder and which, accordingly, will reveal how far this thought disorder can be called schizophrenic.

It is mainly this latter approach which Lyman Wynne and Margaret Singer have adopted and developed. They thus succeeded in thoroughly studying and differentiating various forms of thought disorders.

Wynne and Singer did not only study the thought disorders of patients who were diagnosed as schizophrenic. They studied also the thinking and communicational styles of these patients' parents. These parents, they realized, communicated in disturbed ways—with each other and with strangers—although they (the parents) had never thought of seeking psychiatric help for themselves. Wynne and Singer became so impressed with this phenomenon that they devised a remarkable research strategy: They tried to predict blindly the quality and severity of the schizophrenic disturbance in these parents' offspring simply by paying attention to the thought disorders of the parents. Wynne and Singer were highly successful in these predictions. Their initial sample consisted of thirty-five families with schizophrenic offspring. Nearly all of their predictions turned out to be correct. By now such predictions have been carried out with several hundred families in different centers in this country. Wynne and Singer observed these parents in relatively unstructured transactional settings. Relatively "open" projective test situations (as, e.g. provided in Rorschach and TAT tests) and similarly unstructured interview and family therapy sessions served this purpose. These settings allowed microscopic exploration of these persons' "structure in action."

The authors did not, it must be noted, use Rorschach, TAT, and other procedures in the conventional manner, but modified these tests in a way which brought to light microscopic defects and deviances in their communications with each other and with the tester. It was—and this is important—not content features such as shared religious delusions and preoccupations, but formal features (that is, stylistic characteristics of their thinking and communication) which made the successful predictions possible.

At this point I cannot elaborate on the scope and the various implications of Wynne's and Singer's still ongoing research. This would require another monograph. However, I shall give a short over-view of the principles by which they distinguish between different kinds of thought disorders in the seemingly normal parents of schizophrenic offspring. Along therewith I shall present some of the examples which these authors adduce. These examples, in a sense, are richer and more illustrative than those we might get from schizophrenic patients themselves. At the same time, they highlight that dialectical turning point where we can see quantity turn into quality; that is, where we can see the seemingly normal communication take on a schizophrenic coloring. And not only do these principles and examples convey some idea of the family context out of which schizophrenia may arise, but they also serve as an inventory of how language may fail as a reconciling medium. We are in a better position to realize how thought disorders—even if this is not immediately apparent —reflect cognitive and relational styles which are inimical to a positive, spirally expanding mutuality. And we may, finally, better understand how the schizophrenic, in his disturbed ways, is "much more human than otherwise" (Sullivan). We get some notion as to how his survival strategies, formed in his dawn of knowing individuation, protect as well as damage him further in that difficult interpersonal field wherein he finds himself compelled to live.

The following principles and examples of Wynne's and Singer's work evolved from the Rorschach protocols of parents who had schizophrenic children. However, the same principles apply to the evaluation of almost any sample of their (the parents') verbal transactions. For example, Gary Morris and his associates could gather similar examples of disturbed communications by simply studying the taped unstructured conversations or research interviews of such parents. They also were able to predict, on the basis of such material, the type and severity of the offsprings' schizophrenic disorders.

With specific reference to what may transpire in a Rorschach test situation, Wynne and Singer distinguish between three main categories of disturbed communication. These, like the following sub-categories, are interrelated, yet can be identified, and hence scored, by carefully examining each response and each comment a person may give. The three main categories are *Closure problems, disruptive behavior,* and *peculiar language and logic.* Let us take up one at a time.

Closure problems may be reflected in nine major subcategories. These reflect ways "in which parents of young adult schizophrenics cause a listener to be uncertain about whether closure over an idea, a response, or a part of an exchange has occurred. The status of meaning that the speaker seemingly was attempting to discuss and share is unclear. He may have trouble in assigning any meaning, or may assign meaning in tentative and contradictory ways, or may disqualify his ideas while or after giving them." Closure problems, therefore, indicate a "vague wooliness and the failure to develop meaning and point." This contrasts with the more dramatic disruptions of ideas and task-sets as dealt with under the second main category called "disruptive behavior."

A person with closure problems may heavily use speech fragments. "The speaker casts loose words, nonword sounds, partially formed statements, and bits of fragmented associations into his remarks. He . . . makes a series of bids for the listener's attention, only to drop each idea before completely grasping it himself; the way in which he tosses out bits of ideas indicates that the listener should attend, but at the same time he indicates that he is not committed to these ideas himself, or that his attention and commitment are only incipient, partial, or ephemeral."

These would be examples:

"This lower central part, uh, is a slight local duh. . . ."
"Two figures, very definitely there, the head, the torso, and they're bent, ah, mmm, well, I dunno why, you bet, ah."

Other responses or comments are simply unintelligible, like this one:

"An abstract. (In the inquiry:) Well, it's not white cotton, I mean I don't think that I think it's plain, you know."

A person may have an unstable inner percept and that makes it difficult for the listener to share a focus with him, as in this example:

"When I first looked at it, it looked like a woman standing on her head, but when I look at it more, I don't see anything."

In other cases the listener is unsure whether the speaker intends him to heed his remarks since the speaker himself takes a nebulous, tentative, uncommitted stance toward what he says, as in this statement:

> "I don't see anything except much the same as the other, except that they have spilled the ink in the fore and aft department."

Responses in negative form ("It doesn't look like a sheep"), subjunctive "if" responses ("If I were sick and upset, I'd say it resembled a person"), and question responses ("That looks like a goose. Is that what you call 'em?") all bring into the transaction a tentative, nebulous element which hinders the sharing of a common focus.

Closure problems exist, further, when contradictory information, inconsistent references, and incompatible alternatives are presented. For example, a statement such as "I've never seen a bat. . . . Last summer a bat got into our cabin," is clearly contradictory.

Disqualifications represent the final major sub-category of closure problems. "Disqualifications cause a listener to have a sense of unsureness about whether the speaker has given or left standing his commitment to a response."

Such disqualifications may be conveyed in a disparaging remark ("That might represent two people, look mighty goofy to me") or it may be reflected in a nihilistic comment in a particular response (". . . it really isn't anything . . .") or on the testing procedure in general ("How can inkblots mean anything?"). Further, a person may be unable to verify his own response ("Looks like a bat coming out of Carlsbad Caverns, but I've never seen a bat"), or he may retract, deny or forget what he said previously.[6]

---

[6] About the possible relation of closure problems of parents to a schizophrenic thought disorder in their children, Wynne and Singer have this to say: ". . . problems of closure are often not easily recognized by a listener *while they are occurring;* they are more *elusive* and *covert* ways of hindering the attainment of shared foci of attention and shared meaning. We believe that their seeming intangibility makes them have a

Disruptive behavior, as falling under the second main category, comprises verbal and non-verbal interruptions of the examiner's speeches. The person who seemingly was invested in finding a response may ask: "Did Mrs. Smith take this test?"; he may respond in an odd or tangential way, he may yawn, swear, hop around while questions are being asked, flatly reject a card, or do something else that rather dramatically breaks or slants the transaction. References to "They" and to the intent of others appear particularly important, since they disrupt the task-set and sidetrack attention, as in these examples: "They wanted to let you know this is medical." "They intended that to be the head."

Peculiar language and logic, the third major category, comprise instances of peculiar word usages, constructions, and pronunciations. For example, ordinary phrases are used oddly ("I pronounce this the same as I saw before") or private terms are introduced without warning ("A poisoned butterfly"); further we may find mispronounced words ("That's an ogray"—instead of ogre), cryptic remarks (*"Semper fidelis"*), clang associations ("Lamb's skin, ram's skin"), abstract global terms ("There are a pair of beings"), unnecessary reiteration ("That's a pig, looks like

---

more disastrous impact upon a listener than do the more sharply defined, vivid, and easily noticed disruptions.

"We reason that a child probably would be very puzzled and bewildered over the subtle, unclear things that occur in transactions that we label as 'closure problems.' In a fast-moving conversation with these parents a person must repeatedly emerge uncertain and unclear about what has been going on.

"The child . . . has to depend on his parents for much of his original experiencing and learning of how to understand things. We reason that parents whose communication is decimated by closure problems . . . are likely to have devastating effects upon a child, especially if the parental involvement with the child has been intense or complicated. Such a child is likely, we hypothesize, to grow up with unusual difficulties in trusting and interpreting both his own perceptions and judgments and those he hears reported by others."

a pig, yeah, a pig"), peculiar logic ("Here's a bird. Got a head on both sides"), and nonsequitur reasoning ("Can't be a female, because there is no head").

In applying the above-described principles and findings, Wynne and Singer came to classify the schizophrenic thought disorder along the three general dimensions mentioned earlier: They differentiated "core" schizophrenia from what I have called tangential schizophrenia. And this tangential schizophrenia, in turn, they conceived as reflecting either amorphousness or extreme types of closure.[7]

Each type of thought disorder, thus differentiated, reflects a cognitive and relational style. Each of these styles is inimical to a positive, spirally expanding mutuality. But the scope and quality of such enmity is different in each instance.

Such differing negative potentials are most evident in the manner in which each type of thought disorder impedes or facilitates the *sharing of a common attentional focus*. This is the crucial issue.

It is such sharing of a common focus from which any new relational movement must take off. In the words of Wynne: "A process which has begun with the focusing of attention, becomes manifest in communication, and can result in shared meaningful experience." The sharing of a common focus, therefore, is the sine qua non for any new positivity in the relationship. Given such sharing, the reality principle will get a new chance. The partners themselves can hope to struggle together. There may be "misunderstandings at the base," but these cannot become too malignant. There is now room for a meeting of minds, for the eventual correction of divergent viewpoints and expectations and hence for a matching and meeting of mutual needs. There is, along therewith, the chance that, in the forward thrust of the positive mutuality, cathexis and structure may so interplay as to give rise to more

[7] Wynne presently is directing a major thrust of his research work at establishing firm distinctions and transitions between these more general types of thought disorders.

solid neutralizations of instinctive energies than existed before.

Compared to normal and neurotic individuals, Lyman Wynne has shown that the attainment of a shared focus seems badly amiss in each of the above three types of thought disorders, yet with these important differences: In states of extreme amorphousness such sharing of a common focus seems jeopardized on a most basic level. These patients simply seem to drift past and around each other. Thus, they seem highly unable to provide a takeoff point for any kind of positive relational movement.

In the fragmented types of thought disorder—and hence in the cases of "core" schizophrenia—the relational mode of conflictual entanglement still seems operative. There is a sharing of sorts of a common focus, a sharing which seems under the spell of double binds, a lopsided, qualified, split kind of sharing. Still, in these instances there seems to be a much better chance for a new, corrective positive mutuality to get under way than seems true for the foregoing situation.

In cases of extreme conceptual closure (as, for example, represented in certain kinds of stabilized paranoid individuals), a policy of self-sufficient restriction appears inflexibly entrenched. Such closure then has become ego- and character-syntonic. It has become a routine way of life and of communication, in which the individual has come to feel at home. There is no longer a feeling of conflict or dissatisfaction about this.[8] This makes for a kind of fixed attentional distortion which bodes ill for a successful sharing of a focus and hence for any new relational expansion.

C. *The Challenges to the Structure:* Schizophrenia as failure to meet due adaptational tests.

Any of the above described transactional settings presents such a test. Its observation therefore allows us to

---

[8] Such ego- and character-syntonic entrenchment of disturbed styles of communication seems typical of many parents of schizophrenic children.

gauge how an individual may stand up in other challenging situations. But in order to come to valid conclusions—and thus make full use of the inferential leverage of the concept schizophrenia—we must, finally, more deeply inquire into the nature of the real challenge. What then presents the critical challenge to the structure?

Most cases of "core" schizophrenia—that is, fragmented, middle-of-the-center schizophrenia—become manifest in late adolescence and early adulthood. I shall therefore sum up those features of this life phase which—in line with the so far developed viewpoints—highlight its critical, crossroads-like character in any individual's life.

With the maturation of the apparatus of adult genitality and, hence, the awakening of the lust dynamism (Sullivan), adolescence marks a period of intense biologic reorganization. It marks the final great spurt of differentiation-integration of any individual's life. Thereafter, differentiation-integration will proceed gingerly, braked and overshadowed by the approaching organismic decay and death.

Along with such biologic growth, the intra-psychic structure must be reshuffled. It must become more complex. Oedipal conflicts and passions, until now in a state of relative slumber, are reactivated. Deep intra-psychic changes become necessary. Adolescence thus is a period of critical defensive juggling and experimentation.

Anna Freud, Edith Jacobson, Erik H. Erikson, Peter Blos, among others, have traced many important features of this intra-psychic upheaval and rearrangement of defenses and identities.

Adolescence is, consonant with these biologic and intra-psychic developments, a period of critical social expansion. The individual must dare to step beyond the family field: New decisive relational diversifications await him. In particular, he must find a clear-cut sexual identity.

Adolescence thus will excessively strain whatever reconciling power an individual may have won. Biologic, intra-psychic, and social changes will deeply reverberate into the nuclear layers of the adolescent personality. Adolescence, specifically, will put to a severe test his powers at self-polarization and self-demarcation and further, it will put to the test the reconciling power of language. This language by now must allow him to cope with a greatly expanding realm of intra- as well as interpersonal experiences. Thus, it allows him to give masturbatory and homosexual urges and experiences a place in his experiential cosmos so as to divest them greatly of their uncanny quality, including their power to make him anxious and guilty. Language thus allows him to dream—and thereby to exploit and expand his imagination playfully—and also, to be realistic and goal-directed.

But adolescence—and this truly makes it a decisive challenge—in the wake of due biologic and intra-psychic upheavals, also leaves room for corrective movements as this seems never possible later: It offers an almost physiological opportunity for a reintegration at the base. This is the main reason why the often stormy identity diffusions of adolescence, as described by Erikson, seem to have their own reintegrative momentum.

An individual, it seems, can procrastinate in his adolescence. He can try to avoid its various challenges and thus carry adolescence with him far into adulthood. But at one point, sooner or later, it will catch up with him. He can no longer postpone interpersonal movements and expansions which are age-appropriate. He will be pressured to live outside his family, find a post-Oedipal partner, make his own occupational career. And it is then, that his crucial challenge will come.

VIII
PSYCHOTHERAPY OF SCHIZOPHRENIA

Schizophrenia, as earlier defined, is only one possible form of psychosis. And within schizophrenia, we saw, the differences as to form and intensity of the disturbance can be great. Any attempt at therapy, therefore, would have to take into account these differences. There cannot be one common approach or "technique."

Still, I shall outline some general viewpoints which derive from my previous considerations. These viewpoints chiefly apply to "core" schizophrenia, as delineated against tangential schizophrenia. I shall, this means, focus on the fragmented type, with typical loosening of associations, as predicated on a symbiotic conflictual entanglement with the mother and as clearly manifested sometime during late adolescence or early adulthood. Yet, to a degree, the following considerations will have meaning for the therapy also of other types of schizophrenia and psychosis. They will, in addition, put into a wider perspective the analysis of neurotic disorders as earlier described.

In the above sense, the typical schizophrenic patient has been unable to meet the challenges of adolescence. In breaking with reality, he has highlighted this failure. He possibly has won a chance for a reintegration at the base, but his respite from the pressures of time is precarious. The more time passes the more his developmental lag will increase. Already he has to cope with the consequences of earlier developmental imbalances and of missed experiences. If no integrative movement gets under way these consequences will further accrete.

Because of his break with reality, he badly seems in need of help and, hence, psychotherapy. But, compared to most neurotic patients, he seems poorly equipped to make use of such help. He no longer is a free agent in the sense that he could contract for analysis. In becoming hospitalized, he still remains dependent on and conflictually entangled with his family although, as a rule, in a more covert and mediated manner than previously. But most important: He has maneuvered himself into a situation in which any new mutuality seems bound to become negative. Extremely unsure of his own needs, of his own capacities, and of his own identity, he is most dependent on the reflective appraisal of others. But, at the same time, he is least likely to get such appraisal. For he fails in the most rudimentary prerequisite for getting it: in the trustful sharing of a common attentional focus from whence meaningful communication and reciprocally enriching experience could emerge. What then, in this situation, is required of a therapist to get under way and sustain a positive mutuality with this patient?

In a sense the therapist seems required to be both mother and analyst. He should be that kind of mother whom the patient needed and did not have; he should be that kind of analyst who expertly can handle the patient's complex psychodynamics. He should reconcile roles and functions that are motherly as well as analytic, that bear the imprint of the mother-child relationship as well as of the psychoanalytic situation.

Is such a reconciliation possible? Or is the very attempt at such reconciliation bound to flounder in important respects? Is not the analyst, in trying to be like a mother, bound to be less of an analyst? And in trying to be more of an analyst, will he not be less of a mother?

I shall, in the following, try to find an answer to this difficult question. I shall do so by viewing the psychotherapy of schizophrenic patients in the light of the five central dichotomies elaborated in the opening chapter. Thus I hope to illuminate the nature as well as possible limits of the required reconciliation.

I shall begin with the first balance.

MOMENT-DURATION

This balance is crucial, but its reconciliation seems particularly difficult. In order that the relationship can become solid and meaningful, in order that the moment can be made to count, the therapist must adopt a long time perspective. He must commit himself. Only thus can he ensure that the other balances will unfold on a wide scope, that they will gain their needed, full momentum. Only thus can there develop a *real* relationship between two *real* people. Only thus can the same object be experienced from ever new angles, distances, moods. Only thus can be made available a frame of reference which allows the confluence of many data that consensually and transactionally have been or will be validated. This dimension of duration and commitment seems most important to counteract the schizophrenic's tendency to live in an isolated moment, to be led astray into a shadowy relational emptiness by his fragmented shifting attention. Otto Will, Frieda Fromm-Reichmann and many others have emphasized and exemplified in their work the importance of realness and commitment in the psychotherapeutic relationship with the schizophrenic.

But this over-all commitment of the therapist must allow for an often needed loosening and sometimes even termination of the relationship. Because of his backlog of developmental imbalances and unlived experiences, and because of his need to live these experiences at the "wrong" time, the schizophrenic patient, more than the neurotic, needs to experiment with life. He must have leeway for trial and error, and, having learned from, and grown through them, he must know he can return to this therapist. The therapist cannot exactly know the timetable for this experimentation and growth. He is not in the position of a mother who is reminded by society when to let her child go to school, when to let him have a date, etc. The schizophrenic patient, in his spurts at new experience and reintegration, must dictate his own pace. The therapist must gear the whole relationship to this pace.

This is one reason why, in the classical analytic situation as well as in the therapeutic situation with schizophrenics, symptomatically similar behavior may have to be evaluated differently. In the analytic situation it might indicate "acting out" and hence a form of resistance: The patient disperses in action what should be contained and verbalized in the analytic relationship. On the other hand, in the latter situation such action may be a belated effort to clear away an experiential backlog, to gain new life experiences, awkward and out of place as such effort may seem.

The therapist, thus, must reconcile a deep and lasting commitment with a recognition of the patient's need of experiences and relations which may lead him away from the therapeutic relationship. They may cause him to withdraw for a short or a long time, and they also may lead him away for good. Should this be so, the therapist must come to grips with the fact that he could be no more than one (though possibly important) link in the chain of relationships which hopefully edge the patient toward an ever more positive mutuality.

SAMENESS-DIFFERENCE

In breaking with reality, the patient, in a most radical sense, has made himself different from others. He now is crazy, the others are sane. In many ways such difference is bound to be dramatized and confirmed in his daily life. It will mark his existential condition and it will tend to make him even lonelier, more estranged from himself and others.

A therapist, in trying to work with such patients, cannot deny this difference. For it will deeply color all aspects of the relationship. But instead of simply and crudely emphasizing this difference and instead of thus further confirming the patient in his "otherness," he will put this difference in perspective. He will trace it to its more apparent roots: to the manner in which the patient distorts, negates, and impedes the actions and attitudes of others. And this means specifically: How he, through these actions and attitudes, prevents the sharing of a common focus, how he, through his slanted and shifting attentional processes, prevents an expanding mutuality.

It is in thus putting difference into perspective, in tracing and examining how it arises and how far it extends, that the therapist comes to focus on what *really* happens in the transaction. This brings to light another difference in this situation as compared to the analytic relationship. The blatant, conventional significance of the patient's attitudes and behavior much more directly must be confirmed and called to the patient's attention. In the analytic situation with neurotics such conventional significance can generally be taken for granted and the main work be directed to uncovering the more covert defensive meanings and past origins of the present transactions.

But—and this is important—such confirmation and tracing of differences between patient and therapist must be so executed as to reveal a basic sameness. The patient, in becoming aware of how he differs also must learn that he "is much more human than otherwise." He must be able to realize that his distorting maneuvers, his difference-producing mechanisms are the outgrowth of needs, conflicts, anxieties which he shares with others and with which, therefore, his therapist, "one of the others," can and does empathize.

Thus establishing sameness the therapist, for example, empathizes with the patient's fear of losing his boundaries, with his excessive (but in the light of his subjective past: justified) distrust, with his underlying despair and loneliness, in short, with his craziness. When the patient finds that his craziness is understood, he is reassured. "My craziness cannot be so bad after all," he will think. "The therapist, in being able to understand me, must have my form of craziness also within himself. We are made of the same human material."

Such discovery, though, will not reassure the patient until he can believe that the therapist is like him merely in some respects, that the sameness is qualified. Like the mother in my earlier description, the therapist must be a citizen of two worlds: he must comfortably live in the world of conventional reality *and* also share in the unconventional world of his patient. In order that he make therapeutic the balance of sameness-difference, he must, in his own person, have successfully reconciled its two poles.

Such successful reconciliation will allow the therapist not to deter the patient by his difference—his achievements and power. He will avoid "being always smarter than the patient," a point which Frieda Fromm-Reichmann often has stressed. He will be able to synchronize his own growth with that of the patient, to let himself, in an essential respect, be guided by the latter's advances. He will, in a natural, uncondescending manner, allow the patient to point out his (the therapist's) shortcomings and mistakes. This is the same thing a good mother, assured of her self-worth, can afford to do.

But also, such successful reconciliation will allow the therapist, if need arises, to "overwhelm" the patient with his power. The patient then will be strongly confronted with the therapist's integrated difference, his forceful stand in reality. Such "over-powering" of the patient often appears necessary in order to counteract his intense withdrawal, negativism, and compensating grandiosity. Haley, among others, has made this point. And John Rosen, for example, in offering himself as an absolving God, in dramatically displaying to the patient his (Rosen's) power over the patient, over his own therapeutic team, and over the patient's family, seems to have made such overpowering a part of his therapeutic strategy. A child, similarly, is reassured when his parents, firmly and matter-of-factly, establish who is the stronger person, thus making appear absurd the child's magical and frightening notions as to his own omnipotence. (Much of the schizophrenic's symptomatology, according to Rosen, reflects a kind of "acted-out daydream" in which a magical omnipotence is prominent.[1])

[1] The following are some illustrative statements by which Rosen describes his treatment approach to schizophrenics: "The direct psychoanalyst and his assistants always try to focus the attention of the psychotic upon the direct psychoanalyst himself, who asserts his authority and preeminence by explicitly regarding the psychotic's behavior as obedience or disobedience of him personally. The direct psychoanalyst says, 'I order you'; he does not say, 'we order you.'

"During the 'formal' treatment session, the direct psychoanalyst sits close to or beside the psychotic, with the assistants nearby. Interruptions, intrusions, and distractions are kept at a minimum while the 'therapeutic dialogue' between the direct psychoanalyst and the psychotic is going on. The assistants, usually, do not speak unless they are brought into the 'dialogue' by the direct psychoanalyst; he might say, 'Have you been "crazy" today?' and, if the psychotic does not respond, he might then turn to one of the assistants and ask, 'Has "Sam" been acting "crazy" today? He doesn't seem to know whether he has been or not.' The assistant would then describe 'Sam's' recent behavior to the direct psychoanalyst, who would then question 'Sam' on the basis of the assistant's report.

"The assistants themselves look forward to the arrival of the direct psychoanalyst, regarding him as the prime mover in the total therapeutic effort directed toward the psychotic. Unconsciously, they look to him for gratification of their own needs for parental direction and approval.

"The treatment session is not a quiet or formal conversation. It is sometimes the occasion for extremely emotional or actually violent behavior on the part of the psychotic. In response to this, or on his own initiative, the direct psychoanalyst may also show strong feelings, with appropriate gestures and actions. For example, he may act as if he is 'furious' at a female psychotic who 'wants to be a boy,' and 'angrily' insist that she is acceptable to him only as a daughter, whom he can love. Or, the direct psychoanalyst might get down on his knees with the psychotic and the assistants, and pray for forgiveness for the psychotic's blasphemous assertion that he is Christ the Lord."

ing the dawn of knowing individuation. Bodily functions and states will gain greater meaning for both partners. Much of what is important seems to be a matter of elusive empathic crosscurrents. The therapist must make great use of the non- and preverbal skills of a mother. He must be able to be attentive and yet relaxed. He must know how to comfort and "hold" the patient without great ado, how to provide that kind of gratification which means both warmth and security.

But frustration must be reconciled with this all-important gratification. And such reconciliation now seems even more difficult than in the earlier described mother-child relationship. For the fact is the patient, in essential respects, no longer is a child. Although important symbiotic features can be enacted in the present relationship, the patient now cannot but experience them differently than would have been the case earlier. Many of the needed gratifications he now must accept on a symbolic level. Thus, Renée, Mme. Sechehaye's patient, must accept an apple instead of the maternal breast. True: Into this apple are condensed Mme. Sechehaye's love and devotion for Renée, her unstinting attention, her willingness to listen to Renée, to share her difficulties and miseries—and yet such gratification, by necessity, must remain much more "mediated" than would be the case during the natural, age-appropriate, and culturally sanctioned period of a symbiotic oral eroticism.

The gratifications which now are possible always seem tainted by the threat of awkwardness and humiliation. The patient, in thus being gratified, cannot help being reminded that these gratifications are not quite the real thing. Also, he will be reminded how far he still has to go. In this sense, frustrations appear inbuilt into the patient's very gratifications in a manner that is not typical for the early mother-child relationship. And yet—just as was the case with the mother in this early relationship—the therapist is now called upon to let gratification win out over frustration. He can succeed in doing so only by always addressing himself to the patient's over-all situation, by seeing in him, each moment, not only the frustrated child but also the sensitive adult. Frieda Fromm-Reichmann, more than others, has emphasized this needed dual orientation in the therapist.

But further, to the degree that a working capital accumulates and earlier relational modes are outgrown, the patient, like the growing child, must learn to cope with frustrations which are both growth-adequate and growth-fostering. In this sense, the patient—like the child—must learn to endure the sting of frustration in whose pain his ego can grow stronger. The therapist must know when and how much the patient may be able to bear frustrations of this kind. The time for such frustrations may have come when a loosening and transformation of the relationship, as described above, is also due. To a degree, such necessary transformation of the relationship in itself is bound to be felt as frustration—to the patient as well as to the therapist. Whether this frustration will be timely and tolerable will depend on how it is balanced by earlier and simultaneous gratifications.

STIMULATION-STABILIZATION

Stabilization, in this relationship, appears no less important than gratification. It enters into the patient's gratification in various ways. The therapist's reliably anticipated presence gives proof and substance to his commitment and devotion. The more the patient's attitudes and expectations drift and tend to contradict one another, the more this stability of the therapist is needed. This stability, in the long run, must absorb and buffer the patient's confusing needs and messages, it must prevent his (the patient's) ambivalence from becoming too strongly aroused. It must be soothing and sobering, though not rebuffing. It must prove as unwarranted the patient's fear of abandonment as this inevitably will grow to the degree that new hopes are kindled, new needs aroused, new dependencies awakened. It will provide the patient, in his amorphous universe, with a familiar point of reference and anchorage in time and space. And most importantly, it will stake out a relational framework within which a needed reintegration at the base might be attempted. The patient, thus, in exposing himself to intense, disintegrating anxiety will know that his therapist will be with him in his turmoil, empathizing with it but *not* overthrown by it.

Clearly, more demands will be made on this stability of the therapist than seems to be the case in either the psychoanalytic or the mother-child relationship. But also, this stability must be reconciled with a kind of stimulation which resembles yet deviates from that which is needed in both these latter situations.

To the degree that the patient needs to experiment with life, he also will need some guidance as to how to experiment. The therapist will have to give some of this guidance. But more important, the therapeutic relationship in itself, as with any other unfolding dialogue, must serve as a basic testing and training ground for new skills. A varied and selective stimulation must form part of such testing and learning. Again, neither a rather clear-cut developmental timetable (as guiding stimulation in the mother-child relationship) nor a rather clear-cut analytic method and situation (as dosing stimulating in the psychoanalytic relationship) will advise the therapist as to when and how much he should stimulate. All that is clear is that he, in one way or another, must succeed in reconciling stimulation and stability.

CLOSENESS-DISTANCE

The weight appears to be on the side of distance. The therapist's respect for distance and his ability to handle it must match the vulnerability of the patient's boundaries. The patient, easily feeling himself encompassed, intruded upon, engulfed, often will need to be spatially removed from the therapist. Therefore, it will make a difference as to whether the therapist sits away five, eight, or ten feet from his patient. If the therapist sits too close, the patient may so tense up as to become inaccessible. If the therapist sits removed enough from the patient, the latter may be able to so relax as to make communication possible and meaningful. The comparison to the violation of an animal's "individual distance," as earlier indicated, is obvious. Staehelin has described how chronic schizophrenic patients in the Swiss hospital of Friedmatt have reacted with either intense fight or flight to any transgression of their "advanced body boundaries."

The therapist's expertness at handling distance can be seen as compensating for the patient's ineptitude to do so. The latter's capacity to establish and change distance smoothly and flexibly in accord with changing and unfolding relationships is disturbed, as Wynne and Singer have clearly shown. His distancing apparatus seems to work jerkily. Since he, in many respects, appears to need distance so badly, he often tries to enforce it rigidly and thus loses sight of whether this is warranted. This ineptitude at proper distancing both constitutes and mirrors his difficulties in sharing a common focus with the therapist.

The therapist, further, needs to structure and watch distance for the same reasons an anlyst must observe it: Only in keeping distance can he hope to examine and understand objectively, to listen, to remain clearheaded, to guard an analytic attitude—all this seeming even more necessary in this therapeutic situation than in the classical psychoanalytic setup.

And yet distance must be reconciled with closeness. Again, such reconciliation seems difficult to achieve. The patient, surely, in all his strained efforts at enforcing distance, will be starved for closeness. But his longings for closeness, dammed up so long, will frighten him to the degree that new hopes for their fulfillment have been aroused. For this closeness, desperately longed for, now threatens to overthrow totally his fragile boundaries. He will consequently fight ever more vehemently to ensure distance. He will show more distrust, hostility; he will attempt to wreck the relationship, and so on.

The relationship, in order to expand positively, must move toward closeness and intimacy despite these difficulties. And the model of this sought-for closeness seems provided by the early mother-child relationship—problematical as this model seems in some respects. The trusting intimacy and near-fusion of this early relationship, which is immediate, which is sustained and warmed by organismic undertows, seems to indicate optimal conditions, under which a needed reintegration at the base may occur. It seems to allow for the greatest possible sharing, for the most perfect coincidence of gratification and security, for the relaxed expression and discharge of a wide variety of affects and needs within one and the same relationship.

The dialectic of this balance "closeness-distance" will have different features, depending on a given patient and on the phase of therapy. I shall illustrate this need for a differing dialectic by briefly mentioning two patients of mine, Annabelle S. and Susan J. Both have been diagnosed as chronic schizophrenic patients of long standing, and both had, prior to their admission to the hospital where I worked, long experiences with hospitalization, with electroshock, and insulin treatment. Both are very precariously related to the world around them, but their balance of distance and closeness poses different problems to their therapist. He, in order to let an increasingly authentic closeness develop, must, so to speak, focus his attention on opposite poles of their balance of closeness and distance.

Annabelle S. is forty-three years old. At times she appears lively, looks young and attractive; at other times she is disheveled, preoccupied, and lost in a fog of confusion. Since her adolescence she has had "mystical experiences." She likes to read difficult and obscure mystical and philosophical books, the more obscure, the more intriguing. In her livelier states, she tends to get quickly lost in her talk, which is highly picturesque and has a distinct literary tinge. Her excitement seems to feed on her words; they seem to fire her to even greater excitement. While talking more and more rapidly she seems to approach a state resembling orgastic bliss, but she is, at the same time, in a race against increasing disorganization. Her words have less and less understandable meaning, she contradicts herself within seconds. She feels influenced by everybody. Her brain is taken out, her intestines are chopped up. Everybody knows her thoughts and feelings. "I am public property. You, Dr. Stierlin, are now inside me. I am all over the place. I am parachuted into outer space."

Annabelle has the receptivity, sensitivity, and drive for a stimulating interchange with other people. But, being unable to maintain separateness vis-à-vis so much drive toward fusion, her sensitivity is not organized into distinct experiences. Her intake of colorful impressions and sexual stimulation cannot be stored and channeled into a love relationship to one person. Past experiences cannot be evaluated against future plans. Past, present, future are experienced as one undifferentiated continuum. Within a few seconds she is the person to whom she talks, then a baby, a man, a woman, "intruded upon and spread all over the place." Her excitement appears shallow and her talk often sounds like a meaningless hebephrenic rambling. Although seemingly involved with others much of the time, this involvement is like shadow-boxing. Unable to structure distance, she also cannot meaningfully experience closeness. Her particular balance of closeness and distance, in other words, allows only very limited relatedness. In reshuffling this balance in the direction of growing authentic closeness, the therapist, above all, must help her to structure distance and separateness. By focusing on actual sequences within her life and therapeutic experience, by identifying and then challenging cloudiness and vagueness in her talk, by providing a relationship of dependable sameness and reliability, he may in this, as well as in many other ways, be helpful in letting Annabelle find a greater sense of structure and separateness. And out of such individuation greater authentic closeness in her relationship to her therapist, as well as to other human beings, can follow.

Susan J., the other patient, is a fifty-eight-year-old spinster. A lonely child and adolescent, she failed to live up to the unrealistic expectations of her socially ambitious mother. As a remedy against feelings of insecurity and failure, Susan's mother preached "will power" and "integrity." The way of life of a lonely and increasingly eccentric girl gradually merged into that of a paranoid schizophrenic woman. She was always busy with some pet project whose significance she grandiosely inflated. Her preoccupations and projects became more and more delusional. In her early thirties she spent many lonely months in a library, doing research in earth radiation. Thereafter she was almost continuously hospitalized. Increasingly she became alienated from her own feelings and needs. She did not perceive her failings in interpersonal skills as such. Instead, she blamed others for all her misfortunes. And to the degree that she considered herself full of integrity and faultless, others were seen as dishonest and mean. She became a subtle detective of meanness in others: The lines of a hand, the shape of a nose, and similar clues allowed her quickly to deduce another person's dishonest intentions.

Susan's paranoid and rigid righteousness, entrenched during many years of eccentric living, has become her shield to maintain distance. It is a formidable weapon against the threat of (and wish for) closeness, which the therapeutic relationship poses. For it invites counter-righteousness and counter-indignation, and in such a head-on collision of wills, the chance for experiencing and subsequently exploring more varied personal feelings is quickly lost. The rigidity and easy availability of this distance-enforcer—her paranoid righteousness—limits greatly all possible experiences of closeness. In order to make therapy useful, this shield has to be eroded, but also has to be respected as long as it is needed. This erosion might be furthered, for example, by addressing oneself to the patient's sense of humor, to that part in her which can be amused by the contradictions in our world and life. It can be eroded by casually personalizing the relationship, by providing through the relationship an example of the values of compromise and the admission of fault in the dealings of two humans with each other. In brief: In order to reshuffle this patient's rigid and limiting balance of distance and closeness in the direction of greater authentic closeness, we have to encourage her tendencies toward near-fusion while eroding her rigid armor of paranoid distance.

That is the very opposite procedure from the one which was indicated in Annabelle's case. Annabelle, in order to develop a greater capacity for authentic closeness, above all needed to structure more definite distance, to check disorganizing drives toward near-fusion.

Sullivan, more than others, has made operative the balance of closeness-distance in the psychotherapy of schizophrenic patients. For this balance, in the case of the schizophrenic, could have no dynamic thrust as long as the psychiatrist's distance was upheld by the notion of the schizophrenic's fundamental difference. As long as the schizophrenic was considered a peculiar human specimen, who was only crazy, who was hallucinating, "who had symptoms," etc., the distant observer could not become a participant observer, and distance could not become reconciled with closeness in a forward-moving dialectic. Sullivan made the schizophrenic appear "much more human than otherwise" and he thus "unleashed" the balance closeness-distance. Sullivan also, in doing so, made much more difficult the psychiatrist's task. He exposed the psychiatrist to the problem of unendingly working toward closeness by observing distance and of establishing distance by recognizing closeness—and this on ever new levels of interpersonal complexity.

TRANSFERENCE IN THE PSYCHOTHERAPY OF SCHIZOPHRENICS

The schizophrenic patient, even more than the neurotic, seems bound to misexperience the present in terms of the past and hence to bring about transferences. This is a consequence of his ego breakdown. Greatly deprived of his ego's modulating and integrating capacities, his relational strategies will remain frozen, unadaptive, inflexible. But also, these strategies often are uninvested. The patient shies away from others. Therefore, the transference impact of these strategies is not brought to bear on others. And further, though basically rigid, his transference patterns seldom reflect a coherent, integrated Gestalt. His shifting and slanted attention, mirroring his fragmentation also, in a sense, breaks and scatters these rigid patterns and thus makes them difficult to recognize.

The developing therapy will highlight these features of his transference. Often the therapist must observe and attentively listen a long time before seemingly confusing, bizarre, and contradictory attitudes and messages of the patient begin to make sense. There is not the intense head-on rush of transferences that is observable in very early stages of the analysis of neurotic patients.

For this reason, it seems, in this psychotherapy it is more difficult to both raise and break the waves of transference, as this was found necessary and typical in the psychoanalytic situation. The transferences of the schizophrenic patient, as a rule, seem both more elusive and more recalcitrant than those of the neurotic. In order that they can be revealed, worked through and outgrown, the five above balances must unfold and be reconciled expertly and on a large scope.

Characteristically, in such forward-moving dialectic, many of the most uncanny, disturbed relational patterns of the patient will have their strongest transference impact relatively late in therapy. In the experience of Otto Will and others, a schizophrenic patient will reenact (and outgrow) in the transference his early conflictual entanglement with his mother only after he has revealed and worked through attitudes which reflect his relatively more "healthy" relationships—such as his ties to his father, to his siblings, etc. But this is only a matter of degree. In any intense analytic and psychotherapeutic work, transferences relating to all layers and ties of the patient's past tend to overlap and to combine in diverse forms of behavior.

The very recalcitrance of the schizophrenic's transferences makes it appear important that the relationship be trusting and gratifying. *"Übertragung,"*[2] in the above scope and depth, seems to require a strong *"Tragung,"* that is, "holding" or carrying of the patient. In this sense, it requires a bond which, in important respects, seems closer to the mother-child than to the analytic relationship. It implies a kind of vital strengthening of the patient in which the elements of gratification, stability, and closeness, as described earlier, play a decisive part.

Such vital strengthening of the patient, however, in reflecting and fostering a growing together of therapist and patient, instead of facilitating and resolving transferences, may also push these underground. They are lost sight of in the growing intimacy of the relationship. The therapist, unwittingly, tends to sacrifice distance and professionalism. There may develop elements of auto-transference, as earlier described: Relational patterns that originated and were warranted in earlier phases of the therapeutic relationship are inappropriately carried over to its later stages. The over-all result may be a smooth, yet expansive matching and collusion of needs and expectations, satisfying to a degree though causing malaise. Sooner or later the relationship will die.

The case of Esther Z., an unmarried, twenty-four-year-old woman, may give an idea of what may happen. For five years, Esther had been hospitalized with a diagnosis of schizophrenia, undifferentiated type. Three series of electroshock treatments had not visibly changed her condition. She remained near-mute, occasionally laughed in a silly fashion, and yet appeared seductive in a cold, contemptuous manner. She had had several tries with psychotherapy, but seemed unreachable. Then Dr. R. began to see her. Dr. R. felt challenged by her and he was more

---

[2] "Transference" in German denotes "trans-holding," "trans-carrying."

daring and more self-sacrificing than Esther's previous psychotherapists. He spent many hours in her room while she scrutinized him icily or even assaulted him. He took Esther for rides in his car, although she resisted him, at first strongly, later less so. She finally began to change. She spoke more in a coherent manner, dressed herself attractively, and resumed playing the piano, which she had given up six years before. Esther thus seemed to move and Dr. R. was hopeful about the further course of therapy.

However, this movement slowly lost momentum. Esther seemed to settle on a plateau of limited improvement. She clearly was much better off than she had been, but she continued to speak little and much of the time she seemed preoccupied with inner voices. It was evident she had come to rely on her therapist, on his taking the initiative, on his telling her what to do and how to do it. The therapist, to a degree, appeared gratified by Esther's dependence on him: This dependence reflected how much he had helped her and how much he meant to her. Being himself of an active temperament, he seemed to enjoy leading Esther on. But this enjoyment became increasingly infected with doubts. Gradually he grew disappointed about Esther's apparent lack of progress. He seemed unable to shift the gears in the relationship, and neither did Esther. They continued to see each other in many sessions. Thus they became more and more a part of each other's lives. Their relationship seemed to run on low but reliable steam, reminiscent of many married couples who carry on chiefly out of habit, inertia, and a vaguely felt need for security.

Esther, finally, began to show signs of slipping back into the condition she showed prior to her therapy with Dr. R. At this time Dr. R. started to think about leaving the hospital staff. As it turned out, Dr. R. and Esther left the institution about the same time. Dr. R. devoted himself to private practice. Esther, upon the insistence of her family, entered a hospital in another part of the country.

RESISTANCE IN THE PSYCHOTHERAPY OF SCHIZOPHRENICS

At the beginning, the schizophrenic patient often has neither the motivation nor the power to seek help. Unlike the neurotic, he cannot, out of his own will, and driven by his suffering, enter into a relationship with a therapist. Therefore, his resistance will not be qualified like that of the neurotic patient in psychoanalysis who "resists" but who also, with the support of his cooperative and observant ego, helps to turn his resistance into fuel for insightful change.

Instead, the schizophrenic's initial resistance can be expected to be unqualified. Thus he will resist his therapist in a rejecting, undifferentiated, all-out way. He will resist the man, called therapist, whom others have forced upon him and he will resist the notion that he himself may be confused, helpless, crazy. He may never budge in this initial all-out resistance, particularly so when his fragmentation has given way to a rather stable, ego-syntonic paranoid structure allowing him to feel at home in his restriction.

But once this patient has established some trust in his therapist, his initially unqualified resistance will tend to become qualified. It will then more resemble the resistance of a neurotic patient. It will then reflect the patient's investment and skills at maintaining his defensive structure, but also will provide some leverage for corrective changes.

Yet the schizophrenic patient, more than the neurotic, has reason to fear such changes, and hence has reason to resist. The changes required of him seem far-reaching and threatening. He already, in a manner unknown to the neurotic, has had his experiences with the anxiety of disintegration. And these experiences were terrifying.

A schizophrenic patient of Christian Müller had been a resistance fighter in the French Maquis. As such, he had come to face a German firing squad. All preparations for the execution had been carried out, but at the last moment he was freed. In telling about this experience later, he stated he would many times prefer reliving it than once more suffer the anxiety of another psychotic disintegration.

While in a fragmented state, a schizophrenic patient may still experience some of the anxiety that goes with psychotic disintegration. But he has taken certain defensive measures against this anxiety—glaringly insufficient as these measures may appear. He will desperately cling to his costly and patched-up defensive structure. He will resist its breakdown—necessary as such breakdown may seem in the light of a needed reintegration at the base.

The patient's resistance must also be seen in the light of his uneven development. More than any neurotic patient this schizophrenic may resist new steps in his growth. Just as a child, in giving in to regressive needs, may resist such steps, so may this patient. He has good reasons: These overdue steps, as we saw, imply a learning and experimenting at the "wrong" time. They now require more efforts and are more likely to expose him to humiliating situations than would have been the case at the "right" time. The therapist will have to empathize with such resistance, which is born out of fear and despair. He cannot push his patient into growth and yet he must hold out certain expectations. There is no simple formula to handle this resistance.

THE THERAPIST'S SPECIAL POSITION

As was seen earlier, the psychoanalytic situation exposes the analyst to unusual temptations as well as frustrations. To counter these, three interdependent systems come into play. First, the analytic situation itself, which seems tailored to "hold" the analyst in his dual position as both participant and chief analytic pacesetter. Second, the analyst's non-analytic life-situation, as an additional system of checks and balances, and third, his personal qualifications.

The therapist of schizophrenic patients also faces singular temptations as well as frustrations. Some of these frustrations have been discussed: The therapist will be exposed to an anxiety which is unusually intense, yet often uncannily elusive. He will feel double-binds in his viscera, that is, feel the impact of conflicting, confusing messages. He will, as the therapy drags on, possibly be confronted with a sense of all-pervasive meaninglessness. He will have to endure unusual hostility, distrust, but also uncommon apathy and stagnation. He will often find himself in situations for which he has no ready answers. Often he will have to ask himself whether his patient's apparent lack of progress indicates "latent" progress or no progress at all, and whether this lack of progress is due to some shortcoming or unsolved counter-transference problem of his own. He will—Leslie Farber has described it—be exposed to despair.

The temptations inherent in such psychotherapy are less easily recognized. I shall mention a few of them. There is the temptation to defy conventional reality by deeply identifying with the unconventional schizophrenic. Or, more likely, such defiance may soften into a fascinated sharing of the schizophrenic's fragmented, but complex and intriguing world. This world of hidden, unsuspected meanings, of provocative absurdity somehow may seem "truer" than the conventional world of meanings. This world may seem intrinsically related to many aspects of modern art where conventions are boldly overthrown, and absurdities, dissonances, and infantilisms, unfamiliar and yet "true," seem to come closest to revealing the essence of our disjointed times. There is, along with the spell exerted by absurdity, the temptation inherent in ambiguity. This ambiguity may entice the therapist to see in the schizophrenic patient all he wants to see, to find in him confirmation for his pet theories and ideologies. Somehow, the schizophrenic, in what he says and does, seems to prove them all. There is the temptation of power, the temptation to impose one's will on a most recalcitrant object. The therapist may seek the triumph of "breaking through" where others failed, of doing the impossible. And there is, finally, the temptation of becoming symbiotically enmeshed with an utterly dependent human being. There may appear the promise of a kind of intimacy, troubling and yet gratifying, which in his normal life seems unattainable.

To a point, all these temptations, when given in to, may not prove harmful to therapy and patient. But this point easily is overstepped. The classical analytic situation, as earlier described, appears not adequate to "hold" the therapist vis-à-vis such a combination of frustrations and temptations. A different situation seems required, one that must incorporate essential elements of the classical psycho-analytic situation, but at the same time, must transcend it. What would this different situation be like?

In pondering this question, I began to reflect about Chestnut Lodge, where, as a therapist, I worked for more than five years. This small sanatorium, now operating fifty-two years, for several decades has geared itself to the intensive psychotherapy of mainly schizophrenic patients. Sullivan and Frieda Fromm-Reichmann, besides its director, Dexter Bullard, crucially shaped its tradition, structure, and orientation.[3]

Chestnut Lodge, in recent years, seems to have opened itself to more diverse and currently popular trends in the therapy of schizophrenics, such as group and milieu therapies, heightened contacts with families, etc. But it is the intense, analytically oriented relationship between two people—doctor and patient—which, over the years, has remained the axis of therapy around which anything else only tangentially seems to cluster. This personal relationship has become the pivot of its therapeutic setting and ideology. And this relationship, in a kind of ongoing experimentation, seems to have become adapted to the schizophrenic's therapeutic needs. (This is not to imply that other settings could not be as well, or even better suited to help schizophrenic patients. But, as of the moment, there seem to exist few, if any, other places with a

[3] Stanton and Schwarz (the one a psychiatrist, the other a sociologist) have based their book *The Mental Hospital* on their observations and experiences at Chestnut Lodge.

comparable tradition and experimental knowledge as regards their psychotherapy.)

What then are the specific features of the therapist's position at Chestnut Lodge which allow him to let unfold the five above balances on a wide and meaningful scope and which, at the same time, help him to cope with the unusual frustrations and temptations inherent in his position?

These features I have described in an earlier paper[4] as a characteristic balance of sensitizing and stabilizing factors. These factors can be seen as constituting a wider therapeutic situation which seems to contain and accentuate the core features of the wider analytic situation outlined in the opening chapter. These factors, in a most general sense, seem to make for an unusually intense entanglement with the schizophrenic patient but also they seem to ensure that this entanglement, again and again, can be mastered, desymbiotized and be put into perspective.

An important sensitizing factor—which tends to promote a deep entanglement with the schizophrenic patient—is, first of all, the very selection and implicit support of the therapists chosen. These are therapists who definitely want to work with schizophrenic patients. Whatever their conscious and unconscious motives for wanting to do so, these therapists can be expected to be enough like their patients to empathize strongly with them. But these therapists also seem more vulnerable to the above described or similar temptations. They seem, particularly when young, entanglement-prone.

Another sensitizing factor, highly important, is the small case load of each therapist and the typically long duration of each treatment. Each therapist at Chestnut Lodge cares for no more than five or six patients, seeing these, over years, in one-hour sessions four or five times weekly. The stage is set for an unusually close and meaningful tie, with strong feelings and expectations invested in the patient.

[4] "Techniques of psychotherapy in a small hospital setting." *Bull. Menninger Clinic*, 27: 96–104, 1963.

Further: The hospital setting, in often elusive ways, seems to foster an intense involvement. For example, within the relatively closed culture of the hospital, a therapist's relationship with his patients will be thoroughly appraised by other members of the therapeutic team. It is difficult for a therapist, particularly when he is still inexperienced and relatively unsure of himself, not to find his own growth and progress staked on the growth and progress of his patients. This is a climate where a therapist's dependence on and competition with other staff members is bound to be activated. Inevitably his patients become affected, in manifold ways by such conflictual, but highly charged, feelings. Problematical as these feelings may appear, they tend to increase further the patient's importance for the therapist, that is, they tend to sensitize the therapist to his patient.

But stabilizing factors of no lesser strength seem inbuilt into the Chestnut Lodge setting. They tend to counteract and balance such sensitization and involvement.

Chestnut Lodge, as an institution, in many ways backs and shields the therapist. In Chestnut Lodge it seems taken for granted that involvements with schizophrenic patients must be deep and unconventional and that they must sir up anxiety. The therapist, in exposing himself to entanglement and anxiety, finds himself supported by others who are in the same boat. But, in addition to being supported by a shared culture and ideology, more specific stabilizing factors operate. The young therapist will have most of his cases supervised by a more experienced staff member. He will meet two times a week with a small group of his colleagues where he can discuss with relative safety difficult counter-transference problems. He will have his personal analysis outside the sanatorium—further helping him to disentangle possible entanglements with his patients and to see these in the perspective of his own psychodynamics and their history. He will, in many ways, be pressured to clarify his own position and feelings vis-à-vis a given patient, and hence to gain distance. He must prepare for regular conferences in which he—in an organized, thought-through manner—must disclose what he does in therapy, where he stands with his patient. He will, most likely, have a research interest which further promotes his detachment and objectivity.

The therapist's personal qualifications, finally, must sustain and balance the impact of this—and any other—therapeutic situation with schizophrenic patients. This is in line with my previous considerations about the psychoanalytic and mother-child relationship.

Much has been written about the qualifications of a therapist of schizophrenics. His devotion, courage, unconventionality, endurance, and the ability to grow himself have been particularly mentioned. Again, I should like to focus on the reconciling power he needs. The therapist of schizophrenic patients must combine the qualities of an analyst who can endure related loneliness as well as a mother who pre-reflectively can adapt herself to her infant's needs and can separate herself from him when this is necessary.

Combining these qualities certainly seems no easy matter. But the accomplishments of such therapists as Mme. Sechehaye, Frieda Fromm-Reichmann, Otto Will, Christian Müller, and many others indicate it is possible.

THE SCHIZOPHRENIC'S SPECIAL POSITION

This position, in many respects, seems more to resemble that of a child than that of an analytic patient, as earlier discussed. But just as a child, despite all his lacking capacities, was seen as an active participant in a dialectic of mutual growth, so must the schizophrenic, sooner or later, through his active participation contribute to the expanding mutuality. And he must, further, strive toward a point in the relationship where his position will more resemble that of an analytic patient than that of a child. No therapist, not even the most devoted, can be expected to work continually without positive response, without being confirmed himself. Without such confirmation, all psychotherapy will reach its limits.

A few years ago Hanna Green published a novel about the life and psychotherapy of an adolescent schizophrenic girl in a small mental hospital. The patient, we realize, was the author herself and the hospital was Chestnut Lodge. This is a rare, perceptively written document. It tells us what the schizophrenic experience can be like, what demands it makes on the hospital and its staff, and what may—and may not—be achieved through psychotherapy. Frieda Fromm-Reichmann, the girl's psychotherapist, provided the title of the book when she once told the author: "I never promised you a rose garden."

I should like to conclude this study on the sobering and hopeful note struck by this message. As never before in human history researchers and therapists are focusing on schizophrenia. In so doing, they meet with problems of staggering complexity. These problems point to man's most frightening potentialities—loneliness, disintegration, destructiveness; but also, they reflect on his capacity to grow in the face of interpersonal adversity. These are the core problems of human existence and relatedness, which again and again, on many levels of experience and thought, reveal conflict and require reconciliation.

SELECTED BIBLIOGRAPHY

Abraham, K., *Clinical Papers and Essays on Psychoanalysis.* London: Hogarth Press, 1955.

Alexander, F., *The Psychoanalysis of the Total Personality.* New York and Washington: Nervous and Mental Disease Publications, 1930.

Arendt, H., *The Human Condition.* Chicago: University of Chicago Press, 1958.

Arlow, J., and Brenner, C., *Psychoanalytic Concepts and the Structural Theory.* New York: International Universities Press, 1964.

Artiss, K., *Milieu Therapy in Schizophrenia.* New York: Grune & Stratton, 1962.

Bachmann, I., "Wittgenstein: Zu einem Kapital der jüngsten Philosophiegeschichte." In: *Beiheft, Ludwig Wittgenstein/Schriften.* Frankfurt am Main: Suhrkamp, 1960.

Bak, R., "Regression of Ego-orientation and Libido in Schizophrenia." *International Journal of Psycho-Analysis,* 20: 64–71, 1939.

Balint, A., *The Early Years of Life.* New York: Basic Books, 1954.

Balint, M., "Early Developmental States of the Ego. Primary Object Love." *International Journal of Psycho-Analysis,* 30: 265–73, 1949.

——, "Changing Therapeutical Aims and Techniques in Psycho-analysis." *International Journal of Psycho-Analysis,* 31: 117–24, 1950.

——, "Pleasure, Object and Libido." *British Journal of Medical Psychology,* 29: 162–67, 1956.

——, "Die drei seelischen Bereiche." *Psyche, 11:* 321–44, 1957, pp. 334–35.

Bateson, G., *et al.*, "Toward a Theory of Schizophrenia." *Behavioral Science, 1:* 251–64, 1956.

Becker, E., *The Birth and Death of Meaning: A Perspective in Psychiatry and Anthropology.* New York: The Free Press of Glencoe, 1962.

———, *The Revolution in Psychiatry.* New York: The Free Press of Glencoe, 1964.

Benedek, T., "Parenthood as a Developmental Phase." *Journal of the American Psychoanalytic Association,* 7: 389–417, 1959.

Benedetti, G., "The Psychotherapy of a Schizophrenic Patient." In: *Modern Psychotherapeutic Practice* (Burton, A., ed.). Palo Alto: Science and Behavior Books, 1965, pp. 37–57.

Benjamin, J., "Predictions and Psychopathologic Theory." In: *Dynamics of Psychopathology in Children* (Jessner, L. and Pavenstedt, E., eds.). New York: Grune & Stratton, 1959.

———, "Further Comments on Some Developmental Aspects of Anxiety." In: *"Counterpoint," Libidinal Object and Subject* (Gaskill, H., ed.). New York: International Universities Press, 1963, pp. 121–53.

Beres, D., "Ego Deviation and the Concept of Schizophrenia." *The Psychoanalytic Study of the Child, 11:* 164–235. New York: International Universities Press, 1956.

———, "Vicissitudes of Superego Functions and Superego Precursors in Childhood." *The Psychoanalytic Study of the Child, 13:* 324–35. New York: International Universities Press, 1958.

Bettelheim, B., *The Informed Heart: Autonomy in a Mass Age.* New York: The Free Press, 1960.

———, *The Empty Fortress. Infantile Autism and the Birth of the Self.* New York: The Free Press, 1967.

Bion, W., "Differentiation of the Psychotic from the Non-psychotic Personalities." *International Journal of Psycho-Analysis, 38:* 266–75, 1957.

———, *Experiences in Groups.* New York: Basic Books, 1961.

Bion, W., *Learning from Experience*. New York: Basic Books, 1963.

Bleuler, E., "Kritik der Freudschen Theorien." *Allgemeine Zeitschrift für Psychiatrie*, 70: 665–718, 1913.

——, "Störung der Assoziationsspannung/Ein Elementarsymptom der Schizophrenie." *Allgemeine Zeitschrift für Psychiatrie*, 74: 1–21, 1920.

——, *Textbook of Psychiatry* (Translated by A. A. Brill from *Lehrbuch der Psychiatrie*, 4th edition). New York: Macmillan, 1924.

——, *Dementia Praecox or the Group of Schizophrenias*. New York: International Universities Press, 1950.

Bloch, E., *Subjekt-Objekt. Erläuterungen zu Hegel*. Frankfurt am Main: Suhrkamp, 1962.

Boss, M., *Psychoanalyse und Daseinsanalytik*. Bern-Stuttgart: Huber, 1957.

Boszormenyi-Nagy, I., "A Theory of Relationships: Experience and Transaction." In: *Intensive Family Therapy* (Boszormenyi-Nagy, I. and Framo, J., eds.). New York: Hoeber, 1965.

Bowen, M., "Family Relations in Schizophrenia." In: *Schizophrenia* (Auerback, A., ed.). New York: The Ronald Press, 1959, pp. 147–78.

Bowlby, J., *Maternal Care and Mental Health*. Geneva: World Health Organization, 1952.

——, "The Nature of the Child's Tie to His Mother." *International Journal of Psycho-Analysis*, 39: 350–73, 1958.

Boyer, L., and Giovacchini, P., *Psychoanalytic Treatment of Characterological and Schizophrenic Disorders*. New York: Science House, 1967.

Brenner, C., *An Elementary Textbook of Psychoanalysis*. New York: Doubleday Anchor Books, 1957.

——, "The Nature and Development of the Concept of Repression in Freud's Writings." *The Psychoanalytic Study of the Child*, 12: 19–46. New York: International Universities Press, 1957.

Brody, S., *Patterns of Mothering*. New York: International Universities Press, 1956.

Brown, R., *Words and Things*. Glencoe: The Free Press, 1958.

Broyer, L., "Office Treatment of Schizophrenic Patients by Psychoanalysis." *The Psychoanalytic Forum, 1*: 338–56, 1966.

Bruch, H., "Transformation of Oral Impulses in Eating Disorders." *Psychiatric Quarterly, 35*: 458–81, 1961.

——, "Falsification of Bodily Needs and Body Concept in Schizophrenia." *Archives of General Psychiatry, 6*: 18–24, 1962.

Bruch, H., and Palombo, S., "Conceptual Problems in Schizophrenia." *Journal of Nervous and Mental Disease, 132*: 114–17, 1961.

Buber, M., *I and Thou*. (Translated by Ronald Gregor Smith.) Edinburgh: T. & T. Clark, 1937.

Bühler, K., "Les Lois Generales d'Evolution dans le Language de l'Enfant." *Journal de Psychologie, 12*: 597–607, 1926.

——, *Die geistige Entwicklung des Kindes*. Jena: Fischer, 1929.

——, *Kindheit und Jugend*. Genese des Bewusstseins. Leipzig: Hirzel, 1931.

——, "Forschung zur Sprachteorie." *Archiv für die gesamte Psychologie, 94*: 401–12, 1935.

Bullard, D. (Ed.), *Psychoanalysis and Psychotherapy: Selected Papers of Frieda Fromm-Reichmann*. Chicago: University of Chicago Press, 1959.

Burnham, D., "Separation Anxiety. A Factor in the Object Relations of Schizophrenic Patients." *Archives of General Pyschiatry, 13*: 346–58, 1965.

Carnap, R., "Überwindung der Metaphysik durch logische Analyse der Sprache." In: *Erkenntnis*, Vol. II, Leipzig, 1931.

Dewey, J., *Human Nature and Conduct. An Introduction to Social Psychology*. New York: Henry Holt, 1922.

——, *Experience and Nature*. London: Open Court Publication Co., 1925.

——, *The Quest for Certainty*. New York: Milson-Balch, 1929.

Edelson, M., *Ego Psychology, Group Dynamics and the Therapeutic Community*. New York and London: Grune & Stratton, 1964.

Eissler, K., "Limitations to the Psychotherapy of Schizophrenia." *Psychiatry, 6:* 381–91, 1943.

——, "Remarks on the Psychoanalysis of Schizophrenia." *International Journal of Psycho-Analysis, 32:* 139–56, 1951.

——, "The Effect of the Structure of the Ego on Psychoanalytic Technique." *Journal of the American Psychoanalytic Association, 1:* 104–43, 1953.

Elrod, N., *Zur Phänomenologie der Besserung*. Basel: Karger, 1957.

Erikson, E., *Childhood and Society*. New York: Norton, 1950.

——, *Identity and the Life Cycle*. New York: International Universities Press, 1956.

Escalona, S., and Heider, G., *Prediction and Outcome: A Study in Child Development*. New York: Basic Books, 1959.

Fairbairn, W., *An Object-Relations Theory of the Personality*. New York: Basic Books, 1952.

Farber, L., "The Therapeutic Despair." *Psychiatry, 21:* 7–20, 1958.

Federn, P., *Ego Psychology and the Psychoses*. New York: Basic Books, 1952.

Fenichel, O., *The Psychoanalytic Theory of Neurosis*. New York: Norton, 1945.

——, *Early Stages of Ego Development. The Collected Papers of Otto Fenichel, 1:* 363–72. New York: Norton, 1955.

Ferenczi, S., *Bausteine zur Psychoanalyse*. Wien: Internationaler Psychoanalytischer Verlag, 1927.

——, "Confusion of Tongues between the Adult and the Child." *International Journal of Psycho-Analysis, 30:* 225–30, 1949.

Flavell, J., *The Developmental Psychology of Jean Piaget*. Toronto, New York and London: D. Van Nostrand, 1963.

Freeman, T., *et al.*, *Chronic Schizophrenia*. London: Tavistock, 1958.

——, *Studies on Psychosis*. London: Tavistock, 1965.

French, M., and Fromm, E., *Dream Interpretation. A New Approach*. New York: Basic Books, 1964.

Freud, A., *The Ego and the Mechanisms of Defence*. New York: International Universities Press, 1946.

——, "Regression as a Principle in Mental Development." *Bulletin of the Menninger Clinic*, 27: 126–39, 1963.

——, *Normality and Pathology in Childhood*. New York: International Universities Press, 1965.

Freud, S., (1896) "Further Remarks on the Neuro-Psychoses of Defence." *Standard Edition*, 3: 159–88. London: Hogarth Press, 1962.

——, (1900) "The Interpretation of Dreams." *Standard Edition*, 4 & 5. London: Hogarth Press, 1953.

——, (1901) "The Psychopathology of Everyday Life." *Standard Edition*, 6: 1–279. London: Hogarth Press, 1960.

——, (1905) "Three Essays on the Theory of Sexuality." *Standard Edition*, 7: 122–243. London: Hogarth Press, 1953.

——, (1911) "Formulations on the Two Principles of Mental Functioning." *Standard Edition*, 12: 213–26. London: Hogarth Press, 1958.

——, (1911) "Psycho-Analytic Notes on an Autobiographical Account of a Case of Paranoia." *Standard Edition*, 12: 3–84. London: Hogarth Press, 1958.

——, (1915) "Repression." *Standard Edition*, 14: 141–58. London: Hogarth Press, 1957.

——, (1916–17) "Introductory Lectures on Psycho-Analysis." *Standard Edition*, 15 & 16. London: Hogarth Press, 1963.

——, (1920) "Beyond the Pleasure Principle." *Standard Edition*, 18: 3–66. London: Hogarth Press, 1955.

——, (1923) "The Ego and the Id." *Standard Edition*, 19: 3–68. London: Hogarth Press, 1961.

——, (1924) "Neurosis and Psychosis." *Standard Edition*, 19: 149–56. London: Hogarth Press, 1961.

Freud, S., (1924) "The Loss of Reality in Neurosis and Psychosis." *Standard Edition, 19:* 183–90. London: Hogarth Press, 1961.

——, (1926) "Inhibitions, Symptoms and Anxiety." *Standard Edition, 20:* 77–178. London: Hogarth Press, 1959.

——, (1932) *New Introductory Lectures.* New York: Norton, 1933.

——, (1940) *An Outline of Psychoanalysis.* New York: Norton, 1949.

Friedman, T., *et al., Psychotherapy for the Whole Family.* New York: Springer, 1965.

Fromm-Reichmann, F., *Principles of Intensive Psychotherapy.* Chicago: University of Chicago Press, 1950.

Gehlen, A., *Der Mensch, seine Natur und seine Stellung in der Welt.* Berlin: Junker & Dünnhaupt, 1940.

Goldfarb, W., *Childhood Schizophrenia.* Cambridge: Harvard University Press, 1961.

Goodrich, D., "Possibilities for Preventive Intervention During Initial Personality Formation." In: *Prevention of Mental Disorders in Children* (Kaplan, C., ed.), New York: Basic Books, 1961, pp. 249–64.

——, "Recent Research in Early Family Development and Child Personality." Paper presented at the meeting of the Third Institute on Preventive Psychiatry, State University of Iowa, April 21–22, 1961.

Green, H., *I Never Promised You a Rose Garden.* New York: Holt, Rinehart & Winston, 1964.

Greenson, R., Series of papers on "Variations in Classical Psychoanalytic Technique." *International Journal of Psycho-Analysis, 39:* 200–42, 1958.

Guntrip, H., *Personality Structure and Human Interaction.* New York: International Universities Press, 1961.

Hall, E., *The Silent Language.* New York: Doubleday, 1959.

Hartmann, H., "Comments on the Psychoanalytic Theory of Instinctual Drives." *Psychoanalytic Quarterly, 17:* 368–88, 1948.

——, "Comments on the Psychoanalytic Theory of the

Ego." *The Psychoanalytic Study of the Child*, 5: 74–96. New York: International Universities Press, 1950.

——, "Psychoanalysis and Developmental Psychology." *The Psychoanalytic Study of the Child*, 5: 7–17. New York: International Universities Press, 1950.

——, "Technical Implications of Ego Psychology." *Psychoanalytic Quarterly*, 20: 31–43, 1951.

——, "Contribution to the Metapsychology of Schizophrenia." *The Psychoanalytic Study of the Child*, 8: 177–98. New York: International Universities Press, 1953.

——, "The Development of the Ego Concept in Freud's Work." *International Journal of Psycho-Analysis*, 37: 425–38, 1956.

——, *Ego Psychology and the Problem of Adaptation*. Journal of the American Psychoanalytic Association, Monograph Series No. 1. New York: International Universities Press, 1958.

Hartmann, H., and Loewenstein, R., "Comments on the Formation of Psychic Structure." *The Psychoanalytic Study of the Child*, 2: 11–38. New York: International Universities Press, 1946.

——, "Notes on the Theory of Aggression." *The Psychoanalytic Study of the Child*, 3 & 4: 9–36. New York: International Universities Press, 1949.

Hayward, M., and Taylor, J., "A Schizophrenic Patient Describes the Action of Intensive Psychotherapy." *Psychiatric Quarterly*, 30: 211–48, 1956.

Hediger, H., *Skizzen zu einer Tierpsychologie im Zoo und im Zirkus*. Zürich: Buechergilde Gutenberg, 1954.

Hegel, G., *The Phenomenology of the Mind*. Translated by J. B. Baillie (with introduction and notes). London: Swann Sonnenschein, 2 vols., 1910.

——, *Sämtliche Werke: Jubiläumsausgabe in 20 Bänden* (Glockner, H., ed.). Stuttgart: Frommann, 1927–30.

Heidegger, M., *Sein und Zeit*. Halle: Niemeyer, 1927.

——, "What Is Metaphysics?" In: *Existence and Being* (Brock, W., ed.). Chicago: Regnery, 1949.

Hill, L., *Psychotherapeutic Intervention in Schizophrenia.* Chicago: University of Chicago Press, 1955.

Inhelder, B., and Piaget, J., "The Growth of Logical Thinking." In: *From Childhood to Adolescence* (Translated by Anne Parsons and Stanley Milgram). London: Routledge & Kegan Paul, 1958.

Jacobson, E., "Denial and Repression." *Journal of the American Psychoanalytic Association,* 5: 61–92, 1957.

——, *The Self and the Object World.* New York: International Universities Press, 1964.

Jaspers, K., *General Psychopathology.* Chicago: University of Chicago Press, 1963.

Kallmann, F., "The Genetic Theory of Schizophrenia. An Analysis of 691 Schizophrenic Index Families." *American Journal of Psychiatry,* 103: 309–22, 1946.

Kanner, L., "Early Infantile Autism." *American Journal of Orthopsychiatry,* 19: 416–26, 1949.

Kaufmann, W., *A Critique of Philosophy and Religion.* New York: Harper, 1958.

——, *Hegel: Reinterpretation, Texts and Commentary.* New York: Doubleday, 1965.

Kety, S., *Biochemical Theories of Schizophrenia,* Parts I & II of a two-part critical review of current theories and of the evidence used to support them. *Science,* 129, 1959.

——, "A Biologist Examines the Mind and Behavior." *Science,* 132: 1861–70, 1960.

——, "Current Biochemical Research in Schizophrenia," Chapter 11 in: *Psychopathology of Schizophrenia.* New York: Grune & Stratton, 1966.

——, "Current Biochemical Approaches to Schizophrenia." *New England Journal of Medicine,* 276: 325–31, 1967.

Klein, M., *Contributions to Psychoanalysis, 1921–45.* London: Hogarth Press, 1948.

——, *Developments in Psycho-Analysis.* London: Hogarth Press, 1952.

——, (1932) *The Psycho-Analysis of Children.* London: Hogarth Press, 1952.

——, *New Directions in Psycho-Analysis.* New York: Basic Books, 1956.

——, *Envy and Gratitude.* New York: Basic Books, 1957.

Kolb, L., "The Body Image in the Schizophrenic Reaction." In: *Schizophrenia* (Auerback, A., ed.), New York: The Ronald Press, 1959.

Kraepelin, E., *Clinical Psychiatry: A Textbook for Students and Physicians,* abstracted and adapted from the 7th German edition of Kraepelin's *Lehrbuch der Psychiatrie.* New York and London: Macmillan, 1907.

——, *One Hundred Years of Psychiatry.* New York: Philosophical Library, 1962.

Kretschmer, E., *Medizinische Psychologie,* 9th edition. Stuttgart: G. Thieme, 1947.

Kringlen, E., "Schizophrenia in Twins. An Epidemiological-Clinical Study." *Psychiatry, 29:* 172–84, 1966.

——, "Hereditary and Social Factors in Schizophrenic Twins. An Epidemiological-Clinical Study." Paper presented at the First Rochester International Conference on Schizophrenia, University of Rochester, New York. March 29–31, 1967.

Kris, E., "Neutralization and Sublimation: Observations on Young Children." *The Psychoanalytic Study of the Child, 10:* 30–46. New York: International Universities Press, 1955.

Laing, R., *The Divided Self: A Study of Sanity and Madness.* London: Tavistock Publications, 1960.

——, *The Self and Others, Further Studies in Sanity and Madness.* London: Tavistock Publications, 1961.

——, *The Politics of Experience.* New York: Random House, 1967.

Laing, R., and Esterson, A., *Sanity, Madness and the Family. Vol. I: Families of Schizophrenics.* London: Tavistock Publications, 1964.

Lidz, T., *The Family and Human Adaptation.* New York: International Universities Press, 1963.

——, "August Strindberg: A Study of the Relationship between His Creativity and Schizophrenia." *Interna-*

tional Journal of Psycho-Analysis, 45: 399–410, 1964.

Lidz, T., *et al.,* "Schizophrenic Patients and Their Siblings." *Psychiatry, 26:* 1–18, 1963.

——, *Schizophrenia and the Family.* New York: International Universities Press, 1965.

Lincke, H., "Einige Bemerkungen zur Triebentwicklung." *Psyche, 11:* 353–73, 1957.

Lorenz, K., *King Solomon's Ring.* New York: Crowell, 1952.

——, *On Agression.* New York: Harcourt, Brace & World, 1966.

McGill, V., *August Strindberg, The Bedeviled Viking.* New York: Brentano's, 1930.

Macnab, F., *Estrangement and Relationship.* London: Tavistock, 1965.

Mahler, M., "On Child Psychosis and Schizophrenia: Autistic and Symbiotic Infantile Psychoses." *The Psychoanalytic Study of the Child,* 7: 286–305. New York: International Universities Press, 1952.

——, "Autism and Symbiosis, Two Extreme Disturbances of Identity." *International Journal of Psycho-Analysis,* 39: 77–83, 1958.

——, "Certain Aspects of the Separation-Individuation Phase." *Psychoanalytic Quarterly, 32:* 1–14, 1961.

——, "On the Significance of the Normal Separation-Individuation Phase: With Reference to Research in Symbiotic Child Psychosis." In: *Drives, Affects and Behavior* (Schur, M., ed.). New York: International Universities Press, 1965, pp. 161–89.

Morris, G., and Wynne, L., "Schizophrenic Offspring and Parental Styles of Communication. A predictive study using excerpts of family therapy recordings." *Psychiatry, 28:* 19–44, 1965.

Müller, C., "Über Psychotherapie bei einem chronischen Schizophrenen." *Psyche, 9:* 350–69, 1955.

Navratil, L., *Schizophrenie und Sprache/Zur Psychologie der Dichtung.* Munich: Deutscher Taschenbuch Verlag, 1966.

Nunberg, H., "The Synthetic Function of the Ego." *In-*

ternational Journal of Psycho-Analysis, 12: 123–40, 1931. Reprinted in *Practice and Theory of Psychoanalysis,* New York: International Universities Press, 1960.

Parker, B., *My Language Is Me.* New York: Basic Books, 1962.

Parsons, T., "Psychoanalysis and the Social Structure." *Psychoanalytic Quarterly, 19:* 371–84, 1950.

——, *Social Structure and Personality.* Glencoe: The Free Press, 1964.

Parsons, T., and Bales, R., *Family, Socialization and Interaction Process.* Glencoe: The Free Press, 1955.

Piaget, J., *The Language and Thought of the Child.* New York: Harcourt, Brace, 1926.

——, *The Construction of Reality in the Child.* Translated by Margaret Cook. New York: Basic Books, 1954.

——, *Play, Dreams and Imitation in Childhood.* New York: Norton, 1962.

Popper, K., *The Open Society and Its Enemies.* London: Routledge & Kegan Paul, 1952. 2 vols.

Provence, S., and Lipton, R., *Infants in Institutions.* New York: International Universities Press, 1962.

Provence, S., and Ritvo, S., "Effects of Deprivation on Institutionalized Infants: Disturbances in Development of Relationship to Inanimate Objects." *The Psychoanalytic Study of the Child, 16:* 189–205. New York: International Universities Press, 1961.

Rahmer, S., *August Strindberg: eine pathologische Studie.* Grenzfragen der Literatur und Medizin, 6. Munich: Reinhardt, 1907.

Rangell, C., "Beyond and Between the No and Yes." In: *"Counterpoint," Libidinal Object and Subject* (Gaskill, H., ed.), New York: International Universities Press, 1963.

Rapaport, D., "Cognitive Structures in Contemporary Approaches to Cognition." *A Symposium.* Cambridge: Harvard University Press, 1951, pp. 157–200.

——, "Consciousness: A Psychopathological and Psychodynamic View." In: *Problems of Consciousness, Transactions of the Second Conference.* March 19–20, 1951. New York: Josiah Macy, Jr., Foundation, pp. 18–57.

——, "The Theory of Ego Autonomy: A Generalization." *Bulletin Menninger Clinic, 22:* 13–55, 1958.

——, "On the Psychoanalytic Theory of Motivation." In: *Nebraska Symposium on Motivation* (Jones, Marshall R., ed.). Lincoln: University of Nebraska Press, 1960, pp. 173–247.

Reichard, S., and Tillman, C., "Patterns of Parent-Child Relationships in Schizophrenia." *Psychiatry, 13:* 247–57, 1950.

Reichenbach, H., *Experience and Prediction. An Analysis of the Foundations and the Structure of Knowledge.* Chicago: University of Chicago Press, 1938.

Renée (pseudonym), *Autobiography of a Schizophrenic Girl,* with analytic interpretation by Marguerite Sechehaye. New York: Grune & Stratton, 1951.

Rheingold, H., "The Measurement of Maternal Care." *Child Development, 31:* 565–75, 1960.

Rimland, B., *Infantile Autism.* New York: Appleton-Century Crofts, 1964.

Ritvo, S., and Solnit, A., "Influences of Early Mother-Child Interactions on Identification Processes." *The Psychoanalytic Study of the Child, 15:* 215–32. New York: International Universities Press, 1958.

Rosen, J., *Direct Psychoanalytic Psychiatry.* New York: Grune & Stratton, 1962.

Rosenfeld, H., *Psychotic States. A Psychoanalytical Approach.* New York: International Universities Press, 1965.

Rosenthal, D., "Familial Concordance by Sex with Respect to Schizophrenia." *Psychological Bulletin, 59:* 401–21, 1962.

——, *The Genain Quadruplets.* New York: Basic Books, 1963.

——, "An Historical and Methodological Review of Genetic Studies of Schizophrenia." Paper presented at the first Rochester International Conference on Schizophrenia, University of Rochester, March 29–31, 1967.

———, "The Heredity-Environment Issue in Schizophrenia: Summary of the Conference and Present Status of our Knowledge." Unpublished manuscript, 1967.

Ryckoff, I., et al., "Maintenance of Stereotyped Roles in the Families of Schizophrenics." AMA Archives of General Psychiatry, 1: 93–98, 1959.

Sapir, E., Language. An Introduction to the Study of Speech. New York: Harcourt, Brace, 1921.

Schachtel, E., Metamorphosis: On the Development of Affect, Perception, Attention and Memory. New York: Basic Books, 1959.

Schaffer, L., et al., "On the Nature and Sources of the Psychiatrist's Experiences with the Family of the Schizophrenic." Psychiatry, 25: 32–45, 1962.

Schilder, P., The Image and Appearance of the Human Body. New York: International Universities Press, 1950.

Schmideberg, M., "Method of Approach to Infant's Mind. A Study of His Ego Activities." Nervous Child, 6: 278–83, 1947.

Schultz-Hencke, H., Lehrbuch der analytischen Psychotherapie. Stuttgart: Georg Thieme, 1951.

Schwing, G., A Way to the Soul of the Mentally Ill. New York: International Universities Press, 1954.

———, Collected Papers on Schizophrenia and Related Subjects. New York: International Universities Press, 1965.

Searles, H. "The Schizophrenic's Vulnerability to the Therapist's Unconscious Processes." Journal of Nervous and Mental Disease, 127: 247–62, 1958.

———, "Integration and Differentiation in Schizophrenia." Journal of Nervous and Mental Disease, 129: 542–50, 1959.

———, "Positive Feelings in the Relationship between the Schizophrenic and His Mother." International Journal of Psycho-Analysis, 39: 1–18, 1959.

Searles, H., *The Nonhuman Environment*. New York: International Universities Press, 1960.

———, "Transference Psychosis in the Psychotherapy of Schizophrenia." *International Journal of Psycho-Analysis*, *44*: 249–81, 1963.

Sechehaye, M., *Symbolic Realization: A New Method of Psychotherapy Applied to a Case Schizophrenia*. New York: International Universities Press, 1951.

———, *Symbolic Realization*. New York: International Universities Press, 1960.

Segal, H., "Some Aspects of the Analysis of a Schizophrenic." *International Journal of Psycho-Analysis*, *31*: 268–78, 1950.

Siirala, M., *Die Schizophrenie des Einzelnen und der Allgemeinheit*. Göttingen: Vandenhoeck und Rupprecht, 1961.

Singer, M., and Wynne, L., "Differentiating Characteristics of Parents of Childhood Schizophrenics, Childhood Neurotics, and Young Adult Schizophrenics." *American Journal of Psychiatry*, *120*: 234–43, 1963.

———, "Thought Disorder and Family Relations of Schizophrenics. III. Methodology Using Projective Techniques." *Archives of General Psychiatry*, *12*: 187–200, 1965.

———, "Thought Disorder and Family Relations of Schizophrenics. IV. Results and Implications." *Archives of General Psychiatry*, *12*: 201–12, 1965.

———, "Principles for Scoring Communication Defects and Deviances in Parents of Schizophrenics: Rorschach and TAT Scoring Manuals." *Psychiatry*, *29*: 260–88, 1967.

Spitz, R., "Hospitalism: An Inquiry into the Genesis of Psychiatric Conditions in Early Childhood." *The Psychoanalytic Study of the Child*, *1*: 53–74. New York: International Universities Press, 1945.

———, "Anaclitic Depression: An Inquiry into the Genesis of Psychiatric Conditions in Early Childhood." *The Psychoanalytic Study of the Child*, *2*: 313–42. New York: International Universities Press, 1946.

———, "The Primal Cavity: A Contribution to the Genesis

of Perception and its Role for Psychoanalytic Theory." *The Psychoanalytic Study of the Child*, 10: 215–40, 1955.

——, "Transference: The Analytic Setting and Its Prototype." *International Journal of Psycho-Analysis*, 37: 380–385, 1956.

——, *No and Yes: On the Genesis of Human Communication*. New York: International Universities Press, 1957.

——, *Die Entstehung der ersten Objektbeziehungen*. Stuttgart: Ernst Klett, 1957.

——, *Field Theory of Ego Formation and Its Implications for Pathology*. The Freud Anniversary Lecture Series, The New York Psychoanalytic Institute. New York: International Universities Press, 1958.

——, "Life and the Dialogue." In: *"Counterpoint," Libidinal Subject and Object* (Gaskill, H., ed.). New York: International Universities Press, 1963, pp. 154–76.

——, *The First Year of Life*. New York: International Universities Press, 1965.

Staehelin, B., Gesetzmaessigkeiten im Gemeinschaftsleben schwer Geisteskranker. *Schweizer Archiv für Neurologie und Psychiatrie*, 69: 436–43, 1952.

Stanton, A., and Schwarz, M., *The Mental Hospital*. New York: Basic Books, 1954.

Stierlin, H., "Contrasting Attitudes toward the Psychoses in Europe and the United States." *Psychiatry*, 21: 141–47, 1958.

——, "The Adaptation to the 'Stronger' Person's Reality." *Psychiatry*, 29: 143–52, 1959.

——, "Individual Therapy and Hospital Structure." In: *Psychotherapy of the Psychoses* (Burton, A., ed.). New York: Basic Books, 1961.

——, "Existentialism Meets Psychotherapy." *Philosophy and Phenomenological Research*, 24: 215–39, 1963.

——, "Techniques of Psychotherapy in a Small Hospital Setting." *Bulletin of the Menninger Clinic*, 27: 96–104, 1963.

——, "Aspects of Relatedness in the Psychotherapy of

Schizophrenia." *Psychoanalytic Review*, 51: 19–28, 1964.

——, Die frühe Mutter-Kind-Beziehung. *Medizinische Klinik*, 51: 1141–44, 1964.

——, "Bleuler's Concept of Schizophrenia in the Light of Our Present Experience." Third International Symposium, *Psychotherapy of Schizophrenia*, Lausanne, 1964. New York: Karger, 1965, pp. 42–53.

——, L'Aggressivité: Essai sur Quelques Aspects Psychiatriques. *L'Evolution Psychiatrique*, 93–105, 1966.

——, "Bleuler's Concept of Schizophrenia: A Confusing Heritage." *American Journal of Psychiatry*, 123: 996–1001, 1967.

Storch, A., "August Strindberg im Lichte seiner Selbstbiographie: eine psychopathologische Persönlichkeitsanalyse." *Grenzfragen des Nerven und Seelenlebens*. Monograph III, 1921, pp. 1–75.

Strindberg, A., (1879) *The Red Room*. (Translated by E. Schleussner.) London: Latimer, 1913.

——, (1886) *The Son of a Servant*. (Translated by C. Field.) London: Rider, 1913.

——, (1887) *The Confessions of a Fool*. (Translated by E. Schleussner.) London: Latimer, 1912.

——, (1888) *Miss Julie*. In: *Six Plays of Strindberg* (Translated by E. Sprigge.) Garden City: Doubleday Anchor Books, 1955.

——, (1897) *The Inferno*. (Translated by C. Field.) London: Rider, 1912.

——, (1897–98) *Legends*. London: Melrose, 1912.

Sullivan, H., *Conceptions of Modern Psychiatry*, Second Edition. New York: Norton, 1953.

——, *The Psychiatric Interview*. New York: Norton, 1954.

——, *The Interpersonal Theory of Psychiatry*. New York: Norton, 1955.

——, *Clinical Studies in Psychiatry*. New York: Norton, 1956.

Szasz, T., *The Myth of Mental Illness: Foundations of a Theory of Personal Conduct*. New York: Hoeber-Harper, 1961.

——, *The Ethics of Psychoanalysis*. New York: Basic Books, 1965.

Tarachow, S., *An Introduction to Psychotherapy*. New York: International Universities Press, 1963.

Tienari, P., "Psychiatric Illness in Identical Twins." *Acta Psychiatrica Scandinavica*, Suppl. 171, 39: 9–195, 1963.

Uppvall, A., *August Strindberg: A Psychoanalytic Study with Special Reference to the Oedipus Complex*. Boston: Badget, 1920.

Wallerstein, R., "The Current State of Psychotherapy: Theory, Practice, Research." *Journal of the American Psychoanalytic Association*, 14: 183–225, 1966.

Weigert, E., "Existentialism and Its Relations to Psychotherapy." *Psychiatry*, 12: 399–412, 1949.

Weismann, A., *The Existential Core of Psychoanalysis: Reality Sense and Responsibility*. Boston: Little, Brown, 1965.

Wender, P., "Dementia Praecox: The Development of the Concept." *American Journal of Psychiatry*, 119: 1143–51, 1964.

Werner, H., *Comparative Psychology of Mental Development*. New York: International Universities Press, 1957.

Werner, H., and Kaplan, B., *Symbol Formation*. New York: Wiley, 1964.

Whitaker, C. (ed.), *Psychotherapy of Chronic Schizophrenic Patients*. Boston: Little, Brown, 1958.

——, *et al.*, "Countertransference in the Family Treatment of Schizophrenia." In: *Intensive Family Therapy* (Boszormenyi-Nagy, I. and Framo, J., eds.). New York: Hoeber, 1965, pp. 323–41.

White, R., "Competence and the Psychosexual Stages of Development." In: *Nebraska Symposium on Motivation* (Jones, M., ed.). Lincoln: University of Nebraska Press, 1960, pp. 97–141.

——, *Ego and Reality in Psychoanalytic Theory. A Proposal Regarding Independent Ego Energies*. New York: International Universities Press, 1963.

Whorf, B., *Language, Thought and Reality*. Selected Writings of Benjamin Lee Whorf (Caroll, J., ed.). New York: M.I.T. and Wiley & Sons, 1956.

Will, O., "Process, Psychotherapy and Schizophrenia." In: *Psychotherapy of the Psychoses* (Burton, A., ed.). New York: Basic Books, 1961.

——, "Schizophrenia and the Psychotherapeutic Field." *Contemporary Psychoanalysis*, 1: 1–29, 1964.

Winnicott, D., "Psychoses and Child Care." *British Journal of Medical Psychology*, 26: 68–74, 1953.

——, "Transitional Objects and Transitional Phenomena: A Study of the First Not-Me Possession." *International Journal of Psycho-Analysis*, 34: 89–97, 1953.

——, *Mother and Child: A Primer of First Relationships*. New York: Basic Books, 1957.

Wittgenstein, L., *Schriften, Tractatus logico-philosophicus, Tagebücher, 1914–16. Philosophische Untersuchungen*. Frankfurt: Suhrkamp, 1960.

Wolff, P., *The Developmental Psychologies of Jean Piaget and Psychoanalysis*. New York: International Universities Press, 1960.

Wolstein, B., *Transference, Its Structure and Function in Psychoanalytic Theory*. Second Edition. New York: Grune & Stratton, 1964.

Wynne, L., "Object Loss and the Unfolding of the Identification Process." Unpublished paper.

——, "Schizophrenics and Their Families: Recent Research Findings and Etiologic Implications." Paper presented to the Mental Health Research Fund Lecture, London, England, February 21, 1968 (In Press).

Wynne, L., *et al.*, Pseudo-Mutuality in the Family Relations of Schizophrenics. *Psychiatry*, 21: 205–20, 1958.

Wynne, L., and Singer, M., "Thought Disorder and Family Relations of Schizophrenics. I. A Research Strategy." *Archives of General Psychiatry*, 9: 191–98, 1963.

——, "Thought Disorder and Family Relations of Schizophrenics. II. A Classification of Forms of Thinking." *Archives of General Psychiatry*, 9: 199–206. 1963.

INDEX

ANCHOR BOOKS

EDUCATION

LINGUISTICS AND LANGUAGE